Hermann Marcus Kottinger

The Youth's Liberal Guide for their Moral Culture and Religious Enlightenment

Hermann Marcus Kottinger

The Youth's Liberal Guide for their Moral Culture and Religious Enlightenment

ISBN/EAN: 9783337253257

Printed in Europe, USA, Canada, Australia, Japan

Cover: Foto ©Lupo / pixelio.de

More available books at **www.hansebooks.com**

Liberal Guide

—— FOR THEIR ——

Moral Culture

—— AND ——

Religious Enlightenment.

—— BY ——

PROF. H. M. KOTTINGER, A. M.

(Translated from the Revised German Edition.)

"*Fathers! Mothers! Let us live for our children!*"
Fred. Froebel,
Founder of the "Kindergarten."

MILWAUKEE:
TRAYSER BROS., BOOK AND JOB PRINTERS, GRAND OPERA HOUSE, 62 ONEIDA STREET.
1877.

Entered according to Act of Congress, in the Year 1877,
By Prof. H. M. KOTTINGER, A. M.,
In the Office of the Librarian of Congress, at Washington, D. C.

TO

B. F. UNDERWOOD, ESQ.,

THE TRUE FRIEND OF

Free Thought and Religious Progress,

Who recommended this Book to the

LIBERAL PUBLIC,

IT IS RESPECTFULLY DEDICATED

BY ITS AUTHOR,

PROF. H. M. KOTTINGER.

PART FIRST.

MORAL CULTURE.

"As with the physical, so with the ethical. A belief, as yet fitful and partial, is beginning to spread amongst men, that here also there is an indissoluble bond between cause and consequence, an inexorable destiny, a law, which altereth not."

H. SPENCER, "Social Statics."

PREFACE.

Every attentive observer of the tendency which the culture of our Age follows, must have noticed that the old religious ideas are in conflict with the new. While natural science, philosophy, and, in general, civilization in every branch of life advance, the denominations of the Church are still constantly uttering the old watchword: "Cling to the orthodox faith!" In every province of human knowledge the use of reason is permitted, except in the domain of religion. In the Old World an ecclesiastical council decrees the infallibility of the Pope; in the New, the churchmen try to fetter liberty of conscience by introducing the Bible into the public schools, and building on its authority the Constitution of our country. That is not the way to advance. Let us strike at the root of the evil; let us give to youth a liberal education! In this rests the hope of our country, the future of humanity.

Five years ago the author published a Text Book for the Sunday Schools of the German Free Religious Congregations in America ("Leitfaden für den Unterricht in den Sonntagsschulen Freier Gemeinden, Milwaukee, Wis."). It was authorized by their Supreme Board, and has been since in general use in most of those schools. This work having subserved so valuable a purpose in the liberal education of the German youth, the author was encouraged to attempt the publication of an English edition. It is a liberal guide for the moral education and mental enlightenment of children. It aims at the destruction of erroneous theological views, and is adapted to the principles and development of liberal science. It contains: First—A doctrine of human duties and rights, established upon the nature of human reason, and illustrated by examples collected from standard English and American authors, both in prose and verse. Secondly—The history of the principal religions. Thirdly—A criticism of the most important liberal narratives. Fourthly—Views of the Universe, represented in the liberal writings of the English, French, German and American natural philosophers, such as Darwin, Huxley, Tyndall, Spencer, La Place, La Marck, Humboldt, Buechner, Feuerbach, Feike, etc.

The Text Books of the Sunday Schools, and, in general, juvenile literature, disseminate much superstition in the unprotected minds of youth. The impressions which they receive from these books they are very apt to carry with them through life. "It is worthy of remark that a belief constantly inculcated during the early years of life, whilst the brain is impressible, appears to acquire almost the nature of an instinct; and the very essence of an instinct is that it is followed independently of reason."—Darwin. "All the machinery of the Church is constantly employed in corrupting the reason of children. In every possible way they are robbed of their own thoughts and forced to accept the statements of others. Every Sunday School has for its object the crushing out of every germ of individuality."—R. Ingersoll.

Zealots will accuse me of demolishing the old temple, without building up a new edifice on its ruins. But I destroy only that part of the old structure which rests on sand; the Christian religion is also partly founded on solid ground, e. g., on the principle (called "the Golden Rule"): "All things whatsoever ye would that men should do to you, do ye even so to them."—(Matth. 7, 12.)

The Morals and Views of the Universe are represented in the Socratic method, in order to better adapt their contents to the capacity of children. Every child of average capacity can easily answer most of the questions proposed in these sections of the book.

Though competent American scholars have reviewed and corrected the translation, the author is afraid that it is still redolent of his mother tongue, and far from perfect conformity with the true genius and idiom of the English language, but he hopes for the kind indulgence of the readers. Should there be a second edition, this book will be supplied. He is told that a similar book, written expressly for children, is, so far, not yet extant in American literature; therefore he trusts that liberal parents will give it a fair trial, until they find a better guide for the moral education and mental enlightenment of their children.

Finally, the author gratefully acknowledges the kind assistance of many ladies and gentlemen in the English edition of the book. Mrs. Cronyn, Mrs. Sara Underwood, Mrs. McCaig and Mrs. Spencer, Miss A. Chamberlain, Messrs. Cronyn, Pfister, McClellan, J. L. Hatch and Dr. J. Spencer have corrected different sections; Mr. Hatch, Mr. B. F. Underwood, Dr. Spencer, Prof. Allen and J. J. Owen have perused and commended the manuscript, and encouraged the author to publish it. To all of them he offers his most sincere and heartfelt thanks.

THE AUTHOR.

SECTION FIRST.

MORALS IN EXAMPLES.

"Verba movent, exempla trahunt."—Latin Proverb.
(Words induce; examples impel.)

CHAPTER FIRST.

MORALS, (in the Stricter Sense.)

I. Duties Towards Ourselves.

1. Bad Habits of the Blackamoor.

A certain man having bought a blackamoor, was so simple as to think that the color of his skin was only dirt and filth, which he had contracted for want of care under his former master. This fault he fancied might easily be removed. So he ordered the poor black to be put into a tub, and was at a considerable charge in providing ashes, soap and scrubbing-brushes for the operation. To work they went, rubbing and scouring his skin all over, but to no manner of purpose, for when they had repeated their washings several times, and were growing quite weary, all they got by it was that the wretched blackamoor caught cold and died.

It is a very difficult task to get rid of inveterated bad habits.—*Esop, ab. 550 A. C.*

2. Bad Results of Bad Actions—Nails in the Post.

There was once a farmer who had a son, named John, a boy very apt to be thoughtless, and careless as to doing what he was told to do. One day his father said to him: "John, you are so careless and forgetful, that every time you do wrong, I shall drive a nail into this post, to remind you how often you are naughty, and every time you do right I will draw one out." His father did as he said he would, and every day he had one, and sometimes he had a great many nails to drive in, but very seldom one to draw out.

At last John saw that the post was quite covered with nails, and he began to be ashamed of having so many faults. He resolved to be a better boy; and the next day he was so good and industrious that several nails came out; the day after it was the same thing, and so on for a long time, till at length only one nail remained. His father then called him, and said: "Look, John, here is the very last nail, and now I am going to draw this; are you not glad?" John looked at the post, and then, instead of expressing his joy, as his father expected, he burst into tears. "Why," said his father, "What's the matter? I should think you would be delighted; the nails are all gone." "Yes," sobbed John, "the nails are gone, but *the scars* are there yet."

So it is with our faults and bad habits; we may overcome them, but the scars remain.

3. Modesty—Pride—Content.

(a)—A Modest Wit.

A supercilious nabob of the East,
Haughty, being great—purse-proud, being rich—
A governor, or general, at the least,
I have forgotten which—
Had in his family a humble youth,
Who went from England in his patron's suite,
An unassuming boy, and in truth
A lad of decent parts, and good repute.
This youth had sense and spirit;
But yet, with all his sense,
Excessive diffidence
Obscured his merit.

One day at table, flushed with pride and wine,
His honor, proudly free, severely merry,
Conceived it would be vastly fine
To crack a joke upon his secretary.
"Young man," he said, "by what art, craft or trade
Did your good father gain a livelihood?"
"He was a saddler, sir," Modestus said,
"And in his time was reckon'd good."
"A saddler, eh! and taught you Greek,
Instead of teaching you to sew!
Pray, why did not your father make
A saddler, sir, of you?"

Each parasite, then, as in duty bound,
The joke applauded, and the laugh went round.
At last Modestus bowing low,
Said (craving pardon, if too free he made),
"Sir, by your leave, I fain would know
Your father's trade!"
"My father's trade! By heaven that's too bad!
My father's trade? Why, blockhead, are you mad?
My father, sir, did never stoop so low—
He was a gentleman, I'd have you know."

"Excuse the liberty I take,"
Modestus said, with archness on his brow,
"Pray, why did not your father make
A gentleman of *you?*"

(b)—The Horse and the Ass.

The horse, adorned with his great war saddle, and champing his foaming bridle, came thundering along the way, and made the mountains echo with his loud, shrill neighing. He had not gone far, before he overtook an ass, who was laboring under a heavy burthen, and moving slowly on in the same track with himself. Immediately he called out to him, in a haughty, imperious tone, and threatened to trample him in the dirt, if he did not break the way for him. The poor, patient ass, not daring to dispute the matter, quickly got out of the way as fast as he could, and let him go by. Not long after this, the same horse, in an engagement with the enemy, happened to be shot in the eye, which made him unfit for show, or any military business; so he was stript of his fine ornaments, and sold to a carrier. The ass meeting him in this forlorn condition, thought that now it was his time to insult; and so says he: "Hey-day, friend! is it you? Well, I always believed that pride of yours would one day have a fall!"—*Esop.*

(c)—The Monkey Tourist.

A monkey clad in cloth-of-gold
(So in the proverb we are told)
Will be a monkey still. The aim
Of this new fable is the same;
Pray, listen while I tell in rhyme
The tale how, once upon a time,
A monkey, dressed in garments bright,
With gaudy colors such as might
Become a harlequin, set out—
To show her finery, no doubt—
Upon her travels. In what way,
By ship or coach, I cannot say;
'Tis only known her journey ran
As far abroad as Setuan:
A country—as I understand—
On maps set down as "Monkey-land";
And widely famous as the place
Where most abound the Simian race,
They're in their own skins simply clad.
Here—as the reader may suppose—
Our lady-tourist proudly shows,
With many a change, her gay attire,
Which all the natives much admire;
And think the wearer must possess
A mind as brilliant as her dress,
And, thereupon, the stranger made
Their leader in a coming raid
For forage, in the country round,
Where monkey-provender was found.

Alas, the day! her clothing proved
An obstacle where'er she moved;
And when the weary day was done,
Her gaudy garments,—every one,—
That in the morning looked so fine,
Were strewn in rags along the line
Through which the expedition led;
And she, worn out and nearly dead,
At night was but the scoff and scorn

Of those who hailed her "queen" at morn!
    A thousand instances confess
That judging people by their dress,
As bright or brave, is a mistake,
That men as well as monkeys make!
                        —*J. Godfrey Sax-*

(d)—**The Mountain and the Squirrel.**

The mountain and the squirrel
Had a quarrel;
And the former called the latter "Little Prig."
Bun replied:
"You are doubtless very big;
But all sorts of things and weather
Must be taken in together,
To make up a year
And a sphere.
And I think it no disgrace
To occupy my place.
If I am not so large as you,
You are not so small as I,
And not half so spry.
I'll not deny you make
A very pretty squirrel track;
Talents differ; all is well and wisely put;
If I cannot carry forests on my back,
Neither can you crack a nut."
                        —*R. W. Emerson.*

4. Temperance.

(a)—The Washingtonian's Story.

Liquor is the subject of my story;
I can not tell what *you* and *other* folks think
Of getting drunk, but for my single self,
I had as lief *not* be, as live *and be*
The poor, degraded wretch that sucks the bottle.
I was born free and sober; so were *you!*
We have no need of brandy. We endure
The winter's cold, and summer's heat, the best,
Without its use.
            I do remember well,
That once, upon a raw and piercing day,
A toper came, and challenged me to work
In open air, that he might try the strength

Of *alcohol* against pure, clear, cold water.
Upon the word, shouldering my burnished ax,
I started with the fellow for the woods,
He took with him a jug well filled with rum,
I slacked my thirst with water from the spring.

   We toiled with vigor, and the air around
Answered in echoes to our sounding steel;
But, ere the sun had reached its noonday point,
The liquid in the jug was well-nigh spent.
A mist now gathered on the toper's eyes
And strength forsook his arm. His feeble blows
Fell harmless against the mighty oaks and pines,
That seemed to *smile* to see the uplifted ax
Strike sideways, glance, and *cleave the frozen earth.*
The effect was irresistible. I laughed
To bursting nigh;—and yet *I should have wept.*
My dinner-time had come, and hunger keen,
That sure attendant upon useful toil,
Turned my thoughts homeward, where the viands hot
Awaited my arrival.

     I spoke
To my companion, he answered me,
But scarce had strength to make speech audible.
We started on together for our homes,
My pace was *even*, for my limbs were *strong:*
My heart was happy; and my head was clear.
My friend fared not so well. His trembling legs
Appeared unwilling to support his weight:
They tottered, reeled, and made "Virginia fence."

  He said "all Nature had conspired against him;"
The *trees* themselves were quarrelsome, and struck
Him right and left, at every step. The *stumps* grew
Turbulent, and stumped him to a fight. He was
No *coward;* but he saw the odds were much
Against him; so he passed along,—
And though his enemies provoked him sore,—
Oft rising up to strike him in the face,
He journeyed on, and uttered but the threat,
"*You'll catch it when I catch you all alone.*"

  The *fences* now began to dance around him;
The *earth* piled up in mountains in his path;
The *stones* came rolling 'gainst his feet, and knocked
His legs from under him; and then the *ground*,

Taking advantage of his helpless plight,
Most cowardly, threw dirt into his face.
At length, he saw his *house* approaching him,—
Whirling, it flew towards him. Windows, doors,
Sides, roofs, foundations, by enchantment moved,
Changed places constantly.
      The cellar door
Attacked him first,—it oped, let him in,
And there I left him,
Covered with *dirt* and glory,—sound asleep.

(b)—Alexander and Clitus.

The sad consequences of anger and intemperance are described in every Reader. They are here illustrated by a notorious example, taken from the history of *Alexander*, King of Macedonia, whom they call the Great, because he has conquered the immense dominions of the Persian monarchy; still he was not able to conquer his own passions, especially *anger* and *intemperance* He had trusted Clitus, his general and personal friend, with the government of one of the most important provinces of his Empire, and ordered him to set out the next day. Before his departure, Clitus was invited in the evening to an entertainment, in which the King, after drinking immoderately. began to celebrate his own exploits, depreciating the warlike acts of his Generals, and even those of his father Philip, King of Macedonia. His discourse displeased several guests, especially Clitus. He, who also was intoxicated, began to relate the glorious actions of Philip, preferring them to those of Alexander, and with eyes sparkling with wine and anger said to him : "It is nevertheless this hand (extending it at the same time) that saved your life at the battle of the Gravicus." Clitus, so far, was right ; for at that battle, as Alexander was fighting bareheaded, and a Persian had his arm raised in order to strike the King behind, Clitus covered Alexander with his shield, and cut off the Persian's hand. Alexander commanded Clitus to leave the table. "He is in the right," said Clitus, as he rose up, "not to bear, free-born men at his table, who can only tell him truth. He will do well, to pass his life among barbarians and slaves." But the King, not longer able to suppress his rage, snatched a javelin from one of his guards, and would have killed Clitus on the spot, had not the courtiers withheld his arm, and Clitus been forced out of the hall. He, however, returned into it by another door, singing with an air of insolence verses reflecting highly on Alexander, who, seeing the General near him, struck him with his javelin, and laid him dead at his feet, crying out at the same time: "Go now to Philip and his friends!"

The King's anger being in a manner suddenly extinguished in the blood of Clitus, his crime displayed itself to him in its blackest light. He had murdered a man who indeed abused his patience, but then he had always served him with the utmost zeal and fidelity, and saved his life. He had punished, by a horrid murder, the uttering of some indiscreet words, which might be imputed to the fumes of wine. Beside Hellenice, sister of Clitus, had nursed Alexander when he was a little child. With what face could he appear before her, and offer her a hand imbrued in her brother's blood?

Upon this he threw himself on his friend's body, forced out the javelin, and would have dispatched himself with it, had not the guards who rushed in upon him, laid hold of his hands, and forcibly carried him into his own apartment. He passed that night and the next day in tears. After these groans and lamentations had quite wasted his spirits, he continued speechless, stretched on the ground, and only venting deep sighs. His friends tried to comfort him; but how weak are all consoling words against the cries of a justly alarmed conscience! He was determined to starve himself; so that it was with the utmost difficulty that his friends prevailed with him to take a little sustenance.

Anger can be compared to thunder; and indeed what havoc does it not make? But how dreadful must it be, when joined with drunkenness? We see this in Alexander.—*Rollin, Ancient Hist.*

(c)—Saint Becky.

A very good man was St. Becky's husband, but with his heart a little too much in his bottle. Port wine—red port wine—was his delight, and his constant cry was a bee's-wing.* Now, as he sat

---

*This word denotes the finest, best kind of wine. It is an English, colloquial expression.

tipsy in his arbor, a wasp dropped into his glass; and the wasp was swallowed, stinging the man inwardly. Doctors crowded, and with much ado the man was saved. Now, St. Becky nursed her husband tenderly to health, and upbraided him not. But she said these words, and they reformed him: "My dear, take wine, and bless your heart with it ; *but wine in moderation.* Else never forget that the bee's-wing of to-day becomes the wasp's sting of to-morrow.—*Douglas Jerrold.*

5. Courage—Temerity—Leap for Life.

Old Ironsides at anchor lay
   In the harbor of Mahon,
A dead calm rested on the bay—
   The waves to sleep had gone,
When little *Hal*, the Captain's son,
   A lad both brave and good,
In sport, up shroud and rigging ran,
   And on the main-truck stood !

A shudder shot through every vein—
   All eyes were turned on high !
There stood the boy, with dizzy brain,
   No hold had he—above, below ;
Alone he stood in air :
   To that far height none dared to go ;—
No aid could reach him there !

The father came on deck :—he gasped,
   "O God ! Thy will be done !"
Then suddenly a rifle grasped,
   And aimed at his son :—
" Jump ! far out, boy, into the wave !
   Jump, or I fire !" he said ;
" That only chance your life can save !
   Jump ! jump, boy !" He obeyed.

He sank, he rose—he lived—he moved—
   And for the ship struck out ;
On board we hailed the lad beloved,
   With many a manly shout.
His father drew, in silent joy,
   Those wet arms around his neck—
Then folded to his heart his boy,
   And fainted on the deck !   —*Morris.*

6. Application—Inertness.

(a)—The Panorama Boy.

Some years ago a boy was sitting with folded hands, in a tiny skiff, on the bosom of the mighty Mississippi. The setting sun was shining on the water and on the beautiful banks of the river, rich with variously colored foliage. So full was the mind of the boy with wonder and delight that the boat glided on unheeded, while he still sat gazing on the banks of the river. He had heard that America was richer in beautiful scenery than any other country in the world, and as he looked around him, he believed the saying, and then came into his mind the desire and resolve to become an artist, that he might paint the magnificent scenes of his native land.

This boy's name was *Barnard*, and the resolution he made to paint the largest picture in the world was never given up till it was accomplished. When his father died, John was left a poor, friendless lad, and obtained employment with a druggist; but so fond was he of sketching the likenesses of those about him, on the walls, with chalk or coal, that his master told him he made better likenesses than pills; so poor John lost his situation. He then tried other plans, and met with many disappointments; but at last succeeded in obtaining as much money as he thought would enable him to paint his great picture.

He had to go through much danger and trouble, before he could take all his sketckes, spread over a distance of 3000 miles.

Having bought a small skiff, he set off alone on his perilous adventure. He traveled thousands of miles, crossing the Mississippi backward and forward to secure the best points for making his sketches. All day long he went on sketching, and when the sun was about to set, he either shot wild fowl on the river, or hauling the little boat ashore, went into the woods with his rifle to shoot game. After cooking and eating his supper, he turned his boat over on the ground, and crept under it, rolling himself up in a blanket to sleep for the night. Sometimes for weeks together he never spoke to a human being. In this manner he went on sketching for more than four hundred days before the necessary drawings were finished, and then he set to work in good earnest to paint the picture

He had only made sketches in his wanderings. After these were completed, there were colors and canvas to be bought, and a large wooden building to be erected, where he might finish his work without interruption. When the panorama was finished, it covered three miles of canvas and represented a range of scenery three thousand miles in extent.

(b)—The Ant and the Grasshopper.

In the winter season a commonwealth of ants was busily employed in the management and preservation of their grains, which they exposed to the air, in heaps, round about the avenues of their little country habitation.

A grasshopper who had chanced to outlive the summer, and was ready to starve with cold and hunger, approached them with great humility, and begged that they would relieve his necessity with one grain of wheat or rye. One of the ants asked him how he had disposed of his time in summer, why he had not taken pains, and laid in a stock, as they had done. Alas, gentlemen, says he, I passed away the time merrily and pleasantly, in drinking, singing and dancing, and never once thought of the winter. If that be the case, replied the ant, laughing, all I have to say is, that they who drink, sing and dance in the summer, must starve in the winter.—*Æsop.*

(c)—The Village Blacksmith.

Under the spreading chestnut-tree
The village smithy stands;
The smith, a mighty man is he,
With large and sinewy hands;
And the muscles of his brawny arms
Are strong as iron bands.

His hair is crisp, and black, and long,
His face is like the tan;
His brow is wet with honest sweat,
He earns whate'er he can,
And looks the whole world in the face,
For he owes nothing any man.

Week in, week out from morn till night,
You can hear his bellows blow;
You can hear him swing his heavy sledge
With measured beat and slow,
Like a sexton ringing the village bell
When the evening sun is low.

And children coming home from school
Look in at the open door,
They love to see the flaming forge,
To hear the bellows roar,
And catch the burning sparks that fly
Like chaff from a threshing-floor.

He goes on Sundays to the church,
And sits among his boys,
He hears the parson pray and preach,
He hears his daughter's voice
Singing in the village choir,
And it makes his heart rejoice.

It sounds to him, like her mother's voice
Singing in Paradise!
He needs must think of her once more,
How in the grave she lies;
And with his hard, rough hand he wipes
A tear out of his eyes.

Toiling—rejoicing—sorrowing,
Onward through life he goes,
Each morning sees some task begin,
Each evening sees it close;
Something attempted, something done,
Has earned a night's repose.

Thanks to thee, my worthy friend,
For the lesson thou hast taught!
Thus at the flaming forge of life
Our fortunes must be wrought;
Thus on its sounding anvil shaped
Each burning deed and thought!

—*Longfellow.*

(d)—The Plowman.

Clear the brown path, to meet his coulter's gleam!
Lo! on he comes, behind his smoking team,
With Toil's bright drops on his sunburnt brow,
The lord of earth, the hero of the plow.
First in the field before the reddening sun,
Last in the shadows when the day is done,
Line after line, along the bursting sod,
Marks the broad acres where his feet have trod.

Still, where he treads, the stubborn clods divide,
The smooth, fresh furrow opens deep and wide,
Matted and dense the tangled turf upheaves
Mellow and dark the ridgy cornfield cleaves.
Up the steep hillside, where the laboring train
Starts the long track that scores the level plain.

Through the moist valley, clogged with oozing clay,
The patient convoy breaks its destined way;
At every turn the loosening chains resound,
The swinging plowshare circles glistening round,
Till the wild field one billowy waste appears,
And weary hands unbind the panting steers.

These are the hands whose sturdy labor brings
The peasant's food, and golden pomp of kings:
This is the page, whose letters shall be seen
Changed by the sun to words of living green.
This is the scholar, whose immortal pen
Spells the first lesson hunger taught to men;
These are the lines, O heaven-commanded Toil!
That fill thy dead—the charter of the soil!
—Holmes.

7. Parsimony—Dissipation.
The Young Man and the Swallow.

A prodigal young spendthrift, who wasted his whole patrimony in taverns and gaming-houses, among lewd, idle company, was taking a melancholy walk near a brook. It was in the month of January, and happened to be one of those warm sunshiny days which sometimes shine upon us even in that wintry season of the year. And to make it more flattering, a swallow, which had made his appearance, by mistake, too soon, flew skimming along upon the surface of the water. The giddy youth observing this without any further consideration, concluded that summer was now come, and that he should have little or no occasion for clothes, so went and pawned them at the broker's, and ventured the money for one stake more among his sharping companions. When this too was gone the same way as the rest, he took another solitary walk in the same place as before. But the weather being severe and frosty, had made everything look with an aspect very different from what it did before; the brook was quite frozen over, and the poor swallow lay dead upon the bank of it, the very sight of which cooled the young spark's brain ; and coming to a kind of sense of his misery, he reproached the deceased bird as the author of all his misfortunes : "Ah, wretch that thou wert !" says he, "thou hast undone both thyself and me, who was so credulous as to depend upon thee."—*Esop*.

9. Frugality—Covetousness—Avarice.
(a)—Quintius Cincinnatus.

When the Romans were in any great emergency, it was their custom to create a Dictator,—that is, a supreme officer, who should *dictate* what was to be done, and who was to be instantly and implicitly obeyed. About 460 A. C., Rome was in fear and confusion from the approach of the Aegin, a successful hostile nation ; and as it was necessary to have a Dictator, Cincinnatus was fixed upon, as the wisest and bravest man belonging to the commonwealth. He cultivated a small farm of four acres with his own hands. The Deputies of the Senate found him following his plow, in one of his little fields. They begged him to put on his gown, and hear the message from the Senate. Cincinnatus anxiously asked "if all was well," and then desired his wife to fetch his gown from their cottage. After wiping off the dust and dirt with which he was covered, he put on his robe, and went to the Deputies. They then saluted him as Dictator, and bade him hasten to the city, which was in the greatest peril.

A handsome barge had been sent to carry Cincinnatus over the river ; for his farm lay on the opposite side of the Tiber. His three sons, with his friends and several of the Senators, were ready to receive him when he landed at Rome, and to carry him in a pompous procession to the house prepared for him The very next morning he began to fortify the city and marshal the soldiers for battle, and he very soon gained a great victory, and made the officers of the enemy pass under the jugum, or yoke. This yoke was a kind of gallows, made of three spears ; two firmly fixed upright in the ground, and the third laid across them. To pass under this was considered a very great disgrace. Cincinnatus having completed the duty for which he had been called from his plow, modestly resigned the dictatorship at the end of sixteen days, though he might have held it for six months. But he liked power only whilst it made him useful; he returned again to his plow, well satisfied by the glory of having saved his country.—*Agnes Strickland.*

(b)—Solicitude Caused by Great Fortune.

A young person once mentioned to Benj. Franklin his surprise that the possession of great riches should ever be attended with undue solicitude, and instanced a merchant, who, although in possession of unbounded wealth, was as busy as any clerk in his counting house. The Doctor, in reply, took an apple from a fruit-basket, and presented it to a child in the room, who could scarcely grasp it in his hand. He then gave him a second, which filled the other; and choosing a third, remarkable for its size and beauty, he presented that also. The child, after many ineffectual attempts to hold the three apples, dropped the last on the carpet, and burst into tears. "See," said the Doctor, "there is a little man with more riches than he can enjoy."

(c)—The Man and his Goose.

A certain man had a goose which laid him a golden egg every day. But not content with this, which rather increased than abated his avarice, he was resolved to kill the goose, and cut up her belly, that he might come to the inexhaustible treasure, which he fancied he had within her. He did so, and to his great sorrow and disappointment, found nothing.

Misers who are not contented, when fortune has blessed them with a constant sufficiency, deserve even to be deprived of what they have.—*Æsop.*

(d)—The Oil-Merchant's Ass.

An ass whose customary toil
Was bearing heavy sacks of oil
(The kind which often serves at night,
Our houses, shops, and streets to light),
His labor over for the day,
Straight to his stable took his way;
But, as he sought to enter there,
The grouping donkey, unaware,
Against the door-hasp hit his nose;

Whereat his indignation rose
To such a pitch, he roundly swore,
(As many an ass has done before!)
And thus in wrath expressed his mind :
" By Jove! one might as well be blind,
As break his noddle in the dark
For want of light. A single spark
Had saved my skin; but not a ray
My master gives to light my way.
I, who for others daily toil,
And fill a thousand lamps with oil,
For lack of one—so justice goes!—
Against the door must break my nose!"

    The miser, who, to gather pelf
For thankless heirs, defrauds himself;
The ignoramus, proud to show
His gilded volumes all a-row,—
Such men as these may we not class
(Poor donkeys!) with the oilman's ass?

                                —*J. Godfrey Saxe.*

(e)—The Little Glass Shoe.

"Ho! ho! ha! ha!—what is it I view?"
  John Wilde, the ploughman cried,
As he hit his foot on a little glass shoe
  That lay on the mountain side;
" Some fay has lost it, there's never a doubt,
  And ah! how lucky for me,
The owner will soon be roaming about
  To find where his shoe may be.
And so (said John) I'll carry it home,
  That's just what I will do,
And he will pay me a pretty sum,
  Who buys this little glass shoe!"
And he spread the story far and near,
  For many a mile around,
That the fairy folk might surely hear
  Who the little glass shoe had found.
And soon to John a merchant came,
  Who said he had heard the news;
And would the ploughman sell the same
  To a dealer in little glass shoes?
And he offered John a pretty price

For the shoe that he had found;
But John replied it was much too nice
　To go for a hundred pound;
Then the merchant offered a hundred more,
　But the ploughman still said, "Nay;
The man who buys my shoe (he swore)
　Will dearly have to pay.
There's not so pretty a shoe on earth
　To cover a lady's toes;
And then I happen to know its worth
　Far better than you suppose.
The shoe is one of wondrous price
　(That nobody can deny),
And yet, perchance, there's some device
　May serve the shoe to buy.
If you are able to show me, now,
　When I am ploughing my field,
That every furrow behind my plow
　A shining ducat may yield,—
Why, then to you the shoe I'll give,
　Else I will keep it myself,—
For an ornament, as long as I live,
　To grace my mantel-shelf!"
And so it was the fairy bought
　('Twas he in merchant's guise!)
His own glass shoe, and, quick as thought,
　Away to his home he hies.
And off went John, with much delight,
　As fast as he could go,
By trial to prove that very night
　If the charm would work or no.
And he found the fairy's word as true
　As he promised in the trade;
For a shining ducat came to view
　In every furrow he made!
And again next morning off he went—
　Nor scarce to eat could stop—
To plough again,—he was so intent
　To gather his golden crop.
And so he ploughed, and ploughed, and ploughed,
　And scarce for slumber ceased;
No wonder John was growing proud,
　So fast his wealth increased!

And still he ploughed by day and night,
   When none were looking on,
Till he seemed, indeed, a sorry wight,
   He grew so lean and wan!
And still, when none his work might view,
   He ploughed by night and day;
And still the more his riches grew,
   The more he pined away.
Until, at last, his work was stopped,
   And the ploughman, where was he?
Down in the furrow, alas! he dropped,
   As dead as dead could be!—
Though good is gold, to have and hold,
   My story makes it clear
Who sells himself for sordid pelf,
   Has bought it much too dear!

                    —*J. Godfrey Saxe.*

9. Gambling—The Gambler's Wife.

Dark is the night! How dark! No light! No fire!
Cold on the hearth the last faint sparks expire.
Shivering, she watches by the cradle side
For him, who pledged her love—last year a bride!

Hark! 'tis his footstep!—'tis past: 'tis gone;
Tick! Tick! How wearily the time crawls on!
Why should he leave me thus?—He once was kind!
And believed 't would last—how mad!—how blind!

Rest thee, my babe!—rest on!—'tis hunger's cry!
Sleep!—for there is no food!—the fount is dry!
Famine and cold their wearying work have done,
My heart must break!—And thou!—The clock strikes one.

Hush! 'tis the dice-box! Yes, he's there, he's there,
For this! For this he leaves me to despair!
Leaves love! Leaves truth! His wife! His child- for what?
The wanton's smile—the villain—and the sot!

Yet I'll not curse him. No! 'tis all in vain!
'Tis long to wait, but sure he'll come again.
And I could starve and bless him, but for you,
My child! His child! Oh, friend!—The clock strikes two.

"Hark! How the signboard creaks! The blast howls by!
Moan! Moan! A dirge swells through the cloudy sky!
Ha! 'tis his knock! he comes!—he comes once more!"
'Tis but the lattice flaps! Thy hope is o'er!

Can he desert me thus? He knows I stay
Night after night in loneliness, to pray
For his return,—and yet, he sees no tear!
No! no! It can not be. He will be here.

"Nestle more closely, dear one, to my heart!
Thou 'rt cold! Thou 'rt freezing! But we will not part
Husband!—I die! Father!—It is not he!
Oh God! Protect my child!" The clock strikes three.

They're gone! They're gone! The glimmering spark has sped!
The wife and child are numbered with the dead.
On the cold hearth outstretched in solemn rest,
The babe lay frozen on its mother's breast!
   The gambler came at last—but all was o'er—
Dead silence reigned around—the clock struck *four*.
—*Dr. Coats.*

10. Education and Mental Culture.

(a)—William Cobbett.

William Cobbett was an eminent Englishman, who exerted a great influence in his country and our own. His early life was distinguished by poverty and hardships, and his success was due to a laudable ambition, supported by good sense and a will to work. Speaking of the difficulties under which he labored, he says : " I learned grammar when I was a private soldier on the pay of sixpence a day. The edge of my berth, or that of my guard bed, was my seat to study in ; my knapsack was my book-case, and a bit of board lying in my lap was my writing-table. I had no money to purchase candle, or oil ; in winter time it was rarely that I could get any light but that of the fire, and only my turn even at that. To buy a pen or a sheet of paper, I was compelled to forego some portion of food, though in a state of half-starvation. I had no moment that I could call my own, and I had to read and write amid the talking, laughing, singing, whistling, and bawling of at least half a score of the most thoughtless of men ; and that, too, in hours of freedom from all control. And I say, if I, under circumstances like these, could encounter and overcome the task, can there be, in the whole world, a youth who can find an excuse for the non-performance?"

(b)—Illustrious American Apprentices.

The following are a few of a long list of names that might be given of eminent Americans who commenced life as apprentice boys:

Benjamin Franklin, a printer, acted a principal part in the great drama of the American Revolutionary War, as Ambassador to France, member of the Congress and Governor of Pennsylvania. He was a friend of George Washington.

Stephen A. Douglas, United States Senator from Illinois, was apprenticed to a cabinetmaker, and served diligently till, upon his health failing, he was released from his engagement.

Nathaniel Bowditch was bred to his father's trade, as a cooper, and was afterward bound to a ship-chandler. He became eminent as a mathematician and astronomer.

Andrew Johnson was indentured at ten years of age to the tailor's trade, and served his term of seven years. During his apprenticeship he learned to read, and, after he was married, his wife taught him to write and cipher. He became President of the United States.

Elihu Buritt, the eminent scholar and friend of peace, is known as the "learned blacksmith." He understands a score of languages.

Governor *Jewell*, of Connecticut, was a tanner; Governor *Claflin*, of Massachusetts, was a shoemaker; President *Grant* was a tanner; Vice President *Colfax* was a printer.

(c)—The Nightingale and the Organ.

A nightingale who chanced to hear
  An organ's deep and swelling tone,
Was wont to lend a careful ear,
  That so she might improve her own.

One evening, while the organ's note
  Thrilled through the wood, and Philomel
Sat tuning her melodious throat
  To imitate its wondrous swell,

A twittering sparrow, hopping near,
  Said, "Prithee, now, be pleased to state
What from those wooden pipes you hear
  That you can wish to imitate?

"I do not hesitate to say,
  Whatever the stupid thing can do
To please us in a vocal way,
  That very organ learned from you!

"Of all sweet singers none is greater
  Than Philomel; but, on my word!
To imitate one's imitator,—
  Can aught on earth be more absurd?"

"Nay (said the nightingale), if ought
  From me the organ ever learned,
By him no less have I been taught,
  And thus the favor is returned.

Thus to my singing, don't you see?
  Some needed culture I impart;
For Nature's gifts, as all agree,
  Are finest when improved by Art!"

Whate'er the foolish sparrow thought,
  The nightingale (so Wisdom votes)
Was wise in choosing to be taught
  E'en by an organ's borrowed notes.

And hence the student may obtain
  Some useful rules to guide his course:
Shun self-conceit, nor e'er disdain
Instruction from the humblest source!

—*J. Godfrey Saxe.*

11. Perseverance—Robert Bruce.

The famous *Robert Bruce* of Scotland, having been defeated in battle, was obliged to hide himself sometimes in woods and sometimes in the huts of poor peasants; for his enemies were in pursuit of him, and determined to kill him if they could find him.

One morning, after a sleepless night of anxiety, as he was lying on a heap of straw in a deserted hut, reflecting upon his misfortunes, and nearly discouraged, he saw a spider trying to swing himself by his thread from one beam of the roof to another. He failed, and the thread swung back to its former position. He made another effort, fell back again, but immediately renewed the attempt. The attention of Bruce was now fully aroused, and his feelings enlisted for the success of the little insect. Again and again the little creature failed, but as often renewed the attempt with unabated energy, and after thirteen unsuccessful efforts, succeeded in the fourteenth in reaching the desired position.

The lesson of perseverance taught by the spider roused the desponding hero to new exertion. He went forth from his hiding place, collected his friends, defeated his enemies in a great and decisive battle, and was soon after crowned King of Scotland.

12. Patience—Anger—The Frog and the Mouse.

There was once a great emulation between the frog and the mouse, which should be master of the fen, and war ensued upon it. But the crafty mouse, lurking under the grass in ambuscade, made sudden sallies, and often surprised the enemy at a disadvantage The frog excelling in strength, and being more able to leap abroad and take the field, challenged the mouse to single combat. The mouse accepted the challenge, and each of them entered the lists, armed with the point of a bulrush, instead of a spear. A kite sailing in the air, beheld them afar off, and while they were eagerly bent upon each other, and pressing on to the duel, this fatal enemy descended upon them, and, with her crooked talons, carried off both the champions.

Nothing so much exposes a man's weak side and lays him so open to an enemy, as passion.—*Æsop*.

13. Vocation—The Wolf and the Stray Kid.

A very stupid wolf (they are not all so) found a kid which had gone astray from the fold. "Little friend," said the wolf, "I have met you very seasonably. You will make me a good supper; for I have neither breakfasted, nor dined to-day, I assure you." "If I must die," replied the poor little kid, "please to give me a song first. I trust you will not refuse me this favor—it is the first I have ever asked you. I have heard that you are a perfect musician." The wolf, like a fool, set up a terrible howling, which, of course, was the nearest to a song that he could get, and the shepherd, hearing the noise, ran to the spot with his dogs, and the wolf made off with himself as fast as he could go. "Very well," said he, as he was running, "they have served me right enough; this will teach me to confine myself to the trade of butcher, and not attempt to play the musician."

Become acquainted first with your talents, before you choose a vocation.—*Perrin.*

II. Duties of Benevolence towards Our Fellow-Creatures.

1. Mutual Charity and Philanthropy.

(a)—The Good Samaritan.

A certain lawyer stood up and said to Jesus, "Who is my neighbor?" Jesus answering, said: "A certain man went down from Jerusalem to Jericho, and fell among thieves, who stripped him of his raiment, wounded him, and departed, leaving him half dead. And, by chance, there came down a certain priest that way; and when he saw him, he passed by on the other side. Likewise, a Levite, when he was at the place, came and looked at him, and passed also by on the other side. But a certain Samaritan, as he journeyed, came where he was; and when he saw him, he had compassion on him, went to him, bound up his wounds, pouring in oil and wine, and set him on his own beast; then he brought him to an inn, and took care of him, and on the morrow when he departed, he took out two pence, gave them to the host, and said unto him: 'Take care of him; and whatsoever thou spendest more, when I come again, I will repay thee.'

"Which now of these three, thinkest thou, was neighbor unto him that fell among the thieves?" And he said: "He that shewed mercy on him." Then said Jesus unto him: "Go, and do thou likewise."—*Bible.*

In this parable, the national enemy of the wounded man proved himself a kind, loving, liberal friend, while the careless priest, and the proud Levite of his own kindred and religion, haughtily passed by on the other side. Take every one for your neighbor who wants your mercy!

(b)—The Sick Passenger.

The captain of a boat in Pennsylvania stood by his craft, when the cars rolled up and a few minutes after a party of about half a dozen gentlemen came out, and deliberately walking up to the captain, addressed him, saying: "Sir, we wish to go on East, but our further progress to-day depends on you. In the cars we have just left a sick man, whose presence is disagreeable. We have been appointed a committee by the passengers to ask that you deny this man a passing in your boat. If he goes, we remain; what say you?"

"Gentlemen," replied the captain, "I have heard the passengers through their committee. Has the sick man a representative here?" To this unexpected interrogatory there was no answer; when, without a moment's pause, the captain crossed over to the car, and entering, beheld in a corner, a poor, emaciated, worn-out creature, whose life was nearly gone by consumption. The captain advanced, and spoke to him kindly. "Oh, sir," said the shivering invalid, looking up, "are you the captain, and will you take me? You see, sir, I am dying; but oh! if I am spared to reach my mother, I shall die happy. She lives in Burlington, sir, and my journey is more than half performed. I am a poor painter, and the only child of her in whose arms I wish to die!"

"You shall go," replied the captain, "if I loose every other passenger for the trip." A moment more, and the passengers beheld him coming from the cars with the sick man cradled in his arms. Pushing directly through the crowd with his dying burden, he ordered a mattress to be spread in the choicest part of the boat, where he laid the invalid with all the care of a parent. That done, the captain directed the boat to be prepared for starting.

But a new feeling seemed to possess the astonished passengers— that of shame and contrition at their inhumanity. A purse was made up by them for the sick man, with a "God-speed" on his way home, to die in the arms of his mother.

Do unto others as you would have others to do unto you.

(c)—The Generous Neighbor.

A fire having broken out in a certain village of Denmark, one of the inhabitants, a poor man, was very active in affording assistance; but every endeavor to extinguish the flames was in vain. At length he was told that his own house was in danger from the flames, and that if he wished to save his furniture, not a moment was to be lost. "There is something more precious," replied he, "that I must first save. My poor, sick neighbor is not able to save himself; he will be lost if I do not assist him; I am sure he relies on me." He flew to his neighbor's house, rushed at once at the hazard of his life through the flames and conveyed the sick man in his arms to a place of safety. A society at Copenhagen showed their approbation of his conduct by presenting him with a silver cup, filled with Danish crowns.

(d)—A Brave Boy.

A boy in New Jersey, at various times, saved four lives before he was ten years old. When a little over eight years old, he saw his younger brother break through the ice, where the water was four feet deep. He had to run twelve or fifteen yards to reach the pond; and remembering having heard his mother read a story of a person saving another's life by creeping, because the ice was not strong enough for him to walk upon it, crept to the hole where his brother had broken through, reached into the water, and pulled him out by the hair, after he had sunk for the third time. Creeping backward, he drew the rescued sufferer to the shore.

After this he saved the lives of three boys at the same pond; and in one of these instances showed as much presence of mind, as any grown person could. Seeing the ice was too thin to bear him, he tried to borrow a sled of a boy near by, who refused it; but, pushing the boy over, he seized the sled, and shoved it to the sinking lad, who caught hold of it, and he, holding by the string, pulled him to the shore.

(e)—J. Howard.

John Howard, a wealthy Englishman, at the age of 28, set sail for Lisbon, in order to carry relief to the surviving sufferers of the terrible earthquake that devastated that city in 1755. England and France being at war at that time, the ship in which he sailed was captured by the French, and carried into the port of Brest. Being made prisoner with the officers and crew, he was put into prison, and treated with the utmost cruelty.

This was his first experience of prison life. Upon his release he returned to England. He spent much time and money in schemes of benevolence. Assisted by his noble wife they built improved cottages, established schools, administered to the sick, and relieved the necessitous. In 1773 he was elected Sheriff of Bedford. He thus became officially acquainted with the condition of the prisons of his county. He found them dark, damp, badly ventilated, and cruelly managed. From his own county, he proceeded through England, inspecting the jails, and found them, invariably, in the same state of corruption.

The observation of such misery, and the hope that he could be instrumental in relieving it, determined his course for life. The inspection and reformation of prisons now became his business. From England he traveled over the whole of Europe, seeking admission into the most dismal, loathsome, and dangerous dungeons, that he might report their condition, and have them reformed. His life was the forfeit of his benevolence. He died at Cherson, in the South of Russia, in 1790, from a disease contracted in visiting a prison. The publication of his work on prisons stirred up a spirit of philanthropy.

(f)—The Chieftain's Daughter.

Upon the barren sand
   A single captive stood;
Around him came, with bow and brand
   The red men of the wood.
Like him of old, his doom he hears,
   Rock-bound on ocean's brim;
The chieftain's daughter knelt in tears
   And sobbed and prayed for him.

Above his head in air
   The savage war-club swung,
The frantic girl, in wild despair,
   Her arms around him flung.
Then shook the warriors of the shade,
   Like leaves on aspen limb,—
Subdued by that heroic maid,
   Who breathed a prayer for him.

"Unbind him!" gasped the chief,
"Obey your king's decree!"
He kissed away her tears of grief,
And set the captive free.
'Tis ever thus, when in life's storm
Hope's star to man grows dim,
An angel kneels in woman's form,
And breathes a prayer for him.
—G. P. Morris.

(g)—Thomson and Quin.

When Thomson, author of the Seasons, first came to London, he was in very narrow circumstances, and, before he was distinguished by his writings, was many times put to his shifts even for a dinner. The debts he then contracted lay very heavy upon him for a long time afterwards; and upon the publication of his Seasons, one of his creditors arrested him, thinking that a proper opportunity to get his money. The report of this misfortune happened to reach the ears of the celebrated actor *Quin*, who had indeed read the Seasons, but had never seen their author; and upon stricter inquiry he was told that Thomson was in the bailiff's hands in sponging-house; thither Quin went, and being admitted into his chamber, "Sir," said he, "you don't know me, I believe, my name is Quin." Thomson received him politely and said: that though he could not boast of the honor of a personal acquaintance, he was no stranger either to his name or merit, and Quin then told him he was come to sup with him, and that he had already ordered the cook to provide a supper. Thomson made the proper reply, and the discourse turned indifferently on subjects of literature. When supper was over, Mr. Quin said to him: "It i now time to enter upon business. Sir, I am in your debt. I owe you a hundred pounds, and am come to pay you (laying a bank note of that value before him). Thomson was astonished, and begged he would explain himself. "Why," said Quin, "I'll tell you: Soon after I had read the Seasons, I took it into my head that, as I had something in the world to leave behind me when I died, I would make my will; and among the rest of my legatees I set down the author of the Seasons a hundred pounds; and this day hearing that you were in this house, I thought I might as well have the pleasure of paying you the money myself, as to order my executors to pay it, when perhaps you might have less need of it: and this, Mr. Thomson, is the business I came about." It were needless to express Thomson's grateful acknowledgements, but we leave every reader to conceive them.

(h)—Little and Great.

A traveler through a dusty road
Strewed acorns on the lea;
And one took root, and sprouted up,
And grew into a tree.
Love sought its shade at evening-time,
To breathe its early vows,
And Age was pleased in heats of noon,
To bask beneath its bows;
The dormouse loved its tangling twigs,
The birds sweet music bore;
It stood a glory in its place,
A blessing evermore.

A little spring had lost its way
Amid the grass and fern;
A passing stranger scooped a well
Where weary men might turn.
He walled it in, and hung with care
A ladle at the brink.
He thought not of the deed he did,
But judged that Toil might drink;
He passed again, and lo! the well,
By summers never dried,
Had cooled ten thousand parching tongues,
And saved a life beside.

A dreamer dropped a random thought,
'Twas old,—and yet 'twas new:
A simple fancy of the brain,
But strong in being true.
It shone upon a genial mind,
And lo! its light became
A lamp of life, a beacon ray,
A monitory flame.
The thought was small,—its issue great:
A watchfire on the hill,
It shed its radiance far adown,
And cheers the valley still.

> O germ! O fount! O word of love!
> O thought at random cast!
> Ye were but little at the first!
> But mighty at the last!
>
> —*Chas. Mackay.*

(1)—St. Phillis.

St. Phillis was a virgin of noble parentage, but withal as simple as any shepherdess of curds-and-cream. She married a wealthy Lord, and had much pin-money. But when other ladies wore diamonds and pearls, St. Phillis only wore a red and white rose in her hair. Yet her pin-money bought the best of jewelry in the happy eyes of the poor about her. St. Phillis was rewarded. She lived until four-score, and still carried the red and white rose in her face, and left their fragrance in her memory.—*Douglas Jerrold.*

2. Retribution.

(a)—The Dove and the Ant.

The Ant, compelled by thirst, went to drink in a clear, purling rivulet; but the current, with its circling eddy, snatched her away, and carried her down the stream. A dove, pitying her distressed condition, cropt a branch from a neighboring tree, and let it fall into the water, by means of which the ant saved herself, and got ashore. Not long after, a fowler having a design against the dove, planted his nets in due order, without the bird's observing what he was about; which the ant, perceiving, just as he was going to put his design into execution, she bit him by the heel, and made him give so sudden a start, that the dove took the alarm, and flew away.

One good turn deserves another.—*Æsop.*

(b)—The Hawk and the Farmer.

A hawk, pursuing a pigeon over a wheat-field with great eagerness and force, threw himself into a net which a husbandman had placed there to take the crows; who being not far off, and seeing the hawk fluttering in the net, came and took him; but just as he was going to kill him, the hawk besought him to let him go, assuring him that he was only following the pigeon, and neither intended nor had done any harm to him. To whom the farmer replied: "And what harm had the poor pigeon done to you?" Upon which he wrung his head off immediately.

As we do to others, we are done by them.—*Æsop.*

(e)—"We" and "You."

As two young friends were walking out, one day,
    (So *Florian** has told)
They chanced to see, before them, in the way
    A well-filled purse of gold.
"By Jove! a pretty prize for us!" cried *Ned;*
    While *Tom* with hasty hand
Was pocketing the purse. "For *us?*" he said;
    "I do not understand
Your meaning, sir; for *me*, sir! that's the word!"
    (Joy beaming in his face.)
"Considering how the incident occurred,
    "'*Us*' isn't in the case!"
"Well,—be it so!" the other made reply;
    Although 'tis hardly fair;
I am not anxious, sir,—indeed, not I,
    Your treasure-trove** to share!"
Just then, two robbers plainly they espied
    In waiting to accost
Our travelers,—when Tom, a-tremble, cried,
    "Ah! brother, we are lost!"
"We?" answered Ned, "O, *we* have naught to fear,
    'Tis *you* the rogues must face;
You,—*you*, my boy! To me 'tis very clear
    'We' isn't in the case!"
And at the word away the fellow ran,
    When rushing from the wood,
The thieves attacked the unresisting man,
    Who, pale with terror, stood
The while they robbed him of his precious purse,
    Too weak for flight or strife,—
No friend to aid him—and (O sad reverse!)
    In peril of his life!
So wags the world!—where oft the selfish "*we*"
    Seems fated to forget
The time may come when e'en the humblest "ye"
    May pay a friendly debt.
The prosperous man who but himself regards,
    May chance to change his tone,
When Fortune leaves him to his losing cards,
    Unpitied and alone!
                                      —*J. Godfrey Saxe.*

*A renowned French fablist.
**Derived from the French word "trouve"—the found treasure.

3. Meekness and Forbearance.

(a)—Chang King.

Chang King was President of the High Court of criminal cases, and being obliged to make on the following day his report to the Emperor (of China) upon an affair of consequence, which fell out in the evening, he called for a Secretary, and drew up the writings, which employed him until midnight. Having finished his papers, he was thinking to take repose, when the Secretary, by accident, struck the candle and threw it down. The fire caught the papers, burnt part of them, and the tallow spoiled the rest. The Secretary was exceedingly sorrowful, and fell on his knees to ask forgiveness for the offense. "It is an accident," said the President, mildly, "rise and let us begin anew!"

(b)—The Turkey and the Ant.

In other men we faults can spy,
And blame the mote that dims their eye;
Each little speck and blemish find,
To our own stronger errors blind.

  A turkey, tired of common food,
Forsook the barn, and sought the wood:
Behind her ran an infant train,
Collecting here and there a grain.
"Draw near, my birds! (the mother cries)
This hill delicious food supplies.
Behold the busy negro race,
See millions blacken all the place!
Fear not; like me with freedom eat;
An ant is most delightful meat.
How bless'd, how envied, were our life,
Could we but 'scape the poulterer's knife!
But man, curs'd man, on turkeys preys,
And Christmas shortens all our days,
Sometimes with oysters we combine,
Sometimes assist the savory chine;
From the low peasant to the lord,
The turkey smokes on every board.
Sure men for gluttony are curs'd,
Of the seven deadly sins the worst."

An ant, who climbed beyond his reach,
Thus answer'd from a neighb'ring beach:
" E'er you remark another's sin,
Bid thy own conscience look within;
Control thy more voracious bill,
Nor for a breakfast nations kill!"

—*John Gay.*

4. Politeness—Sham-Politeness.

(a)—Washington.

Captain Stephen Trowbridge tells the following incident of Washington's visit to Milford, N. H., in 1790: "While the latter was walking about the town, attended by a number of his officers, a colored soldier, who had fought under him, and lost a limb in his service, made his way up to the General and saluted him. Washington turned to his colored soldier, shook hands with him, and gave him a present of a silver dollar. One of the attendants objected to the civilities thus shown by the President of the United States to such an humble person, but Washington rebuked him sharply, asking if he should 'permit this colored man to excel in politeness.'"

(b)—Domestic Asides: or, Truth in Parentheses.

" I really take it very kind,
This visit, Mrs. Skinner!
I have not seen you in an age—
(The wretch has come to dinner!)

" Your daughters, too, what loves of girls—
What heads for painters' easels!
Come here and kiss the infant, dears,—
(And give it p'r'aps the measles!)

" Your charming boys I see are home
From Reverend Mr. Russell's;
'Twas very kind to bring them both,—
(What boots for my new Brussels!)

" What! Little Clara left at home?
Well now I call that shabby;
I should have loved to kiss her so,—
(A flabby, dabby, babby!)

"And Mr. Skinner, I hope he's well,
Ah! though he lives so handy,
He never now drops in to sup,—
(The better for our brandy!)

" Come, take a seat—I long to hear
About Matilda's marriage!
You're come of course to spend the day!—
(I thank Heaven, I hear the carriage!)

" What! Must you go? Next time I hope
You'll give me longer measure;
Nay—I shall see you down the stairs—
(With most uncommon pleasure!)

" Good-bye! Good-bye! Remember all,
Next time you'll take your dinners!
(Now, David, mind I'm not at home
In future to the Skinners!")
—*Thomas Hood.*

5. Sacrifice of Life by Charity—Voltamad.

During a violent gale at the Cape of Good Hope, a vessel was dragged from her moorings, driven upon the rocks, and completely wrecked. The crew were seen struggling for their lives, and clinging to the broken spars and rigging. The sea ran fearfully high, and broke over the poor sailors with such a fury, that no boatman dared venture to their assistance.

Meanwhile a planter, by the name of *Voltamad*, who was advanced in years, had rode from the fields to be a spectator of the distressing scene. His heart yearned at the suffering of the unhappy seamen, and knowing the bold spirit of his horse, and his great skill in swimming, he instantly determined to make a desperate effort for their deliverance.

He alighted, and after blowing some spirits into the nostrils of the gallant steed, remounted, and instantly plunged into the midst of the breakers. At first, both disappeared, but were soon after seen swimming for the wreck; on reaching which, he took two of the men, one on each side, and brought them in safety to the shore.

This perilous expedition was repeated seven times, whereby fourteen lives were saved. On returning for the eighth time, the horse being fatigued, and meeting a most formidable wave, the old man lost his balance, and was overwhelmed in a moment. The horse swam to the shore; but his gallant and humane rider was seen no more.

The East India Directors in Holland, on receiving the intelligence of this affair, raised a monument to his memory. They called one of their ships after his name, and wrote to the Regency of the Cape, ordering, that in case Voltamad had left any children, they should be provided with handsome fortunes without delay.

6. Filial Love.

(a)—The Good Indian Son.

Some years ago a gentleman, being on the banks of the Kennebec River, saw an Indian coming across in his canoe He had his family with him, consisting of his wife and a very aged woman, whom he had carefully covered with a blanket. His name was Quenockross; he had been wounded in battle and was lame in one of his feet. When he reached the shore, he kindled a fire, and then took the aged woman out of the canoe in his arms, and laid her down very tenderly by it. He then cooked some food, and gave it to her. This woman was his mother.

(b)—Volney Beckner.

Volney Beckner was a boy of twelve years of age, and was engaged, with his father, on board of an English vessel. One day the child of a passenger, a little girl, fell into the ocean. The father of Volney, who happened to be present, plunged after her, and soon caught her by her clothes, when he saw that he was pursued by a terrible shark. The crew aimed blows at the monster with the harpoon, but did not hit it. At that instant the young Volney plunges into the billows, armed with a sharp sabre, he swims to the shark, glides under him, and plunges the steel up to the handle in his body. His desire to save his father imparts strength to his arm. It is against the boy that the shark now turns his rage. Volney avoids his antagonist, and deals new blows at him.

During the combat some one had thrown several ropes from the deck. The father and son each seized one. The spectators were overjoyed; they believed the three were almost out of danger. But alas! the next moment the furious monster made a last and desperate effort. He plunged down in order to make a more vigorous leap; then, dashing out of the water, and raising his huge jaws he took in half of the body of the young Volney, and separated it from the other half, which remained hanging to the rope! This horrible spectacle froze every heart with terror. Beckner, the father, succeeded in getting on board the vessel, his son having saved his life and that of the child, by perishing himself.

(c)—Self-Sacrifice of a Daughter.

When the ill-fated steamer Henry Clay struck the shore of the Hudson river, 1852, a mother and her daughter (who were on board) were clinging to each other, contemplating with dismay their slender prospect of reaching land from the stern of the boat, which lay far out in the water. As the progress of the flames was driving them to the fatal leap from the wreck, a friend came up and leaning over the daughter—as though to impart to the more youthful of the two the small chance of life which remained—announced that he would do everything in his power to aid them, but that it was scarcely possible for him to save more than one of the two. The noble daughter was neither overcome by the terror nor shaken by the temptation of that trying hour. Her determination was instantly formed. She turned to her mother, and breathing one farewell word, before her intention could be divined, or her action anticipated, she plunged into the river; and thus she perished, resigning her chance of escape to the parent whom she loved better than life.

(d)—The Children's Hour.

Between the dark and daylight,
When the night begins to lower,
Comes a pause in the day's occupations
That is known as the Children's Hour.

I hear in the chamber above me
The patter of little feet,
And the sound of a door that is opened,
And voices soft and sweet.

From my study I see in the lamp-light,
Descending the broad hall stair,
Grave Alice, and laughing Allegra,
And Edith with golden hair.

A whisper, and then a silence,
Yet I know by their merry eyes
They are plotting and planning together
To take me by surprise.

A sudden rush from the stairway,
A sudden raid from the hall!
By three doors left unguarded
They enter my castle wall!

They climb up in my turret
O'er the arms and back of my chair;
If I try to escape, they surround me;
They seem to be everywhere.

They almost devour me with kisses,
Their arms about me entwine,
Till I think of the Bishop of Bingen
In his Mouse-Tower on the Rhine.*

Do you think, O blue-eyed banditti,
Because you have scaled the wall,
Such an old mustache as I am
Is not a match for you all?

I have you fast in my fortress,
And will not let you depart,
But put you down into the dungeon,
In the round-tower of my heart.

And there I will keep you forever,
Yes, forever and a day,
Till the walls shall crumble to ruin,
And moulder in dust away!

—*H. W. Longfellow.*

(e)—Filial Piety.

The Roman history furnishes us with a remarkable example of filial piety. A lady of illustrious birth had for some cause been condemned to be strangled, and was sent to prison in order to be put to death. The jailer, who had received orders to strangle her, was touched with compassion for her beauty and misfortunes, and not being able to resolve to kill her, determined to let her die of hunger. He however consented to allow her daughter to visit her in

---

*Bingen, a German town on the Rhine, where the river is compressed into a narrow strait, between towering rocks. High above them all soars the Mice-Tower (der Maeusethrum), so called from the popular belief that Archbishop Hatto of Metz, who used it as a granary for speculative purposes during times of famine, was gnawed to death there by mice in 969.

the prison, taking care that she brought her mother no food. Many days elapsed, during which the daughter's visits were very frequent. At length the jailer became surprised that his prisoner could exist so long without sustenance. His suspicions immediately rested on the daughter, whom he now determined to watch still more closely. To his utmost astonishment he found that she nourished her mother with her own milk. His amazement at this pious and ingenious invention caused him to inform the Triumvir of the circumstance, who immediately acquainted the Preator with it. The latter, considering it worthy the public attention, related it to an assembly of the people. The result was the pardon of the criminal; and, at the same time, a decree was passed that for the future both mother and daughter should be supported at the public expense. The Romans also raised a temple upon the spot, and dedicated it to *Filial Piety*.

7. Filial Obedience—The Wolf and the Kid.

The goat, going abroad to feed, shut up her young kid at home, charging him to bolt the door fast, and open it to nobody, till she herself should return. The wolf, who lay lurking just by, heard this charge given, and soon after came and knocked at the door, counterfeiting the voice of the goat, and desiring to be admitted. The kid, looking out at the window and finding the cheat, bid him go about his business; for, however he might imitate a goat's voice, yet he appeared too much like a wolf to be trusted.

Children do wisely by obeying their parents.—*Esop*.

8. Love of Brothers and Sisters.
(a)—The Courageous Brother.

A boy in the town of Weser, in Germany, playing one day with his sister, four years of age, was alarmed by the cry of some men who were in pursuit of a mad dog. The boy, suddenly looking round, saw the dog running towards him, but, instead of making his escape, he calmly took off his coat and, wrapping it round his arm, boldly faced the dog. Holding out the arm covered with the coat, the animal attacked it and worried it, until the men came up and killed the dog. The men reproachfully asked the boy why he did not run and avoid the dog, which he could so easily have done.

"Yes," said the little hero, "I could have run from the dog, but if I had, he would have attacked my sister. To protect her, I offered him my coat that he might tear it."

(b)—The Heroine Emma Carroll.

A similar case of heroism occurred in the city of Evansville, Indiana, in which Emma Carroll, a little girl eleven years old, ran through the flames of burning kerosene, and rescued, at the expense of her life, her motherless baby brother, of whom she had the care. In the terrible agony of her dying hours she was consoled with the thought that the baby had escaped unharmed. She had saved him.

(c)—Stanzas, addressed by Lord Byron to His Sister.

Though the day of my destiny's over,
    And the star of my fate hath declined,*
Thy soft heart refused to discover
    The faults which so many could find;
Though thy soul with my grief was acquainted,
    It shrank not to share it with me,
And the love which my spirit hath painted
    It never hath found but in *thee*.

Then when nature around me is smiling,
    The last smile which answers to mine,
I do not believe it beguiling
    Because it reminds me of thine;
And when winds are at war with the ocean,
    As the breasts I believed in with me,
If their billows excite an emotion,
    It is that they bear me from *thee*.

Though human, thou didst not deceive me,
    Though woman, thou didst not forsake,
Though loved, thou foreborest to grieve me,
    Though slander'd, thou never couldst shake,
Though trusted, thou didst not disclaim me,
    Though parted, it was not to fly,
Though watchful, 'twas not to defame me,
    Nor, mute, that the words might belie.

---

*By request of his wife and her friends, he was divorced from her, and also separated from his daughter Ada, by these sad accidents the star of his fate had declined. He exiled himself, and lived in Italy and Greece.

Yet I blame not the world, nor despise it,
  Nor the war of the many with one—
If my soul was not fitted to prize it,
  'Twas folly not sooner to shun;
And if dearly that error hath cost me,
  And more than I once could forsee,
I have found that, whatever it lost me,
  It could not deprive me of *thee*.

From the wreck of the past, which has perish'd,
  Thus much I at least may recall,
It hath taught me that what I most cherish'd,
  Deserved to be dearest of all :
In the desert a fountain is springing,
  In the wide waste there still is a tree,
And a bird in the solitude singing,
  Which speaks to my spirit of *thee*.

(d)—Isabella, the Suitor for a Condemned Brother.

Second Scene of the Second Act in Shakespeare's Play, "Measure for Measure."

ANGELO. Deputy of the Duke of Austria.
ISABELLA, Sister of CLAUDIO.

Isab. I am a woeful suitor to your honor,
Please but your honor hear me.
　　Ang.　　　　　　Well, what's your suit ?
　　Isab. I have a brother is condemn'd to die.
I beseech you, let it be his fault
And not my brother.
　　Ang. Condemn the fault, and not the actor of it ?
Why, every fault's condemn'd ere it is done.
Mine were the very cipher of a function
To fine the faults whose fine stands in record,
And let go by the actor.
　　Isab. O just, but severe law !
I *had* a brother then,—Heaven keep your honor !
Must he needs die ?
　　Ang.　　　　　　Maiden, no remedy.
　　Isab. Yes ; I do think that you might pardon him,
And neither Heaven, nor men, grieve at the mercy.
　　Ang. I will not do't.

---

*Claudio had married a young lady without the consent of an unjust, antiquated law, which was neglected, and out of use since many years ; but the Deputy of the Duke wants it to be executed in the case of Claudio, because he is " newly in seat, and that people may know he can command " According to this law Claudio should die.

  Isab.   But *can* you, if you *would?*
  Ang.   Look; what I *will* not, that I *cannot* do.
  Isab.   But might you do't, and do the world no wrong,
If so your heart were touch'd with that remorse*
As mine is to him?
  Ang.   He's sentenced; 'tis too late.
  Isab.   Too late? Why, no? I, that do speak a word,
May call it back again: well, believe this;
No ceremony** that to great ones 'longs,
Not the king's crown, nor the deputied sword,
The marshal's truncheon, nor the judge's robe,
Become them with one half so good a grace
As mercy does.
If he had been as you, and you as he,
You would have slipp'd like him; but he like you
Would not have been so stern.
  Ang.   Pray you, be gone.
  Isab.   I would to Heaven I had your potency,
And you were I! Should it then be thus?
No, I would tell what 't were to be a judge,
And what a prisoner.
  Ang.   Your brother is a forfeit of the law,
And you but waste your words.
  Isab.   Alas! Alas! How would you be,
If He, which is the top of judgment should
But judge you as you are? O think on that,
And mercy then will breathe within your lips
Like man new made!
  Ang.   Be you content, fair maid.
It is the law, not I, condemns your brother;
Were he my kinsman, brother, or my son,
It should be thus with him: he must die to-morrow.
  Isab.   To-morrow? O that's sudden! Spare him, spare him!
He's not prepared for death. Even for our kitchens
We prepare the fowl of season; shall we serve Heaven
With less respect than we do minister
To our gross selves? Good, Good my lord, bethink you:
Who is it that hath di'd for this offence?
There's many have committed it.
  Ang.   The law hath not-been dead, though it hath slept;
Those many had not dar'd to do that evil,

---

 *Compassion.   **Emblem of power.

It but the first that did th' edict infringe,
Had answer'd for his deed.
  Isab.   Yet show some pity.
  Ang. I show it most of all when I show justice.
            Be satisfied:
Your brother dies to-morrow: be content!
  Isab. So you must be the first that gives this sentence,
And he that suffers. O! it is excellent
To have a giant's strength; but it is tyrannous
To use it like a giant. Could great men thunder
As Jove himself does, Jove would ne'er be quiet;
For every pelting, petty officer
Would use his heaven for thunder;
Nothing but thunder. Merciful Heaven!
Thou rather with thy sharp and sulphurous bolt
Split'st the unwedgeable and gnarled oak,
Than the soft myrtle; but man, proud man,
Dress'd in a little brief authority,
Most ignorant of what he's most assur'd,—
His glassy essence,—like an angry ape,
Plays such fantastic tricks before high Heaven,
As makes the angels weep. Go to your bosom;
Knock there, and ask your heart what it doth know
That's like my brother's fault: if it confess
A natural guiltiness, such as is his,
Let it not sound a thought upon your tongue
Against my brother's life.
  Ang. [*Aside.*]   She speaks, and 't is
Such sense that my sense breeds with it. [*To her.*]
Fare you well.
  Isab. Gentle my lord, turn back.
  Ang. I will bethink me,—come again to-morrow.
  Isab. Hark, how I'll bribe you. Good my lord, turn back.
  Ang. How! Bribe me?
  Isab. Ay, with such gifts that Heaven shall share with you.
Not with fond shekels* of the tested gold,
Or stones, whose rates are either rich or poor,
As fancy values them; but with true prayers
That shall be up at Heaven, and enter there
Ere sun-rise: prayers from preserved souls,

---

*Shekel, a gold coin, which was in use among the Jews.

From fasting maids, whose minds are dedicate
To nothing temporal.
    Ang.   Well; come to me to-morrow.
    Isab.   Heaven keep your honor safe.
    Ang. [*Aside.*]   Amen!
    Isab.   At what hour to-morrow
Shall I attend your lordship?
    Ang.   At any time 'fore noon.
    Isab.   Save your honor! [*Exit.*

9. Friendship.

(a)—Damon and Pythias.

Damon and Pythias (or Phintias) are the names of two celebrated Syracusans, which are always joined as the types of true and noble friendship. They were both Pythagoreans, and united to each other in the strictest ties of friendship they had naturally sworn to observe with inviolable fidelity, which was put to a severe trial.

Pythias was condemned to death by Dionysius, the Tyrant of Syracuse (about 405 a. C.), but petitioned for permission to make a journey into his own country to settle the marriage-contract of his sister, promising to procure a friend to take his place, and suffer his punishment, if he would not return after three days. The King granted his request. Damon generously agreed to be his security, and Pythias set out on his journey. The courtiers, and Dionysius in particular, awaited with impatience the event of so delicate and extraordinary an adventure.

Before the dawning of the third day, Pythias had united the sister with the husband, and made speed to return home, in order to arrive in due time. Meanwhile torrents of rain deluged the country, and carried off all bridges. This and other accidents prolonged his voyage; he did not make his appearance in town at the preconcerted time. The Tyrant derided the rash and imprudent zeal by which Damon had bound himself in such a manner; but far from expressing any fear or concern, Damon replied with tranquility in his looks and confidence in his expressions, that he was assured that his friend would return. At last Pythias arrived at the town-gate, where the cross was already raised, and Damon dragged up. "Stop! hangman!" cried Pythias, " here I am, for whom he was bondsman!" The people were much surprised by the sudden appearance of Pythias. The friends embraced each other, crying from joy and grief. There was no eye empty of tears. The wonderful news was immediately reported to the King; he was struck by sympathy and admiration; softened by the instance of such rare fidelity, he granted Pythias his life, and even desired to be admitted into the union of their friendship.

(b)—The Hare and Many Friends.

Friendship, like love, is but a name,
Unless to one you stint the flame,
True friends are seldom; who depend
On many, rarely find a friend.

A hare who, in a civil way,
Complied with everything, like Gay,*

Was known by all the beastial train
Who haunt the wood or graze the plain;
Her care was never to offend,
And every creature was her friend.

As forth she went at early dawn,
To taste the dew-besprinkled lawn,
Behind she hears the hunter's cries,
And from the deep-mouth'd thunder flies;
She starts, she stops, she pants for breath,
She hears the near advance of death;
She doubles to mislead the hound,
And measures back her mazy round,
Till, fainting in the public way,
Half dead with fear she gasping lay.

What transport in her bosom grew,
When first the horse appear'd in view!
" Let me (says she) your back ascend,
And owe my safety to a friend.
You know my feet betray my flight;
To friendship every burthen 's light."

The horse replied: " Poor honest puss,
It grieves my heart to see thee thus.
Be comforted, relief is near;
For see, the goat is just in rear."

---

* "Gay (the poet of this fable) was of a timid temper, and fearful of giving offence to the great "—Pope. They disappointed the expectations he put in their promises.

The goat remarked her pulse was high,
Her languid head, her heavy eye:
"My bark (says he) may do you harm,
The sheep's at hand, and wool is warm."

The sheep was feeble, and complain'd
His sides a load of wool sustain'd;
Said he was slow; confess'd his fears;
For hounds eat sheep as well as hares.

She now the trotting calf address'd,
To save from death a friend distress'd;
" Shall I (says he), of tender age,
In this important care engage?
Older and abler pass'd you by;
How strong are those, how weak am I!
Should I presume to bear you hence,
Those friends of mine may take offence;
Excuse me, then! you know my heart;
But dearest friends, alas, must part.
How shall we all lament! Adieu,
For see, the hounds are just in view." —*John Gay.*

10. Bad Company—The Husbandman and the Stork.

Bad company is to be avoided!

The husbandman pitched a net in his field to take the cranes and geese who came to feed upon the new sown grain. Accordingly, he took several, both cranes and geese; and among them a stork, who had pleaded hard for his life, and, among other apologies which he made, alleged that he was neither goose nor crane, but a poor, harmless stork, who performed his duty to his parents to all intents and purposes, feeding them, when they were old, and, as occasion required, carrying them from place to place upon his back. " All this may be true," replies the husbandman, " but as I have taken you in bad company, and in the same crime, you must expect to suffer the same punishment."—*Esop.*

11. Gratitude to Benefactors—Ingratitude.

(a)—Thomas Cromwell.

Francis Frescobald, a Florentine merchant, had gained a plentiful fortune, of which he was liberal-handed to all in necessity; which being well known to others, a young stranger applied to him for charity. Signor Frescobald, seeing something in his countenance more than ordinary, overlooked his tattered clothes, and, compassionating his circumstances, asked him what he was, and of which country. "I am," answered the young man, "a native of England; my name is Thomas Cromwell. I left my country to seek my fortune; came with the French army, where I was page to a footman, and carried his pike and burganet after him." Frescobald commisserating his necessities, and having a particular respect for the English nation, clothed him genteelly, took him into his house till he had recovered strength by better diet, and, at his taking leave, mounted him on a good horse, with sixteen ducats of gold in his pockets. Cromwell expressed his thankfulness in a very sensible manner, and returned to England, where he was preferred into the service of Cardinal Wolsey.

After the Cardinal's death, he worked himself so effectually into the favor of King Henry VIII., that this one made him a Baron, Viscount, Earl of Essex, and, at last, Lord Chancellor of England.

In the meantime, Signor Francis, by repeated losses by sea and land, was reduced to poverty, and calling to mind, without ever thinking of Cromwell, that some English merchants were indebted to him in the sum of 15,000 ducats, he came to London to procure payment.

Traveling in pursuit of this affair, he fortunately met with the Lord Chancellor, as he was riding to court; who, thinking him to be the same gentleman that had done him such great kindness in Italy, asked him if he was not Signor Frescobald. "Yes, sir," said he, "and your most humble servant." "No," said the Chancellor, "you are not my servant, but my special friend, that relieved me in my wants, and laid the foundation of my greatness." He immediately alighted, embraced him with tears of joy, and took him in his company to his house. Frescobald having in a few words given him a true state of his circumstances, he led him to his closet, and opening a coffer, first took out sixteen ducats, delivering them to Frescobald, saying: "My friend, here is the money you lent me at Florence, with ten pieces you laid out for my apparel, and ten more you paid for my horse; but considering that you are a merchant, and might have made some advantage by this money in the way of trade, take these four bags, in every one of which are four hundred ducats, and enjoy them as free gifts of your friend.

He next caused him to give him the names of all of his debtors, and obliged them to pay their debts in fifteen days. During this time Frescobald lodged in the Chancellor's house, and was repeatedly invited to continue in England, and was offered a loan of 60,000 ducats for four years, if he would trade there; but he desired to return to Florence.

(b)—The Gardener and his Dog.

A gardener's dog, frisking about the brink of a well in the garden, happened to fall into it. The gardener very readily ran to his assistance; but as he was endeavoring to help him out, the cur bit him on the hand. The man took his ungrateful treatment so unkindly, that he left him to shift for himself, with this expostulation: "Wicked wretch," quoth he, "are you so unreasonable as to injure the hand that comes to save your life! The hand of me, your master, who has hitherto fed and taken care of you! Die as you deserve; for so mischievous and illnatured a creature is not fit to live."

All obligations you lay upon an ungrateful person are thrown away.—*Æsop*.

(c)—The Hart and the Vine.

A hart, being pursued hard by the hunters, hid himself under the broad leaves of a shady spreading vine. When the hunters were gone by, and given him over for lost, he, thinking himself very secure, began to crop and eat the leaves of the vine. By this means the branches, being put into a rustling motion, drew the eyes of the hunters that way, who seeing the vine stir, and fancying some wild beast had taked covert there, shot their arrows at a venture and killed the hart; who, before he expired, uttered his dying words to this purpose: "Ah! I suffer justly for my ingratitude, who could not forbear doing an injury to the vine that so kindly concealed me in time of danger."—*Æsop*.

(d.)—The Countryman and the Snake.

A villager, in a frosty, snowy winter, found a snake under a hedge almost dead with cold. He could not help having compassion for the poor creature, so he brought it home and laid it upon the hearth near the fire; but it had not lain there long before (being revived with the heat) it began to erect itself, fly at his wife and children, filling the whole cottage with dreadful hissings. The countryman hearing an outcry, and perceiving what the matter was, caught up a mattock, and soon dispatched him, upbraiding him at the same time in these words: "Is this, vile wretch, the reward you make to him that saved your life? Die, as you deserve; but a single death is too good for you."—*Æsop*.

12. Tolerance—Fanaticism—Religious Constancy.

(a)—William Penn.

William Penn was well educated and rich. He spent his money freely in aiding those who were punished for conscience's sake; and finally he resolved to found a colony in America, where such persecuted people could take refuge. It happened that his father had left, at his death, a claim for a large sum of money which he had lent to King Charles II., and W. Penn proposed to the King to give him a province in America, instead of the money. This the King was very glad to do. So William became the sole proprietor of a great tract of country which he called Pennsylvania (1682). He permitted every poor emigrant to settle on this land, and secured freedom of thought and speech to all. He called it a "free colony for all mankind," and declared to the people: "You shall be governed by laws of your own making. I shall not usurp the right of any, nor oppress his person. As the liberty of conscience is a right which all men have received of Nature with their existence, it is resolved that nobody will be compelled to assist any kind of public worship. To every one full power is granted to perform freely the public or private exercise of his religion, if he only confesses the belief in God and fulfills his civil duties." He gave the city which he laid out the name "Philadelphia," which means "brotherly love." The people governed themselves, choosing their own officers, and making their own laws. Every man who paid a tax had a right to vote, without regard to religious belief. No oath was required of witnesses in court.

(b)—Thomas Cranmer.

Thomas Cranmer, Archbishop of Canterbury, was the adviser and assistant of King Henry VIII., when he reformed the Church of England. He would neither recognize the supreme authority of the Pope, nor the real presence of Christ in the Holy Supper; and, in a word, he professed, in his writings, the Protestant faith. Therefore Queen *Mary,* who was herself Catholic, and married to the ill-famed Philip II., King of Spain, degraded him from the state of Lordship, deprived him of his Bishopric, and put him in prison. Here she ordered him to recant his heresies; he *did* recant. Nevertheless she sentenced him to be burned at the stake, and to recant once more. But now he did no longer obey her dictate; on the contrary, in his last moment of life, he declared to hold by all that he had written in his books. He was burned. The following scenes are taken from Alfred Tennyson's "Queen Mary," in the fourth act:

Scene Second. CRANMER *in prison.*
THOMAS CRANMER, THIRLBY, *Bishop of Ely.*

Cr. Weep not, good Thirlby.
Th. Oh, my lord, my lord!
My heart is no such block as Bonmer's* is:
Who would not weep?
Cr. Why do you so my-lord me,
Who am disgraced?
Th. On earth; but saved in heaven
By your recanting.
Cr. Will they burn me, Thirlby?
Th. Alas, they will; these burnings will not help
The purpose of the faith; but my poor voice
Against them is a whisper to the roar
Of a spring-tide.
Cr. And they will surely burn me?
Th. Ay; and besides, will have you in the church
Repeat your recantation in the ears
Of all men, to the saving of their souls,
Before your execution. May God help you
Thro' that hard hour!
Cr. And may God bless you, Thirlby! [*Exit Thirlby.*

---
* Edmund Bonmer, who formerly was Cranmer's friend, and had confessed the same doctrine as this, showed him now, when Cranmer was imprisoned, the cold shoulder.

Well, they shall hear my recantation there.
Disgraced, dishonored! Not by them, indeed,
By mine own self—by my own hand!
Fire—inch by inch to die in agony! *Latimer*
Had a brief end—not *Ridley*. *Hooper** burned
Three-quarters of an hour. Will my fagots
Be wet as his were? It is a day of rain.
I will not muse upon it.
My fancy takes the burner's part, and makes
The fire seem even crueller than it is.
No, I not doubt that God will give me strength,
Albeit I have denied him.
     Enter SOTO *and* VILLA GARCIA.
 V. G.   We are ready
To take you to St Mary's, Master Cranmer.
   Cr. And I: lead on; ye loose me from my bonds. [*Exeunt.*
    Scene Third—*St. Mary's Church.*
Father COLE *in the pulpit*, LORD WILLIAMS OF THAME *presiding*. LORD WILLIAM HOWARD, LORD PAGET *and others*. CRANMER *enters between* SOTO *and* VILLA GARCIA, *and the whole choir strike up* "*Nunc Dimittis.*"** CRANMER *is set upon a scaffold before the people.*
   Cole. Behold him! [*A pause; people in the foreground.*
   People. Oh, this unhappy sight.
   Cr. I shall declare to you my very faith
Without all color.
   Cole.   Hear him, my good brethren!
   Cr. I do believe in God, Father of all ;
In every article of the Catholic† faith
And every syllable taught us by our Lord,
His Prophets, and Apostles, in the Testaments,
Both Old and New.
   Cole.   Be plainer, Master Cranmer!
   Cr. And now I come to the great cause that weighs
Upon my conscience more than anything
Or said or done in all my life by me ;
For there be writings I have set abroad
Against the truth I knew within my heart,
Written for fear of death, to save my life,
If that might be; the papers by my hand

---

*These Protestants were burnt, before Cranmer, by Queen Mary.
**These words began a Psalm, and import : " Now, O God, you dismiss your servant by letting him die."
†Cranmer meant the *universal* faith of the primitive Christian Church.

           [*Holding out his right hand.*
Written and sign'd—*I here renounce them all;*
And, since my hand offended, having written
Against my heart, my hand shall first be burnt.
So I may come to the fire.   [*Dead silence.*
 Williams. [*Raising his voice.*]
You know that you recanted all you said
Touching the sacrament in that same book
You wrote against my Lord of Winchester;
Dissemble not; play the plain Christian man!
 Cr. Alas, my Lord,
I have been a man loved plainness all my life,
I *did* dissemble, but the hour has come
For utter truth and plainness; *wherefore I say,*
I hold to all I wrote within that book.
Moreover,
As for the Pope, I count him Antichrist,
With all his devil's doctrines; and refuse,
Reject him, and abhor him. I have said.
  [*Cries on all sides,* " *Pull him down! Away with him!*"
 Cole. Ay, stop the heretic's mouth! Hale him away!
 Williams. Harm him not, harm him not, have him to the fire!
CRANMER *goes out between two Friars smiling; hands are reached to him from the crowd.* LORD WILLIAM HOWARD *and* LORD PAGET *are left alone in the church.*
 Pag. The nave and aisles all empty as fool's jest!
No, here's Lord William Howard. What, my Lord,
You have not gone to see the burning?
 How.   Fie!
To stand at ease, and stare as at a show,
And watch a good man burning. Never again.
I saw the deaths of Latimer and Ridley.
Moreover, tho' a Catholic, I would not,
For the pure honor of our common nature,
Hear what I might—another recantation
Of Cranmer at the stake.
 Pag. You'd not hear that.
  Enter PETERS, *gentleman of* SIR HOWARD.
 How.   See
Peters, my gentleman, an honest Catholic,
Who follow'd with the crowd to Cranmer's fire
Peters, how pale you look! You bring the smoke
Of Cranmer's burning with you

Pet.   Twice or thrice
The smoke of Cranmer's burning wrapt me round.
    How. Peters, you know me Catholic, but English;
Did he die bravely? Tell me that, or leave
All else untold.
    Pet. My Lord, he died most bravely.
    How. Then tell me all.
    Pag. Ay, Master Peters, tell us.
    Pet. You saw him how he past among the crowd;
And ever as he walk'd the Spanish friars
Still plied him with entreaty and reproach;
But Cranmer, as the helmsman at the helm
Steers, ever looking to the happy haven
Where he shall rest at night, moved to his death;
And I could see that many silent hands
Came from the crowd, and met his own; and thus,
When we had come where Ridley burnt with Latimer,
He, with a cheerful smile, as one whose mind
Is all made up, in haste put off the rags
They had mock'd his misery with, and all in white,
His long, white beard, which he had never shaven
Since Henry's death, down-sweeping to the chain,
Wherewith they bound him to the stake, he stood,
More like an ancient father of the church,
Than heretic of these times; and still the friars
Plied him, but Cranmer only shook his head,
Or answer'd them in smiling negatives;
Whereat Lord Williams gave a sudden cry:—
"Make short! Make short!" And so they lit the wood.
Then Cranmer lifted his left hand to heaven,
And thrust his right into the bitter flame;
And crying, in his deep voice, more than once,
"*This hath offended! this unworthy hand!*"
So held it till it all was burn'd, before
The flame had reach'd his body. I stood near—
Mark'd him—he never uttered moan of pain;
He never stirr'd, or writhed, but, like a statue,
Moving in the greatness of the flame,
Gave up the ghost, and so past martyr-like.

(e)—**Roger Williams.**

Roger Williams was a Puritan, and a fugitive from English persecution; but his wrongs had not clouded his accurate understanding; he announced the doctrine of *the sanctity of conscience.* This doctrine would quench the fires that persecution had so long kept burning; would repeal every law compelling attendance on public worship; would abolish tithes and all forced contributions to the maintenance of religion; would give an equal protection to every form of religious faith. In the unwavering assertion of his views he never changed his position; the sanctity of conscience was the great tenet, which, with all its consequences, he defended, as he first trod the shores of New England; and in his extreme old age it was the last pulsation of his heart.

So soon as he arrived in Boston, he found himself among the the New England churches, but not of them. His principles led him into perpetual collision with the clergy and the Government of Massachusetts. The magistrates insisted on the presence of every man at public worship; Williams reprobated the law. The breach by and by widened more and more. Finally, summoned to appear before the General Court, Williams avowed his convictions in the presence of the representatives of the State. The Court pronounced against him the sentence of exile, and resolved to remove him to England in a ship that was just ready to set sail. A pinnace was sent for him; the officers repaired to his house; he was no longer there. Three days before, he had left Salem, in winter snow and inclement weather, of which he remembered the severity even in his late old age. For fourteen weeks he was sorely tossed in a bitter season, not knowing what bread or bed did mean. Often in the stormy night he had neither fire, nor food, nor company; often he wandered without a guide, and had no house but a hollow tree. But he was not without friends. When he came to the cabin of the chief of Pokanoket, he was welcomed by Massasoit. The Indians were "the ravens, who fed him in the wilderness." And in requital for their hospitality, he was ever through his long life their friend and benefactor. In a frail Indian canoe he embarked on the stream (the Seekonk river, called also Narraganset river), with five companions (in June, 1636). To express his unbroken confidence in the mercies of God, he called the place of his landing Providence. "I desired (said he), it might be for a shelter for persons distressed for conscience."— *George Bancroft, History of the United States, I, ch. 9, pp. 376.*

13. Love of Enemies—The Generous Quaker.

A Quaker, of exemplary character was disturbed at night by footsteps around his dwelling. He arose from his bed, and cautiously opened a back door to reconnoitre. Close by was an outhouse, and under it a cellar, near a window of which was a man busily engaged in receiving the contents of the pork barrel from another within the cellar. The old man approached, and the thief outside fled. He stepped to the cellar window and received the pieces of pork from the thief within, who after a little while asked the supposed accomplice, in a whisper, "Shall we take it all?" The owner of the pork said softly: "Yes, take it all," when the man industriously handed up the remainder through the window, and then came up himself. Imagine the consternation, when, instead of greeting his companion in crime, he was confronted by the Quaker. Both were astonished; for the thief proved to be a near neighbor, whom none would have suspected of such conduct. He pleaded for mercy, begged the old man not to expose him, spoke of the necessities of poverty, and promised never to steal again.

"If thou hadst asked me for meat," said the good Friend, "It would have been given thee. I pity thy poverty, thou art forgiven." The thief was greatly rejoiced, and was about to depart, when the old man said: "Take the pork, neighbor!" "No, no," said the thief, "I don't want your pork." "The necessity was so great that it led thee to steal; one-half of this pork thou must take with thee." The thief insisted that he could never eat a morsel of it; the thought of the crime would make it choke him. But the old man was inexorable, and furnished the thief with a bag, and one-half of the pork put therein, and laying it on his back, sent him home with it. He met his neighbor daily for many years afterwards, and their families visited together, but the matter was kept a secret.

CHAPTER SECOND.

RIGHTS AND DUTIES OF JUSTICE.

I. *Private Rights and Duties.*

1. Consequences of Murder—Lady Macbeth.

Macbeth, a Scottish nobleman, being himself the heir apparent to the throne, in case of King Duncan's death, during the minority of his sons, and instigated by his ambitious wife, kills with her aid his kinsman and his sovereign, usurps the crown, rules tyrannically, murders his General Banquo, slaughters the family of Macduff, Thane of Fife, who distrusts him, and is finally slain by Macduff. The consciousness of these foul deeds, of which Lady Macbeth was an accomplice, disturbed her mind and night's rest. Murder will out. Shakespeare illustrates this truth in his eminent tragedy, "Macbeth."

Act Fifth, Scene First.

[*Enter a Physician and a Waiting Gentlewoman.*]

Doctor. I have two nights watch'd with you, but can perceive no truth in your report. When was it she last walk'd?

Gentl. Since his Majesty went into the field, I have seen her rise from her bed, throw her night-gown upon her, unlock her closet, take forth paper, fold it, write upon't, read it, afterwards seal it, and again return to bed; yet all this while in a most fast sleep.

Doc. A great perturbation in nature,—to receive at once the benefit of sleep and do the effects of watching. In this slumb'ry agitation, besides her walking and other actual performances, what at any time have you heard her say?

Gentl. That, sir, which I will not report after her.

Doc. You may to me; and 'tis most meet you should.

Gentl. Neither to you, nor any one, having no witness to confirm my speech. [*Enter* LADY MACBETH, *with a taper.*] Lo you! here she comes, this is her very guise, and upon my life, fast asleep. Observe her; stand close.

Doc. How came she by that light?

Gentl. Why, it stood by her; she has light by her continually; 'tis her command.

Doc. You see, her eyes are open.

Gentl. Ay, but their sense is shut.

Doc. What is it she does now? Look how she rubs her hands.

Gentl. It is an accustom'd action with her to seem thus washing her hands; I have known her continue in this a quarter of an hour.

L. Macbeth. Yet here is a spot*.

Doc. Hark! She speaks. I will set down what comes from her, to satisfy my remembrance the more strongly.

L. Macbeth. Out, damned spot! Out, I say!—One, two; why, then 'tis time to do 't.—Hell is murky!—Fie! my lord, fie! A soldier, and afear'd? What need we fear who knows it, when none can call our power to account?—Yet who would have thought the old man to have had so much blood in him?

Doc. Do you mark that?

L. Macbeth. The Thane of Fife had a wife; where is she now? What, will these hands ne'er be clean?—No more o' that, my lord; no more o' that; you mar all with this starting.

Doc. Go to, go to; you have known what you should not.

Gentl. She has spoken what she should not, I am sure of that: Heaven knows what she has known.

L. Macbeth. Here's the smell of the blood still; all the perfumes of Arabia will not sweeten this little hand. Oh! oh! oh!

Doc. What a sigh is there! The heart is sorely charg'd.

Gentl. I would not have such a heart in my bosom for the dignity of the whole body.

Doc. Well, well, well.

Gentl. Pray God, it be, sir.

Doc. This disease is beyond my practice; yet I have known those which have walk'd in their sleep, who have died holily in their beds.

L. Macbeth. Wash your hands, put on your night-gown; look not so pale. I tell you yet again, Banquo's buried; he cannot come out on's grave.

Doc. Even so?

L. Macbeth. To bed, to bed; there's knocking at the gate. Come, come, come, give me your hand. What's done cannot be undone: to bed, to bed, to bed.** [*Exit.*]

Doc. Will she go now to bed?

Gentl. Directly.

    Doc. Foul whisp'rings are abroad. Unnatural deeds
    Do breed unnatural troubles; infected minds
    To their deaf pillows will discharge their secrets.

---

*After they had murdered Duncan, Lady Macbeth said to her husband: "My hands are of your color; but a little water clears us of this deed." (Act Second.)

**When Lady Macbeth heard the knocking at the door of the castle, she urged Macbeth to get on his night-gown, and to go to bed, "lest occasion call us, and shew us to be watchers." (Act Second.)

More needs she the divine than the physician.
God, God forgive us all! Look after her;
Remove from her the means of all annoyance,
And still keep eyes upon her. So, good night!
My mind she has mated,* and amaz'd my sight.
I think, but dare not speak.
    Gentl.   Good-night, good Doctor.   [*Exeunt.*]

2. Liberty—The Yankee Girl.

She sings by her wheel at that low cottage door,
Which the long evening shadow is stretching before,
With a music as sweet as the music which seems
Breathed softly and faint in the ear of our dreams.

How brilliant and mirthful the light of her eye,
Like a star glancing out from the blue of the sky!
And lightly and freely her dark tresses play
O'er a brow and a bosom as lovely as they.

Who comes in his pride to that low cottage door,—
The haughty and rich to the humble and poor?
'Tis the great Southern planter, the master who waves
His whip of dominion o'er hundreds of slaves.

"Nay, Ella, for shame! Let those Yankee fools spin,
Who would pass for our slaves with a change of their skin,
Let them toil as they will at the loom or the wheel,
Too stupid for shame, and too vulgar to feel!

"But thou art too lovely and precious a gem
To be bound to their burdens and sullied by them,—
For shame, Ella, shame,—cast thy bondage aside,
And away to the South, as my blessing and pride.

"O, come where no winter thy footsteps can wrong,
But where flowers are blossoming all the year long,
Where the shade of the palm-tree is over my home,
And the lemon and orange are white in their bloom!

"O, come to my home, where my servants shall all
Depart at thy bidding and come at thy call;
They shall heed thee as mistress with trembling and awe,
And each wish of thy heart shall be felt as a law."

----
* Astonished.

O, could ye have seen her,—that pride of our girls—
Arise and cast back the dark wealth of her curls,
With a scorn in her eye which the gazer could feel,
And a glance like the sunshine that flashes on steel!

"Go back, haughty Southron! thy treasures of gold
Are dim with the blood of the hearts thou hast sold;
Thy home may be lovely, but round it I hear
The crack of the whip and the footsteps of fear.

"And the sky of thy South may be brighter than ours,
And greener thy landscapes, and fairer thy flowers;
But dearer the blast round our mountains which raves,
Than the sweet summer zephyr which breathes over slaves.

"Full low at thy bidding thy negroes may kneel,
With the iron of bondage on spirit and heel;
Yet know that the Yankee girl sooner would be
In fetters with them, than in bondage with thee!
—J. G. Whittier.

3. Honesty—Fraud—Theft—Indemnification.

(a)—An Honest Boy.

Jean Baptiste Colbert, French Minister, in early life was an apprentice to a woolen-draper. In selling a piece of goods to a Parisian banker, he made through a mistake an overcharge of 630 francs, and received the amount of the bill. His knavish old master, on learning the fact, was delighted, and exclaimed: "You are a fine boy, Baptiste; you will one day be an honor to all your friends; 630 francs profit on the piece! Oh, happy day!" And he agreed to let Baptiste have something of the profits as a reward. But no sooner did the honest boy learn the mistake, and hear this remark of his master, than he replied: "How, godfather, would you take advantage?" and taking up his hat, he continued: "I will go to the gentleman whom I have treated so badly, beg him to excuse me, and return him the money he overpaid." And he immediately accomplished his honest resolution; and for so doing was turned out of employment. But this act of honesty became his first step to distinction. The next day, the rich banker, learning all the facts connected with the conduct of this honest boy, took him into his own banking-house. From that first step his career was upward in the road of usefulness and honor, till he was created "Comptroler General of Finance" by Louis XIV.

(b)—Mercury and the Woodman.

A man was felling a tree on the bank of a river, and by chance let his hatchet slip out of his hand, which dropped into the water, and immediately sunk to the bottom. Being, therefore, in great distress for the loss of his tool, he sat down and bemoaned himself most lamentably. Upon this Mercury appeared to him, and being informed of the cause of his complaint, dived to the bottom of the river, and coming up again, showed the man a golden hatchet, demanding if that were his. He denied that it was. Upon which Mercury dived a second time, and brought up a silver one. The man refused it, alleging likewise that this was not his. He dived a third time, and fetched up the individual hatchet the man had lost. Upon sight of which the poor wretch was overjoyed, and took it with all humility and thankfulness Mercury was so pleased with the fellow's honesty, that he gave him the other two into the bargain, as a reward for his just dealing. The man goes to his companions, and giving them an account of what had happened, one of them went presently to the river's side and let his hatchet fall designedly into the stream. Then sitting down upon the bank, he fell a weeping and lamenting, as if he had been really and sorely afflicted. Mercury appeared as before, and diving, brought him up a golden hatchet asking if that was the hatchet he lost. Transported by the precious metal, he answered: "Yes;" and went to snatch it greedily. But the god detesting his abominable impudence, not only refused to give him that, but would not so much as let him have his own hatchet again.

Honesty—the best policy!—*Æsop.*

(c)—The Starling.

An old huntsman named *Maurice* kept in his room a clever starling, that could speak several words. If e. g. his owner called out: "Starling, where are you?" the starling would always answer: "Here I am." Charles, the little son of a neighbor, had much fun with the bird, and paid him many visits. One day, when he came to see him, the hunter happened to be out of the room, Charles quickly caught the bird, put it in his pocket, and was about to sneak away with him. But at this moment Maurice came into the room. His intention was to give the boy the bird as a present, and, therefore, he called as usual: "Starling, where are you?" The bird called out from the pocket of the boy, as loud as he could: " Here I am !" Charles was forced to deliver the bird, and was roughly turned out of the hunter's house.

Theft, be it ever so slyly committed, often comes to light.

(d)—An Act of Indemnification.

A farmer residing a few miles from a large town, calling on one of the principal merchants in the place, stated that on a certain day, more than eleven years ago, he had passed on him a counterfeit ten-dollar bill. describing the note. The merchant who had always been in the habit of preserving in a small box all counterfeits, as well as the date of their reception, on referring to it, found the bill, as well as the date at which he had received it, corresponding with the farmer's words. The latter, on taking hold of the bill, tore it into fragments with apparent satisfaction, and desired that merchant to calculate the interest, which having been done, he paid the whole amount in good money.

4. Veracity—Lying—The Oath.

(a)—The Boy who Would Not Tell a Lie.

When George Washington was some seven or eight years old, his father gave him a hatchet; and like all boys who are suddenly made the owners of such a desirable possession, he began trying its edge on everything that came in his way. Unfortunately, however, he thoughtlessly chopped down one of his father's favorite young cherry trees, never dreaming of the mischief he had done, until Mr. Washington next day discovered it, and inquired for the culprit. As soon as the boy heard of the loss, and learned how highly his father had valued the tree, he came forward in a manly manner, though with great sorrow pictured on his countenance, and exclaimed: "I did it, father, with my hatchet; I cannot tell a lie." This so touched his father's heart, that he embraced his son most tenderly, while he declared how much more he valued this evidence of truthfulness than all the trees in his garden.

(b)—Gossip.

Said Gossip One to Gossip Two,
  While shopping in the town,
One Mrs. Pry to me remarked,
  "Smith bought his goods of Brown."

Says Gossip Two to Gossip Three,
  Who cast her eyelids down,
" I've heard it said to-day, my friend,
  Smith got his goods from Brown."

Says Gossip Three to Gossip Four,
  With something of a frown,
" I've heard strange news—what do you think?
  Smith took his goods from Brown."

Says Gossip Four to Gossip Five,
  Who blazed it round the town,
" I've heard to-day such shocking news—
  Smith stole his goods from Brown!"

(c)—Sacredness of Oath.

The respect with which the ancient Athenians revered the oath is very remarkable, as was exhibited in the case of *Euripides*. This great poet had introduced in one of his plays a person, who, being reminded of an oath he had taken, replied: " I swore with my mouth, but not with my heart." The impiety of this sentiment set the audience in an uproar; made Socrates leave the theatre with indignation, and gave so great offence that he was publicly accused, and brought upon his trial, as one who had suggested an evasion of what they thought the most holy and indissoluble bond of human society.

5. Love.

(a)—Love Conquers all Obstacles—Quintin Matsys.

Quintin Matsys, who was born near Antwerp in the year 1460, was the son of poor parents. His father was a blacksmith, and when the boy was some fourteen or fifteen years of age, he also learned this trade. After some years he was one of the best blacksmiths in town. When he was about twenty years old, he left this business, and devoted himself to the art of painting. There are several different stories about the reasons for his becoming a painter; perhaps the one nearest the truth is this: He became deeply in love with a lady, while pursuing his trade as a blacksmith, and the lady loved him. He asked her father his consent to their marriage. The old gentleman shook his head. He had nothing against Matsys, he said; "but my daughter must never marry any one who is not an artist. You are not a painter; you are nothing but a blacksmith." The young man's spirit was roused a little by this harsh answer, but he showed no signs of anger. His resolution was soon formed. He determined to become a painter, and then to claim the hand of her whom he loved. This resolution he made known to the young lady, who approved it, and, without informing any one else of his plan, he went to Haarlem, and placed himself under the tuition of a celebrated painter there. His genius and his love—so the story goes—conquered all obstacles, and after some two or three years he returned to Antwerp, and went directly to the house of the old painter, with one of his best pictures under his arm. He first met the lady of his choice. They went together into the studio of her father, who was not in the house at the time. There was hanging up against the wall a picture by the old gentleman, which he valued as one of his best efforts. That picture Matsys took down, drew on the face of one of the figures in it a very accurate representation of a bee, and placed the painting on the artist's easel, where he would be sure to see it, when he came in. Sure enough, he did see it, and eagerly inquired who had painted the bee. Matsys had stepped out of the room, and the daughter said it was done by an artist who had come from Haarlem to see him. "Who is it? Who is it?" he inquired, quite out of breath with impatience. "*Quintin Matsys*," said the daughter. The rest of the story is soon told. The lovers were married, of course.

(b)—Lavinia and Palemon.

The lovely young *Lavinia* once had friends;
And Fortune smiled, deceitful, on her birth.
For, in her helpless years deprived of all,
Of every stay, save Innocence and Heaven,
She, with her widow'd mother, feeble, old,
And poor, lived in a cottage, far retired,
Among the windings of a woody vale;

By solitude and deep surrounding shades,
But more by bashful modesty, conceal'd,—
Her form was fresher than the morning rose
When the dew wets its leaves; unstain'd and pure,
As is the lily on the mountain-snow.
　　　　　A native grace
Sat fair proportion'd on her polish'd limbs,
Veil'd in a simple robe, their best attire,
Beyond the pomp of dress; for loveliness
Needs not the foreign aid of ornament,
But is, when unadorn'd, adorn'd the most.
So flourish'd, blooming, and unseen by all,
The sweet Lavinia; till, at length, compell'd
By strong Necessity's supreme command,
With smiling patience in her looks, she went
To glean *Palemon's* fields. The pride of swains
Palemon was, the generous and the rich;
Who led the rural life in all its joy
And elegance, such as Arcadian song
Transmits from ancient uncorrupted times:
When tyrant custom had not shackled man,
But free to follow Nature was the mode.
He then, his fancy with autumnal scenes
Amusing, chanced beside his reaper-train
To walk, when poor Lavinia drew his eye;
Unconscious of her power, and turning quick
With unaffected blushes from his gaze:
He saw her charming, but he saw not half
The charms her down-cast modesty conceal'd;
And thus in secret to his soul he sigh'd:—
" What pity! that so delicate a form,
By beauty kindled, where enlivening sense
And more than vulgar goodness seem to dwell,
Should be devoted to the rude embrace
Of some indecent clown; she looks, methinks,
Of old Acasto's line; and to my mind
Recalls that patron of my happy life,
From whom my liberal fortune took its rise;
Now to the dust gone down; his houses, lands,
And once fair-spreading family, dissolved.
'Tis said, that in some lone obscure retreat
Urged by remembrance sad, and decent pride
Far from those scenes which knew their better days,

His aged widow and his daughter live,
Whom yet my fruitless search could never find,
Romantic wish! would this the daughter were!"

When, strict inquiring, from herself he found
She was the same, the daughter of his friend,
Of bountiful Acasto; who can speak
The mingled passions that surprised his heart:
And as he view'd her, ardent, o'er and o'er,
Love, gratitude, and pity wept at once.
Confused, and frighten'd at his sudden tears,
Her rising beauties flush'd a higher bloom,
As thus Palemon, passionate and just,
Pour'd out the pious rapture of his soul:
"And art thou then Acasto's dear remains?
She, whom my restless gratitude has sought,
So long in vain? O heavens! The very same,
The soften'd image of my noble friend,
Alive his every look, his every feature,
More elegantly touch'd. Sweeter than Spring!
Thou sole surviving blossom from the root
That nourish'd up my fortune! Say, ah where,
In what sequester'd desert hast thou drawn
The kindest aspect of delighted heaven?—
Ill it befits thee, oh, it ill befits
Acasto's daughter, his, whose open stores,
Though vast, were little to his ampler heart,
The father of a country, thus to pick
The very refuse of those harvest-fields
Which from his bounteous friendship I enjoy.
Then throw that shameful pittance from thy hand,
But ill appli'd to such a rugged task;
The fields, the master, all, my fair, are thine;
If to the various blessings which thy house
Has on me lavish'd, thou wilt add that bliss,
That dearest bliss, the power of blessing thee!"

Here ceased the youth: yet still his speaking eye
Express'd the sacred triumph of his soul,
With conscious virtue, gratitude and love,
Above the vulgar joy divinely raised.
Nor waited he reply. Won by the charm
Of goodness irresistible, and all
In sweet disorder lost, she blush'd consent.

> The news—immediate to her mother brought,
> While, pierced with anxious thought, she pined away
> The lonely moments for Lavinia's fate:
> Amazed, and scarce believing what she heard,
> Joy seized her wither'd veins, and one bright gleam
> Of setting life shone over her evening hours:
> Not less enraptured than the happy pair;
> Who flourish'd long in tender bliss, and rear'd
> A numerous offspring, lovely like themselves,
> And good, the grace of all the country round.
> —James Thomson, "The Seasons—Autumn," v. v. 177—310.

6. Master and Servant.—The Old Hound.

An old hound, who had been an excellent good one in his time, and given his master great sport and satisfaction in many a chase, at last, by the effect of years, became feeble and unserviceable. However, being in the field one day when the stag was almost run down, he happened to be the first that came in with him, and seized him by one of his haunches, but his decayed and broken teeth, not being able to keep their hold, the deer escaped and threw him quite out. Upon which, his master, being in a great passion, and going to strike him, the honest old creature is said to have barked out this apology: "Ah! Do not strike your poor old servant; it is not my heart and inclination, but my strength and speed that failed me. If what I now am displeases, pray don't forget what I have been."

It is inhumane to treat an old servant ill.—*Esop*

II. Public Rights and Duties.

1. Patriotism.

(a)—General J. Reed.

General Joseph Reed, of Pennsylvania, was intensely devoted to the interests of his country. The agents of George III. desired to bribe him to be a traitor to the cause of liberty; so Governor Johnston, one of the three commissioners of the King, secretly offered him £10,000 (about $50,000), and a public office, if he would engage to promote the British interests. To this impudent offer he nobly replied: "I am not worth purchasing, but such as I am, the King of Great Britain is not rich enough to buy me."

(b)—The Last Will.

An old man, of the name of Guyot, lived and died in the town of Marseilles, in France. By the most laborious industry, and the severest habits of abstinence, he amassed a large fortune. His neighbors considered him a miser, and thought he was hoarding up money from mean motives. In his will were found the following words: "Having observed, from my infancy that the poor of Marseilles are ill-supplied with water, which can only be purchased at a great price, I have cheerfully labored the whole of my life to procure them this great blessing; and I direct that the whole of my property shall be laid out in building an aqueduct for that purpose."

(c)—Barbara Fritchie.

Up from the meadows, rich with corn,
Clear in the cool September morn
The clustered fires of Frederick stand,
Green-walled by the hills of Maryland.
Round about them orchards sweep,
Apple and peach trees fruited deep—
Fair as the garden of the Lord
To the eyes of the famished rebel horde,
On that pleasant morn of the early fall,
When Lee marched over the mountain-wall
Over the mountains winding down,
Horse and foot, into Frederick-town.
Forty flags, with their silver stars,
Forty flags, with their crimson bars,
Flapped in the morning wind: the sun
Of noon looked down, and saw not one.
Up rose *Barbara Fritchie* then,
Bowed with her four-score years and ten,—
Bravest of all in Frederick-town.
She took up the flag the men hauled down :
In her attic window the staff she set,
To show that one heart was loyal yet.

Up the street came the rebel tread,
Stonewall Jackson riding ahead,
Under his slouched hat, left and right
He glanced: the old flag met his sight.
"Halt!"—the dust-brown ranks stood fast—
"Fire!"—out blazed the rifle-blast.
It shivered the window, pane and sash;
It rent the banner with seam and gash.
Quick as it fell from the broken staff,
Dame Barbara snatched the silken scarf.
She leaned far out on the window-sill
And shook it forth with a royal will.
"Shoot, if you must, this gray, old head
But spare your country's flag," she said.
A shade of sadness, a blush of shame
O'er the face of the leader came;
The nobler nature within stirred
To life at that woman's deed and word;
"Who touches a hair of yon gray head,
Dies like a dog! March on!" he said.
All day long, through Frederick street,
Sounded the tread of marching feet;
All day long that free flag tossed
Over the heads of the rebel host.
Ever its torn folds rose and fell
On the loyal winds that loved it well,
And through the hill-gaps, sunset light
Shone over it with a warm good-night.
Barbara Fritchie's work is o'er,
And the rebel rides on his raids no more.
Honor to her! And let a tear
Fall, for her sake, on Stonewall's bier!
Over Barbara Fritchie's grave,
Flag of Freedom and Union, wave!

—*J. G. Whittier.*

(d)—**James Lick.**

James Lick was born in Pennsylvania. In his youth he was brought up to the business of cabinet-maker, and served for a while in a pianoforte manufactory in Baltimore, in which business, as principal, he accumulated some $40,000 in Buenos Ayres, to which place he migrated in 1820. He prosecuted his trade in Chili and Peru for several years. He arrived in San Francisco in 1847, and, since that time, accumulated from five to six millions of dollars. He died in 1876, 80 years old. He was a prominent advocate of Thomas Paine, and of free-thinkers generally. Therefore he made a donation of a splendid mill-property in the vicinity of San Jose, California, for purposes of the Thomas Paine Hall, in Boston. In his last will he bequeathed to the University of California $700,000 for the purpose of purchasing land on Mount Hamilton, and for constructing and putting up on that land a powerful telescope, superior to any one ever yet made; and also a suitable observatory connected therewith; besides $25,000 for the Protestant Orphan Asylum of San Francisco; $25,000 for an Orphan Asylum of San Jose, free to all orphans, without regard to creed or religion of parents; $25,000 for the Ladies' Protection and and Relief Society of San Francisco; $10,000 for the purchase of scientific and mechanical works for the Mechanics' Institute of San Francisco; $10,000 to be paid to the trustees of the Society for the Prevention of Cruelty to Animals of San Francisco, accompanied with a hope that these trustees may organize such a system as will result in establishing a similar Society in every city and town in California: to the end that the rising generation may not witness or be impressed with such scenes of cruelty and brutality as constantly occur in this State; and furthermore $100,000 to found an institution to be called the "Old Ladies' Home," to be located in San Francisco, as a retreat for women who are unable to support themselves, and who have no resources of their own; $150,000 for the erection and maintaining in the city of San Francisco of free baths; $60,000 for the erection of a bronze monument (to be placed in the Golden Gate Park of San Francisco) to the memory of Francis Scott Key, author of the song, the "Star Spangled Banner;" $500,000 for founding and endowing an institution to be called "The California School of Mechanical Arts," the object and purpose of which shall be to educate males and females in the practical arts of life, such as working in wood, iron and stone, or any of the metals, and in whatever industry intelligent mechanical skill now is or can hereafter be applied; such institution to be open to all youths born in California; finally the residue of the proceeds of his property for the purchase of a suitable library, natural specimens, chemical and philosophical apparatus, useful in the advancement of science.

2. Heroism.
(a)—Leonidas at Thermopylae.

Xerxes, King of Persia, wanted to conquer also Greece, and invaded this country with an immense army (480 a. C.). Everything gave way before his march, until he came to the pass of *Thermopylae*. On this spot *Leonidas*, one of the reigning Kings o Sparta, with a few thousand brave soldiers, awaited his coming. Xerxes, for four days, expected every moment to hear of the flight of this little band; and then he sent to desire them to give up their arms. "Come and take them!" was the short answer of this true native of Laconia. The bravest Persian troops were ordered out against the forces of Leonidas; but they were always driven back with disgrace. At last, a vile wretch went and informed the King of a secret path by which he could ascend an eminence that overlooked the enemy's camp. The Persians gained this advantageous post during the darkness and silence of night, and the next morning the Greeks discovered that they had been betrayed. Leonidas knew it was in vain to expect his small army could longer resist the endless forces of Xerxes; he, therefore, sent away his allies, and kept with him only his own three hundred Lacedaemonians. Xerxes marched his vast army against this little band. Leonidas fell among the first, bravely fighting, and covered with wounds. Of the three hundred heroes, only one escaped to bear to Sparta the glorious news that her valiant warriors had died in her defense. But this man was spurned as a coward, until, at the battle of Plataea, he proved his extraordinary courage. Afterwards a monument was erected at the narrow pass of Thermopylae to the memory of the brave men who had died there, and these lines were written on it: "Go, passenger, and tell Lacedaemon that we died here in obedience to her laws!"—*Agnes Strickland.*

(b)—Arnold Winkelried.

"Make way for liberty!" he cried;—
Made way for liberty and died.
In arms the Austrian phalanx stood,

A living wall, a human wood!—
A wall, where every conscious stone
Seemed to its kindred thousands grown;
A rampart all assaults to bear,
Till time to dust their frames should wear;
A living wall, a human wood!
Impregnable their front appears,
All horrent with projected spears,
Whose polished points before them shine
From flank to flank one brilliant line,
Bright as the breakers' splendors run
Along the billows, to the sun.
Opposed to these a hovering band
Contended for their native land:
Peasants, whose new-found strength had broke
From manly necks the ignoble yoke,
And forged their fetters into swords,
On equal terms to fight their lords;
And what insurgent rage had gained
In many a mortal fray maintained;
Marshaled, once more, at freedom's call,
They came to conquer, or to fall.
And now the work of life and death
Hung on the passing of a breath;
The fire of conflict burned within,—
The battle trembled to begin.
Yet, while the Austrians held their ground,
Point for attack was nowhere found;
Wher'er the impatient Switzers gazed,
The unbroken line of lances blazed;
The line 'twere suicide to meet,
And perish at their tyrants' feet:—
How could they rest within their graves,
And leave their homes, the homes of slaves?
Would they not feel their children tread
With clanging chains above their head?
It must not be:—this day, this hour,
Annihilates the oppressor's power.
All Switzerland is in the field;—
She will not fly,—she cannot yield;—
She must not fall; her better fate
Here gives her an immortal date.
Few were the numbers she could boast,

But every freeman was a host,
And felt as though himself were he
On whose sole arm hung victory.
It will depend on one, indeed;
Behold him—*Arnold Winkelried!*
There sounds not the trump of fame
The echo of a nobler name.
Unmarked he stood amid the throng,
In rumination deep and long,
Till you might see, with sudden grace,
The very thought come o'er his face,
And by the motion of his form
Anticipate the bursting storm;
And by the uplifting of his brow
Tell where the bolt would strike, and how.
But 'twas no sooner thought than done,
The field was in a moment won.—
"Make way for liberty!" he cried,
Then ran with arms extended wide,
As if his dearest friend to clasp:—
Ten spears he swept within his grasp:—
"Make way for liberty!" he cried,
Their keen points met from side to side;—
He bowed amongst them like a tree,
And thus made way for liberty.
Swift to the breach his comrades fly;
"Make way for liberty!" they cry,
And through the Austrian phalanx dart,
As rushed the spears through Austrian heart;
While, instantaneous as his fall,
Rout, ruin, panic, scattered all:—
An earthquake could not overthrow
A city with a surer blow.
Thus Switzerland again was free;
Thus death made way for liberty.
—*James Montgomery.*

(c)—Marco Bozzaris.

At midnight, in his guarded tent
The Turk was dreaming of the hour,
When Greece, her knee in suppliance bent,
Should tremble at his power:
In dreams, through camp and court he bore
The trophies of a conqueror;

In dreams his songs of triumph heard;
Then wore his monarch's signet ring—
Then pressed that monarch's throne—a king;
As wild his thoughts, and gay of wing,
As Eden's garden bird.

An hour passed on—the Turk awoke;
That bright dream was his last:
He woke, to hear his sentries shriek—
"To arms! They come! The Greek! The Greek!
He woke to die midst flame and smoke,
And death-shots, falling thick and fast,
As lightnings from the mountain-cloud,
And heard, with voice as trumpet loud,
Bozzaris cheer his band:
"Strike—till the last armed foe expires!
Strike!—for your altars and your fires!
Strike!—for the green graves of your sires!
God, and your native land!"

They fought, like brave men, long and well;
They piled that ground with Moslem slain;
They conquered—but Bozzaris fell,
Bleeding at every vein.
His few surviving comrades saw
His smile, when rang their proud hurrah,
And the red field was won:
Then saw in death his eyelids close,
Calmly, as to a night's repose,
Like flowers at set of sun.

Bozzaris! With the storied brave
Greece nurtured, in her glory's time,
Rest thee: there is no prouder grave,
Even in her own proud clime.
We tell thy doom without a sigh;
For thou art *Freedom's* now, and *Fame's*—
One of the few, the immortal names,
That were not born to die.

— F. G. *Halleck.*

(d)—General Wolfe.*

Amidst the clamor of exulting joys,
    Which triumph forces from the patriot heart,
Grief dares to mingle her soul-piercing voice,
    And quells the rapture which from pleasure start.

O, *Wolfe*! to thee a streaming flood of woe,
    Sighing we pay, and think e'en conquest dear;
Quebec in vain shall teach our breast to glow,
    Whilst thy sad fate extorts the heart-rung tear.

Alive, the foe thy dreadful vigor fled,
    And saw thee fall with joy-pronouncing eyes;
Yet they shall know thou conquerest, though dead!
    Since from thy tomb a thousand heroes rise.

                                              —*Oliver Goldsmith.*

(e)—The Battle at Bunker Hill.

General Gage, the royal commander in Boston, was planning to extend his lines and include Bunker Hill, because it commanded the city. So the Americans sent during the night (June 16th, 1775,) a force of one thousand men, under command of Colonel *Prescott*, to erect some earth-works for its protection. His men were mostly farmers; they had no uniforms, and carried fowling-pieces without bayonets. It was decided to fortify *Breed's Hill*, as being nearer to Boston, instead of *Bunker Hill*. The work was soon begun. As day dawned, the newly-made earth-works were seen from the ships, which began to fire at them, as did a battery in Boston, but the Americans went on building their fortifications. Three thousand British soldiers were embarked in boats, and sent across to Charlestown. Prescott placed his men as he best could, behind the half-finished mounds. Without food, without water, and with very little ammunition, the Americans awaited their opponents. Prescott ordered them: "Wait till you can see the whites of their eyes." On came the British, till they were within some ten rods of the redoubt. Then the word "fire" was given, and, when the smoke cleared away, the ground was strewed with British soldiers, and the survivors had already begun to retreat. Twice they advanced, and twice they were driven backwards; then

---

*The English ascended the heights of Quebec (the plains of Abraham), General Wolfe was twice wounded, but continued to lead the charge at the head of his grenadiers, till he received a third and mortal wound. He was conveyed to the rear. Being informed that the French took to flight, "Then (said he), I die contented," and immediately expired. ct. 55.

a third attack was made upon the main fort. General Putnam passed around the ranks, telling his men that, if the British were once more driven back, they would not rally again; and his men shouted: "We are ready for the red coats again." But Putnam knew that their powder was almost gone, and told them to reserve their fire till the British were within twenty yards. Once more they awaited the assailants, who now advanced with fixed bayonets, without firing, and under the protection of batteries of artillery. Most of the Americans had but one round of ammunition left, and few had more than three. Scarcely any had bayonets. Their last shots were soon fired, and there was nothing for them but to retreat as best they could. They lost more men in the retreat than in the battle. Among their losses was the brave General *Warren*, eminent as a physician and as a patriot. He was President of the Provincial Congress, and was there only as a volunteer, not in command. The victory of the British was dearly won, for they lost a thousand men. The American loss was 450.

(f)—Seventy-Six.

What heroes from the woodland sprung,
When through the fresh awakened land,
The thrilling cry of freedom rung,
And to the work of warfare strung,
The yeoman's iron hand!

Hills flung the cry to hills around,
And ocean-mart replied to mart,
And streams whose springs were yet unfound,
Pealed far away the startling sound
Into the forest's heart.

Then marched the brave from rocky steep,
From mountain river swift and cold;
The borders of the stormy deep,
The vales where gathered waters sleep,
Sent up the strong and bold,—

As if the very earth again
Grew quick with God's creating breath,
And from the sods of grove and glen,
Rose ranks of lion-hearted men
To battle to the death.

The wife, whose babe first smiled that day,
The fair, fond bride of yestereve,
The aged sire and matron gray,
Saw the loved warriors haste away,
And deemed it sin to grieve.

Already had the strife begun;
Already blood on Concord's plain
Along the springing grass had run,
And blood had flowed at Lexington,
Like brooks of April rain.

The death-stain on the vernal sward
Hallowed to freedom all the shore,
In fragments fell the yoke abhorred,—
The footsteps of a foreign lord
Profaned the soil no more.
—*W. Cullen Bryant.*

(g)—Abraham Lincoln.*

Oh, slow to smite, and swift to spare,
  Gentle, and merciful, and just!
Who in the fear of God, didst bear
  The sword of power, a nation's trust!
In sorrow by thy bier we stand,
  Amid the awe that hushes all,
And speak the anguish of a land,
  That shook with horror at thy fall.
Thy task is done: *the bond are free;*
  We bear thee to an honored grave,
Whose proudest monument shall be
  The broken fetters of the slave.
Pure was thy life; its bloody close
  Hath placed thee with the sons of light,
Among the noble host of those
  Who perished in the cause of Right.
—*W. C. Bryant.*

(h)—Conflict of Duties—Regulus.

The Carthagenians sent the Roman Consul *Regulus,* whom they had taken prisoner during war, to Rome, to propose an exchange of prisoners. He had been obliged to take an oath that he would return in case he proved unsuccessful. In Rome he declared to

---

*On New Year's Day of 1863, President Lincoln issued the *Emancipation Proclamation*, which declared free all the slaves within the borders of the Confederate States. This manly act caused his premature death, the 14th of April, 1865. John Wilkes Booth assassinated him

the Senate that an exchange of prisoners ought not to be so much as thought of; that such an example would be of fatal consequence to the Republic. The citizens, who had so basely surrendered their arms and persons to the enemy were unworthy of the least compassion; that with regard to himself, as he was so far advanced in years, his death ought to be considered as nothing, whereas they had in their hands several Carthagenian Generals, in the flower of their age, and capable of doing their country great service for many years. The illustrious exile therefore left Rome, in order to return to Carthage, unmoved either by the deep affliction of his friends, or the tears of his wife and children, although he knew too well the grievous torments which were prepared for him. And, indeed, the moment his enemies saw him returned without having obtained the exchange of prisoners, they put him to every kind of torture their barbarous cruelty could invent; lastly they nailed him to a cross, their usual punishment, and left him to expire on it.—*Rollin's Ancient History*.

3. Behavior Towards Animals.

(a)—The Hornets' Nest.

A boy who delighted in torturing animals once discovered a hornets' nest near the woods which skirted the pasture lands of a Mr. Williams. He plagued them from day to day, till they became very cross, and then he got some salt, and called Mr. Williams' horses and cattle in the field, and fed them with it under and around the little tree on which the hornets' nest hung. As soon as they were well engaged in licking the salt, he threw a club against the nest, when out came the hornets upon the horses and cows, and stung them dreadfully. They ran, and snorted, and kicked as though they would kill themselves. But he got punished. He was so much pleased to see the poor horses jump and writhe in agony, that he forgot himself, leaped out from his concealment, hopping up and down, slapping his hands, and laughed and shouted at a great rate. A portion of the hornets were attracted by him, and in the midst of his shouts he felt a dreadful sting inflicted on his face, and, before he could flee, he was stung with much severity several times. Next day his face and his eyes were so swollen that he could not see. It soon became generally known how he had behaved in the matter, and no one felt pity for the cruel boy. His young companions jeered and laughed at him.

(b)—Sir Isaac Newton.

You remember, I suppose, the story of an apple's falling on the head of Isaac Newton, and thus leading him to discover the force of gravitation, which keeps the heavenly bodies in their courses. But did you ever hear the story of Newton, and his little dog Diamond? One day, when he was fifty years old, and had been hard at work more than twenty years studying the theory of light, he went out of his chamber, leaving his little dog asleep before the fire.

On the table lay a heap of manuscript papers containing all the discoveries which Newton had made during those twenty years When his master was gone, up rose little Diamond, jumped up on the table, and overthrew the lighted candle. The papers immediately caught fire. Just as the destruction was completed, Newton opened the chamber door, and perceived that the labors of twenty years were reduced to a heap of ashes. There stood little Diamond, the author of all the mischief.

Almost any other man would have sentenced the dog to immediate death But Newton patted him on the head with his usual kindness, although grief was at his heart. "Oh, Diamond, Diamond," he exclaimed, "thou little knowest the mischief thou hast done!"
—*Nath. Hawthorne.*

SECTION SECOND.

Doctrine of Duties and Rights.

IN QUESTIONS AND ANSWERS.

"Reason, Observation, and Experience,—the Holy Trinity of Science,—have taught us that happiness is the only good; that the time to be happy is now, and the way to be happy is to make others so. This is enough for us."—*Rob. Ingersoll*, "*The Gods.*"

Introduction.

§ 1. Explanations—Man's Moral Faculties.

What does Nature assign to every one of its creatures?

Its peculiar destiny.

By what do we discern the destination of a thing?

By its constitution.

By what do we also discern the destined end of Man?

By his faculties and forces.

What does Man (according to the common usage of language) naturally possess?

He possesses a body, senses, a mind, intellect, reason, conscience, different impulses, etc.

What force is the human *Mind* in the general signification of the word?

It is the force by which we perceive, feel and desire. The force of perceiving is also called *Intellect.*

What do we discern by Intellect and Reason?

By Intellect we discern truth and error; by Reason, what is right and wrong, good and bad.

What is Mind in the stricter sense?

The faculty of the feelings. In this signification we call it also the Heart.

How many classes of feelings are there?

Two, viz: *sensations* and *emotions.*

How do sensations differ from emotions?

Sensations are caused by impressions on the senses e. g., hunger, thirst, heat, and cold. Emotions are occasioned by an excited condition of mind, e. g. love, hatred, gratitude, repentance.

Can Reason also be cultivated?

It can be cultivated, like every other faculty.

In what regard is Reason called *Conscience*?

As far as its verdicts refer to our own actions, and are joined with approbation and content, or with reproach and repentance.

Does Conscience always remain the same?

No; it changes in proportion as we grow better or worse, or attain a higher grade of culture.

What else is Conscience called?

Moral Sense.

What is *human will*?

It is the power of man to commence an act for himself.

Is human will absolutely free?

No, it is only so far free as man can resolve according to what he has perceived to be good or bad, right or wrong.

By what is our will induced to action?

By motives.

Under what kind of necessity does the honest man act?

Under moral necessity.

What do we acquire by our senses?

We acquire by them our notions of objects (see Intuit. of the Univ., §§ 10, 11).

What do the notions of objects write in our mind?

Wishes and desires.

What do, by degrees, spring out of the wishes and desires?

If they are often satisfied, propensities, habits, passions spring out of them.

Is the power of habits strong?

It is almost irresistible; habit becomes a new nature of man.

What impulses did Nature give to Man?

Different impulses; e. g., the impulse to preserve his life, to procure food, property, honor; the impulse of sympathy, which moves us to take interest in the sufferings and joys of our fellowmen, etc.

What is man's highest faculty?

Reason; it is the highest prerogative in which man excels animals.

§ 2. Human Destination.

What is the proper way for man to reach his destination?

The only proper way is to develop harmoniously all his faculties and forces, and to use them according to Nature's laws.

Must he destroy some of them?

He should destroy no faculty,—on the contrary, grant every one its claim; he must only subordinate the lower to the higher ones.

What do Man's nature and constitution teach us to consider as his destination?

Man's nature and constitution teach us that he is destined to promote his own happiness or welfare, and that of his fellow-creatures.

How does man attain this end, viz: his own welfare and that of others?

By satisfying in a natural way all his faculties.[*]

Does experience confirm this view of human destination?

Experience confirms it, for we see that all men endeavor to become happy. Nobody carries his wheat to market with the intention of giving it away, but for the sake of his profit.

But what does *not* constitute human happiness?

Grossly sensual enjoyments do not constitute it; suffice it that our necessary wants are satisfied, that we live free of pain, fear, covetousness, and other base passions; that we enjoy a pure conscience. "Sound health, moderate fortune, and a mind well stored with knowledge; these are the grand ingredients of happiness."—Thales, 643 A. C.[**]

But what confers the highest degree of happiness?

The consciousness of generous actions; e. g., when a mother

---

[*] "Man's happiness can only be produced by the exercise of his faculties." "Happiness consists in the due satisfaction of all the desires, that is, in the due exercise of all the faculties."—*Herb. Spencer, Soc. Statistics, pp. 92, 93.*

[**] *Thales, Solon, Bias, Aristotle, Pittacus, Democritus, Cleobulus,* belonged to the famous Greek philosophers. They lived long before Christ. There is a vulgar notion among Christians that there never were any views of morality before the Bible was composed, and that without this book we should have no idea of right and wrong. This notion is gratuitous and presumptuous. Morality existed before the Bible existed, and will exist when the Bible is obsolete. We can find morality of the highest and purest character in the writings of men who lived a long time before Christ. Morality is perfectly independent of the Jewish and Christian Text Book

joyfully sacrifices her life for her child. Virtue is its own recompense.

But whose aid do we need in order to be happy ourselves?

In order to be happy, we need the aid of other persons; for nobody is able alone to provide for all his wants.

What do people soon find out?

They soon find out whether we are selfish, unjust and uncharitable.

What will they do when this is the case?

They will do to us just as we have done to them.

In what way must we, then, procure the favor of other persons?

By justice and kindness.

How must we, therefore, behave towards them, if we want to be happy?

In order to be happy, we must make also others happy.

Finally, nobody is always happy.*

§ 3. Duties—Virtue and Vice—Their Consequences—Doctrine of Duties.

Who is said to be prudent?

He who for his own advantage is induced to perform any action.

When do we call an action moral?

If man acts according to reason and conscience, his action is called moral, or absolutely good.

What kind of a motive must there be at the bottom of a moral action?

A moral intention must be its motive.

What does Reason command man to do?

Reason commands him to do what is good and right, and to shun what is bad and wrong.

What is Reason, therefore, to his moral life?

Its legislator.

What do we call the laws of Reason?

Duties, which man is obliged to fulfil.

What is virtue?

---

*The principle of the doctrine of Happiness is recognized by the most celebrated philosophers on Morals, e. g., by H. Spencer, who even says: "Human welfare agrees with the Divine will; that's the doctrine of all our Theologians." This remark may put at ease those persons who cannot think that moral conduct without religion is possible.

Virtue is the performance of the laws of Reason.

Whom do we call *virtuous*?

Him who always performs his duties.

What do we call the contrary of virtue and virtuous?

Vice and *vicious*.

Is there only one virtue and one vice?

There are several virtues and vices, e. g., the virtue of temperance, of application, of placability; the vice of avarice, of envy, etc.

Who acts wisely?

He who in order to attain moral purposes, chooses also the aptest means.

What are the consequences of virtue and vice?

Virtue affords man inward content, the respect and love of others, often also prosperity, and at all events the supreme happiness of life. Vice deprives him of peace of mind, racks him with the stings of his conscience, destroys the health of his body and his mental faculties, and heaps the hatred and contempt of others upon him. Every one bears in himself his heaven and his hell.

Why, then, ought we to practice virtue and to shun vice?

Because that creates happiness,—this unhappiness.

What are Morals in Ethics?

They are the science which teaches us the knowledge of human duties.

Why is this science useful?

Because it teaches us to know our duties, upon the practice of which our welfare depends.

Are morals and manners synonymous terms?

No; the latter regard only the outward deportment of man, the way of life according to custom and convenience. Manners change in the course of time, and are very different with diverse nations. But the fundamental laws of Ethics are eternal, immutable and universally valid.

§ 4. First Principles of Ethics.

What are moral principles?

Such propositions as those from which the special precepts of Morals can be derived.

What is the use of principles in Ethics?

They facilitate the knowledge and performance of human duties.

To what may a first principle be compared?

To a standard which, as it were, ought to lead us on in the path of virtue.

Several such principles have been devised by the teachers of moral philosphy. Some of them here are stated:

1. Promote your own welfare, and that of your fellow creatures.
2. Seek after happiness.
3. Seek after happiness by dint of virtue. (The term "happiness" must be understood in the sense which has been pointed out in § 2.)
4. Seek after virtue.
5. Act always in such a manner that your conduct could become the law for all intellectual creatures.
6. Seek after virtue and justice.
7. Try to become useful to yourself and to others.
8. Act always according to Nature's laws.
9. Act according to your perfect conviction of right.
10. Act in accordance with the voice of Reason and Conscience, as far as both these faculties are developed and cultivated. "Make Reason thy guide."—Solon, 638 a. C.

On the last principle it must be remarked that there also is an erroneous, a narrow and lax, a dead conscience. Conscience among different nations permits many actions which are condemned before the tribunal of pure morality. So e. g. savage nations don't consider theft a crime. Among Arabs it is a common practice to rob and ransack travelers. In Turkey, China, and Hindoostan, polygamy rules without causing any scandal. The higher castes in Europe and America consider the duel a matter of honor. On several islands of the Pacific the custom is in vogue of killing old people, even one's own parents, in order to get rid of them. In this way rude people always have acted. Jews, Mohammedans and Christians believed that it was a kind of divine service to exterminate Infidels—as they called their religious antagonists—with fire and sword. Moses and David did not feel any remorse,—the former, when he had ordered to cut down 3,000 Israelites as an expiatory sacrifice to the Lord ; the latter, when he put the inhabitants of the conquered town Rubba under iron saws and choppers, and burned them in brick-kilns (II. Sam., 12-31). The Carthagenians, Phenicians, and Persians were not at all deterred by their conscience from burning alive their own children as sacrifices, etc. Again, men have in different times and countries diverse notions of right and wrong, according as their reason is rude or cultivated.

Is there in man anything like innate conscience?

No! Conscience is the product of education, built up by the lives of millions of men, resting in the bottom of humanity.

How far, then, can Reason and Conscience be supreme legislators for our conduct?

Only as far as they, like other faculties of the mind, have been developed and cultivated.

By what means are they developed and cultivated?

By domestic education, by the instruction of the school, by experience, etc.

Other principles, upon which the precepts of the single divisions of Ethics rest, will be presented in their proper place.

§ 5. Division of Ethics.

How are duties divided?

In order to facilitate the review of the great number of the ethical precepts, duties usually are divided into two branches, into duties : First, towards ourselves (personal duties) ; and second, in duties towards other persons.

How are these duties of the second class subdivided?

Into duties : First, of *Benevolence* (Humanity) ; and secondly, duties of *Justice*.

What kind of duties form the contents of Morals in the stricter sense of the word?

The duties towards ourselves, and the duties of benevolence.

Can the Divine will also be a first principle of Ethics?

No ; for History proves that people often believe or pretend the suggestions of their passions to be God's will. (Cf. Hist. of the Rel , § 16.) Moreover, we do not know by experience any other will than that of man.

What duties form the contents of the doctrine of Justice?
The duties of Justice.

To those two parts of duties often the duties towards God and animals are added. The duties towards God cannot here be considered, because many persons do not believe in the existence of an individual which they call God, though they acknowledge the obligation of moral laws.

CHAPTER FIRST.

ETHICS (in the Stricter Sense).

I. Duties Towards Ourselves (Personal Duties.)

§ 6. First Principles.

1. Endeavor to make yourself happy.
2. Endeavor to preserve yourself.

What impulse of human nature is the strongest?
The impulse of self-preservation.

3. Seek after perfection.
4. Cultivate the faculties of your body, intellect and mind harmoniously.
5. Let this be your device : A sound mind in a sound body!
6. Advance with the Time!

§ 7. General Duties Towards Ourselves.

1. Love yourself!

What does it mean to love ourselves?
To love ourselves means to look for everything which is useful to us, and to keep off everything which is noxious to us.

Why ought we to love ourselves?
Because thereby we obey the instincts of our nature (cf. views of the Univ., § 11).

2. *Respect yourself.*

Why ought every body to respect himself?

Because man is elevated far above the other creatures, and especially because he excels them in his moral faculties, and in his desires for perfection. "Those who respect themselves will be honorable; but he who thinks lightly of himself, will be held cheap by the world."—Chinese Proverb.

3. What should we, therefore, shun?

We should shun all follies and vices.

Why should we shun them?

Because by them we debase ourselves below the animals, hurt the dignity of free rational beings, and therefore act against the respect we owe to ourselves.

For what other reason ought we to avoid follies and vices?

Because they bring about noxious consequences. No folly, no vice remains with impunity. Nature takes vengeance for every trespass on her laws.

4. *We should not be proud and haughty.*

What does pride do?

It overrates one's self, and undervalues or despises others.

Why should we not be proud?

Because all men own the nobility of the same nature, and have the like destination as ourselves.

What are the different kinds of pride?

Pride of money, of caste, of titles, of scholarship, of art, of priesthood, of beauty (vanity), of virtue, of creed, etc.

Why ought we not to be proud of our virtue?

Because nobody is quite perfect and without any moral defect, besides no man is entirely the author of his moral excellence.

Why not of genius?

Because it is a mere gift of Nature.

Why not of knowledge and ability?

Because modesty is the highest ornament of a true scholar and artist.

Why not of money and property?

Money and property do not impart to man an intrinsic value, and are for the most part gifts of Fortune.

Why not of beauty?
Because it is fading away.
What are the sad consequences of pride?
Pride makes man ridiculous and odious to others, and he is often humiliated. A proverb says: Pride goes before fall.

5. On the contrary, we ought to be unassuming and modest.
What consciousness ought to induce us to be modest?
The consciousness that we are yet far from the goal of perfection.

SPECIAL DUTIES TOWARDS OURSELVES.

§ 8. 1.—Duties with Regard to Our Life and Health.

1. What is our first duty towards ourselves?
To take care of our life and health.
For what reason?
Because love of life and its sound condition is innate to man; life and health are the groundwork of happiness, and the first condition to attain moral excellence.

2. What duty follows from that of self-preservation?
Our duty to employ all means tending to this purpose.
What means are subservient to this purpose?
Industry, wholesome articles of subsistence, to which fresh water also belongs, suitable clothing, cleanliness, washings and baths, hardening exercises, rest and sleep, etc.

3. What ought we, therefore, to avoid?
Everything which baffles that purpose.
What should we avoid in particular?
Intemperance in food and drink (gluttony, and propensity to drunkenness), effeminacy, lewdness, foolhardy risks, and the sway of the passions.
What evil consequences follow intemperance and voluptuousness?
Painful and infamous diseases, contempt, and often also the loss of wealth.

4. What is the counterpart of lewdness?
Modesty and chastity.
What does chastity require of us?

It requires us to close our eyes, ears and heart against everything which is impudent and indecent, to shun intercourse with frivolous and vicious persons, and to perform not even in solitude any deed for which our conscience would cause us to blush, if we were sur-surprised at it by respectable persons. "Do nothing shameful, though you are alone."—Democritus, a Greek philosopher, 470 A. C.

5. What mortifications and self-castigations are in vogue among several religious sects?

Fasting, nocturnal watching (vigils), self-flagellation, living in celibacy, etc.

Why should such customs be avoided?

Because they also destroy the forces of the body. All natural instincts are necessary and sacred; none ought to be destroyed. (Cf. Hist. of Rel., § 13: Monasteries.)

6. What does the duty of self-preservation require of us, if we fall sick?

It requires us, in this case, to employ the best and most convenient means to recover our health.

Whom ought we especially to consult?

We ought to consult a competent, skillful physician, and to use carefully the remedies prescribed by him.

Against whom and what ought the patient to be carefully on his guard?

Against quacks and quackery.

7. Is man in no case at liberty to give up life?

There may cases happen in which he is permitted to do so; nay, sometimes it may prove even our duty to sacrifice life, e. g., if our country is threatened by a great danger. "Life is not the highest good of man, but the greatest evil is guilt."—Schiller.

8. Why ought we also to cultivate and improve the faculties of our body?

Because the body is the instrument of mind.

What kind of exercises ought therefore to be introduced in all schools?

Exercise of bodily training (gymnastics).

What are the advantages they afford?

They procure strength, dexterity, and beauty to the body, and dispose the mind to cheerfulness.*

§ 9. 2.—With Regard to Property.

1. What do we want in order to be able to conserve life?

Fortune and property.

To what other ends is property a good help?

To mental culture; also to benefitting others and procuring for ourselves higher comforts of life.

2. In what way is property justly acquired?

By industry, parsimony, and prudence.

What good results follow industry?

It gives us courage, love of life, cheerfulness, and independence. Industry affords honor to man.

What are the consequences of idleness?

Idleness leads to indigence and distress, to shame and contempt, to dejection, dependence upon others, and quite often to crimes, even. " Be not idle, though rich."—Thales.

3. What vices form the counterparts of parsimony?

Prodigality, avarice, and greediness.

What punishment is often inflicted upon the prodigal?

The punishment of poverty; he is brought down to beggary.

Whom do we call avaricious?

We call him avaricious who grudges to both himself and to his fellow-creatures the necessary comforts of life, and values money and riches higher than anything else.

What is the natural chastisement of the miser?

His life is miserable; he is despised and forsaken by others, and he is saving for *laughing* heirs who will not thank him.

Who is called greedy?

He whose desire to acquire fortune knows no limit.

To what crimes are the covetous easily misled?

To fraud and injustice.

What virtue ought we to practice in order to secure a happy life, while we endeavor to gather earth's blessings?

---

*"A School Board should include physical training and drill as part of the regular business of school. It is impossible to insist too much on the importance of this part of education for the children of the poor of great towns I should give no grant to a school in which physical training is not a part of the programme, or, at any rate, offer to pay upon such training."—Huxley, Critiques, p. 41.

In order to secure a happy life, we must practice frugality.

Are riches necessary for a happy life?

No; the necessaries of nature can be satisfied by a small measure of her gifts.

To what transgressions do riches easily mislead man?

To extravagance, haughtiness, laziness, effeminacy and disgraceful debauchery.

How ought the man, who is blessed with riches, to use them?

He ought to use them for his own benefit, and for the welfare of mankind.

§ 10. 3.—With Regard to Mental Culture.

How do we satisfy the desire for getting knowledge?

By mental culture.

What does it mean to cultivate the mind?

To cultivate the mind means to develop its faculties, namely, the intellect, the memory, the feelings, etc. "Learning is the best provision for old age."—Aristotle, 384 A. C.

What kind of knowlege ought we, therefore, acquire?

Such as is either necessary or useful for our life. "The truly learned are not those that read much, but those who read what is useful."—Aristippus, 365 A. C.

From what error ought we to keep ourselves free?

From superstitions, especially from religious superstition.

Who is called superstitious?

He who attributes to an object such forces and effects as it cannot claim by nature's laws.

How does superstition manifest itself?

By the fear of ghosts, of death, of torments in hell, by the belief in miracles, witchcraft, fortune-tellers, etc.

What are the bad effects of superstition?

It assails human health, life, and property; it has cruelly destroyed the lives of millions of men who were called infidels, heretics, and witches. (See Hist. of Rel.)

What means ought we to use in order to cultivate our mental faculties?

Good schools and books, libraries, periodicals, lectures, and such societies as are organized to this end.

What societies are most excellent with regard to religious progress?

The free religious associations and liberal leagues.

How ought we to act towards them?

We ought to side with them, advance their ends, and fear no sacrifice nor persecution for their cause.

What sciences ought we particularly to study, in order to secure us against superstition?

The natural sciences, namely: natural philosophy, natural history, astronomy, geology, etc.

§ 11. 4.—With Regard to Moral Culture.

1. Why ought we to cultivate and improve the mind (the mental faculties)?

Because morality gives man his highest worth.

What are we to do to this end?

We must learn to know and govern ourselves.

What does it mean to know one's self?

It means to know what good and bad qualities, propensities and habits one has. "Kown thyself."—Thales. "Before you go home, think what you have to do; when you come home, examine yourself and consider whether you have done all well."—Cleobulus, 571 A. C.

What does it mean to govern one's self?

It means to subdue one's defective desires and propensities to the law of Reason.

Why ought we to learn to know and rule ourselves?

Because without self-knowledge and self-command there is no progress in virtue possible.

2. In what way do we grow in moral perfection?

By having intercourse with virtuous persons, and by shunning the company of vicious ones.

3. What studies serve this purpose?

The study of Universal History, and the reading of the classic authors of ancient and modern times. History teaches us virtue and justice in examples; the classics ennoble the moral faculties and the human mind.*

Are novels also adapted to this end?

Among the many, only very few are; for generally they foster a morbid sentimentality, fill the imagination with vacant visions, and make man dissatisfied with real life.

But how far can the plays of the stage ennoble the human heart?

So far as they present life as it is, or ought to be, as it were, in a mirror.

4. When do we show constancy of mind?

When we become neither insolent in good fortune, nor desponding in misfortune.

Why ought we never to despair?

Because all accidents of our life are the phenomena of the necessary connection of causes and effects.

§ 12. With Regard to Aesthetical Refinement.

1. Why ought we to provide for our aesthetical culture?

Because by it we satisfy the sense of beauty, which is innate to every man. This culture facilitates the acquirement of virtue, guards often against rude excesses, and is a source of innocent pleasure.

2. By what means is the aesthetic sense cultivated?

By the fine arts, e. g., by drawing, painting, music and dancing.

What does intercourse with Nature afford, also?

Intercourse with her affords many and pure enjoyments; her charms are inexhaustible and ever new.

§ 13. Choice of a Vocation.

What does the expression imply, "*Choose a vocation!*"

It means to choose an occupation to which we will devote our whole life.

Why ought we to select a definite vocation?

In order that our life may be useful to ourselves and to other people.

What have men to do before they select a vocation?

---

*E. g. Shakespeare's tragedies have perhaps promoted morality more efficaciously and more generally than all the sermons of the clergy.

They ought to examine themselves as to whether they possess the faculties and vigor which are required for the profession of their choice.

2. What kind of knowledge and aptitude ought they to acquire? Such as are necessary in order to fulfill their professional duties. What have they to do after the choice? After it they ought to discearge faithfully and cheerfully the duties of their vocation.

Why should we not look down with scorn on the vocations of other persons?

Because every work honors its performer; different ranks are necessary for the welfare of mankind, and therefore men must divide the different tasks among them. Besides, the faculties and propensities of men are very different; therefore every one is not fit for every profession.

II. Duties Towards Our Fellow Creatures (Duties of Benevolence).

§ 14. First Principles.

1. Do unto other men as, according to reason, you wish that they should do unto you.
2. Love your fellow-creatures, as well as yourself.
3. Use other men as independent beings, not as mere means.
4. Be humane to every one.
5. Promote also the welfare of others.
6. Act in conformity with the sympathetic impulse.

§ 15. General Duties.

1. How ought we to behave towards other men?

We should love and respect them, if good, like ourselves; for all men have the same nature, the same faculties, and the same destination; they all are members of the same family. All are as jinks in the chain of human society; they need each other; all help and supply each other. They all wish to be happy. "We are all limbs of one great body. Nature produces us all, as relations to each other. She inspired us with mutual love, and made us social."—Seneca. "The universal, immutable and eternal law of all intelligent beings is to promote the happiness of one another, like children of the same father."—Cicero, 70 A. C.

2. How else ought we to behave towards others?

We ought to be obliging and kind, just and equitable, peaceable, affable and polite towards them.

How should we consider the faults and frailties of other men?

We should not censure them harshly, but judge meekly and equitably. "With what judgment you judge, ye shall be judged; and with what measure you mete, it shall be measured to you again. Why beholdest thou the mote that is in thy brother's eye, but considerest not the beam that is in thine own eye? Or how wilt thou say to thy brother: Let me pull the mote out of thine eye; and behold a beam is in thine own eye? Thou hypocrite, first cast out the beam out of thine own eye, and then shalt thou see clearly to cast out the mote out of thy brother's eye."—Bible.

What does politeness not consist of?

Politeness does not consist of slavish subjection, cringing, flattery and fawning; it ought to be the expression of benevolence.

What do we gain by politeness?

The good will of men.

3. What impulse ought we also to satisfy?

The impulse of sympathy.

How do we satisfy it?

If we take a hearty interest in the sufferings and joys of others.

What should sympathetic feelings produce?

They should produce benevolent actions; our emotions ought not to remain idle.

4. When do we show the highest degree of philanthropy?

When we sacrifice our own weal for our family, for our friends, for our country, or in general for mankind.

5. Why ought we to avoid selfishness?

Because selfishness is the contrary of generosity, and lays claim to every advantage at the expense of others.

SPECIAL DUTIES.

§ 16. 1.—Duties of Children Towards their Parents.

What are the duties of children towards their parents?

1. Children ought to love their parents.

Why?

Because the parents render the children so many benefits.

For what benefits particulary are children indebted to their parents?

For life, nourishment, clothing and protection.

What other benefits do parents confer on their children?

Parents nurse their children when they fall sick; they provide for their education and instruction, and leave them, when they die, the property they have saved in life. "Cherish thy parents! What thou bestowest on them, thou shalt receive from thy children in thine old age."—Thales.

2. Children ought to respect parents.

Why ought they to respect them?

Because the parents are more intelligent, and have more experience than children.

How ought they to behave if the parents commit faults?

They ought to be forbearing, and not despise their parents when they grow old and frail. "Reverence thy parents."—Solon.

3. Children should obey their parents.

For what reasons?

Because parents know the world better than children, and their orders aim at the welfare of the children.

What bad results does disobedience cause?

Disobedient children are disliked and punished, and by disobedience they often injure themselves.

In what manner ought children to obey parents?

They ought to obey them cheerfully, and immediately, and always.

7. They should also be grateful to their parents.

Why?

Because the parents are their greatest benefactors.

In what way do children prove themselves to be grateful?

When they aid their parents as much as they can, in their work, nurse them in their diseases, and support them in their old age and helplessness.

5. Children ought to be true and sincere to their parents.
Why ought they to be true and sincere?
Because the parents are their best friends, and cannot educate them well, unless they know all about the doings of their children.

§ 17. 2.—Duties Towards Brothers, Sisters and Relations.

By what connection are brothers and sisters closely related?
By the connection of blood and family.
How, then, should brothers and sisters mutually behave?

1. They should love each other most dearly,—next to the parents.
2. They ought to be to each other obliging and kind, liberal and compassionate.
3. To deal mutually with candor and trust.
4. To bear small offences patiently, to be peaceable, and prompt to forgive each other.
5. Not to belittle and slander each other to their parents.

What do children owe to their grand-parents and to other relatives?
They owe them love, respect and kindness.

§ 18. 3.—Duties Towards Companions.

How should children behave towards comrades, schoolmates and playmates?

1. They should be kind and accommodating to them.
2. Not scoff at them, nor frighten them for fun, much less ill-treat them.
3. Not cause quarrels and enmity among them.
4. But strive to reconcile them to each other.
5. Not entice each other to evil doings.

Whose company must children avoid?
The company of the wicked.

§ 19. 4.—Duties Towards Teachers.

Why do not parents themselves always teach and educate their children?
Either because they have not the knowledge which is necessary

for their instruction, or because the duties of their vocation prevent them from performing it.

To whom, therefore, do they intrust the children?

To teachers and tutors.

Whom do teachers and tutors represent?

They represent the parents of the children.

To what duties, then, are children in general bound?

They are bound to the same duties towards their teachers and tutors as towards their parents.

How should they behave towards them in particular?

1. They should show them love and respect in their behavior.
2. Be obedient to them.

What does the obedience of the scholars towards their teachers require?

It requires that they receive their instruction with silence and attention, perform diligently their oral and written exercises, and avoid defiance and obstinacy towards the orders of the teachers.

Why ought their obedience to be distinguished by these qualities?

Because without them they cannot have good success at school.

3. They ought also to show themselves grateful towards their teachers.

§ 20. 5 and 6.—Duties Towards Friends and Benefactors.

How ought friends to behave mutually?

1. They ought to be kind and obliging.
2. Sincere and discreet, by confiding their secrets to each other, and by keeping them faithfully.
3. To keep mutually-promised faith inviolate. "The sacrifices we make to a friend we count not sacrifices, but pleasures; we sorrow for his sorrow; we supply his wants, or, if we cannot, we share them. We follow him into exile; we close ourselves in his prison; we soothe him in sickness; we strengthen him in death; nay, if it is possible, we throw down our life for his."—Epicurus in "A Few Days in Athens," by Francis Wright, p. 126 "Be kind to your friends, that they may continue such; and to your enemies, that they may become your friends."—Cleobulus. "Friends are one soul in two bodies."—Aristotle.

What do we owe to our benefactors?

We should pay them particular respect, and be grateful to them.

What must we do in order to be grateful?

We must not only express our gratitude in words, but prove it by our deeds, e. g., by remunerating their favor by similar services, if there be any chance to do so. Ingratitude is the most hideous vice. "Acknowledge thy benefits by return of other benefits, but never revenge injuries."—Confucius, 600 A. C.

§ 21. 7.—Towards Poor, Sick, Frail, and Old People.

How ought we to behave towards such persons?

We ought to treat them with tender care, to assist them, to support them by good advice and actual comfort. Even the rudest warriors usually spare children, old people, and helpless women. "When thou doest alms, let not thy left hand know what thy right hand doeth."—Bible.

How ought children, especially, to deal with aged people?

They must not mock, but esteem them.

Why ought children to do so?

Because they must also grow old; beside, such men have endured many afflictions during their long lives, and experience has enriched their minds with useful knowledge.

§ 22. 8.—Towards Religious Sects.

How did Jews, Christians and Mohammedans deal with each other in former days?

They hated and persecuted each other cruelly.

Has religious hatred now a-days entirely ceased?

No; rather among the Christians themselves the different sects, as Catholics, Lutherans, Methodists, Calvinists, etc , act, frequently, hatefully towards each other.

What are our duties towards persons who do not share our religious views?

1. We ought to love them as human beings; especially, if they are connected with us by the ties of blood and close relationship.

2. We ought to respect them as our fellow-creatures, particularly if they are honest, righteous and good; and such are found in every sect.

3. We ought to be compassionate, obliging and helpful to them. For what reason?

Because we ought to be so towards every one.

What do we demonstrate by such a behavior?

We demonstrate by it that our religious views are more correct than theirs.

By what does genuine piety show its excellence?

By kindness and justice towards others.

4. We ought to be tolerant toward such persons, if we think their creed to be erroneous.

When are we tolerant?

When we do not deride and persecute them on account of their creed, but meekly teach them a better doctrine, also give way in indifferent matters, and not disturb them in the exercise of their religion.

Why ought we to be tolerant?

Because such people think themselves to have the true belief, since they have been trained in it, and have received it from their parents as a dear inheritance. All trees have not the same bark. Error is peculiar to human nature. Again, our religious tenets are not infallible. There is room for all creeds on earth. Without patience there would be no end of quarrels and wars. Moreover, all religions, the Mosaic law, the Koran, the Evangelic, etc., agree in the essential precepts of Morals. "We are all full of weakness and errors; let us mutually pardon each other our follies, —it is the first law of nature. Of all religions, the Christian ought, doubtless to inspire the most toleration, although hitherto the Christians have been the most intolerant of all men."—Voltaire.

5. Nevertheless, we ought to investigate truth, defend it fearlessly, and cling to it, if we are persuaded by its arguments. We ought also to repel hostile aggressions upon our religious rights, and destroy superstitious opinions when we can.

§ 23. 9.—**Duties Towards Personal Enemies.**

What are we *not* obliged to grant to our enemies?

We are not obliged to love them as tenderly as our dearest

friends, nor to suffer injury inflicted by them; still less must we sacrifice our welfare for them.

But how ought we to behave towards them?

We ought to answer calmly their insults, to deal honestly with them, to wish them well, and to do them good, if we can consistently; also to pardon them, when they regret their offence.

Why is such a behavior our duty?

Because it is conforming to our nature. "Forgiveness is more beautiful than vengeance; that is human, this is brutal."—Pittacus, 600 A. C. By meekness and kindness we reconcile our enemies to us most surely, and ennoble ourselves.

CHAPTER SECOND.

DOCTRINE OF JUSTICE (of Duties and Rights, Resting on Reason and Nature).

§ 24. Explanations—Division of Doctrine.

What are the objects of the doctrine of Justice?

Its objects are the mutual rights and duties of mankind.

What corresponds to every right of ours?

A duty which others ought to perform towards us.

What do they call this duty?

Duty of right.

How do duties of right differ from duties of benevolence?

The duties of right differ from those of benevolence in that they may be joined with compulsion, which means that their fulfillment may be *enforced* in case of necessity.

What else, then, are the duties of right called?

They are called *compulsory* duties. e. g., a citizen can be compelled to pay his taxes, when he refuses to do so voluntarily.

What rights and obligations form the contents of the Right of Reason?

Those Rights and obligations, the validity of which is deduced from the decisions of Reason.

What others are called Rights by Reason?

Natural rights.

What do the *positive* or conventional rights teach?

They teach the rights and corresponding duties which in some given State are acknowledged; as, e. g., there is a code of certain rights for the State of Wisconsin, another for the State of New York, of France, Italy, etc.

How are both the natural and the positive rights further divided?

Into public and private rights.

What rights and duties form the object of public rights?

Those rights and duties which subsist between the citizens of a State.

What other name is given to the public rights?

The name of State Rights

What is the object of the doctrine of private rights?

The rights and corresponding duties of individuals and small societies.

What kind of intention should there be at the bottom of an absolute moral action?

Moral intention.

What can be wanting in the performance of a duty of right?

The moral intention.

What do we call an action in which the moral intention is wanting?

We call it a legal action. e. g., The payment of my debt is a legal act when I pay it because I do not like to be sued and compelled by the Court to pay; but it is a moral act if I pay the debt because I am persuaded by my conscience that it is my duty to do so.

What liberty can everybody claim?

The liberty to satisfy all his natural impulses in a rational way.

Why?

Because he cannot be happy without this liberty. (§ 2.)

Is this liberty unbounded when we live in society with other persons?

No: for they must enjoy the same degree of liberty with us.

By what is our liberty in this case limited?

By the equal liberty of others.
What restriction of liberty is only valid by natural right?
The equal restriction of the liberty of all individuals.

I. Private Rights and Duties.

§ 25. First Principles.

1. Every one has the liberty of doing everything, by which he does not infringe upon the equal liberty of others.
2. Bound your liberty by the law of equal rights of others.
3. Give to every one his own.
4. Do right, and be afraid of none.
5. Act honestly and righteously.
6. What you don't like others to do unto you, that, also, do not unto them.
7. Claim from others the same regard for *your* rights, which they claim for *theirs*.

§ 26. Rights and Duties with Regard to Life and Health— Homicide—Right of Self-Defence.

What right has man with regard to his life and health?
He has the right to preserve his life and health.
What duty follows from this right?
The duty to respect the life and health of our fellow-creatures.
What, therefore, ought we not to do?
We should neither destroy, shorten, nor damage their lives.
What is the name of the crime by which one unlawfully destroys another's life?
Murder, man-slaughter, homicide.
Why is man slaughter a crime?
Because the slaughtered is deprived of his rights by his murderer, and also because the murderer does not like to be killed in turn.
2. How can people otherwise injure the life of their fellow-man?

They injure it when they seduce him to perpetrate shameful actions which damage his life, or when they destroy his health by vexation, terror, or violent attack.

3. When are we right in making use of arms and force?

When another attacks us unjustly, and our life is endangered.

What is the defence in this case called?

Self-defence.

How far may self-defence be extended?

Not further than it is necessary for the preservation of our own lives and property.

§ 27. 2.—With Regard to Our Personal and Religious Liberty.

1. What right should every man claim with regard to his person?

Every one should claim the liberty of his person; for Reason teaches us that all men, without distinction of color, sex, station, and caste, are born with the same inalienable rights, and that the earth is the common mother of all.

Can a man, then, by right become the serf or slave of others?

None can by right become the serf or slave of others, either by inheritance, or by purchase and sale, or by birth or violence.

From what other law can the injustice of slavery be deduced?

From the law of equal rights, which all enjoy; for the slave is not as free as his oppressor (Cf. § 24).

2. Is there no other kind of freedom to which every man is entitled?

Yes; *the mental and religious liberty.*

What are the rights of mental and religious liberty?

The right to freely investigate truth, and especially the first cause of the Universe; also to freely confess and practice the religion to which we are devoted by conscientious conviction. All dissidents in religious opinions ought to enjoy equal rights.

3. Why is every one entitled to mental and religious liberty?

Because truth and religious knowledge are the most precious gifts to mankind, without which it cannot attain its destination.

4. What duty is equally incumbent upon others?

The duty of respecting our right concerning our mental and religious liberty.

5. What are they, on that account, forbidden to do?
They are forbidden to persecute and injure others for the sake of peculiar religious opinions, or to compel them to embrace their creed.

6. What right is ours in such a case?
We have the right to repel the aggressions made on our religious freedom.

7. Must we be content to be only *tolerated* by the condescension of the established churches?
No! "All men are equally entitled to the free exercise of religion, according to the dictates of conscience."—James Madison.

§ 28. 3.—With Regard to Property—Theft—Robbery—Fraud—Indemnification.

1. What do we want for the preservation of our life?
Property.
To what, then, is every man entitled besides?
To possession and property.

2. Why ought we to respect the property of other people?
Because we desire, also, to keep the possession of our own.
What crimes must we therefore shun?
Theft, robbery, and fraud.
Who makes himself guilty of these crimes?
Any one makes himself guilty of theft, who secretly deprives others of their property; of robbery, he who seizes violently on it; of fraud, he who withdraws it from them by means of designed deceit or illusion.
To what regard ought we, especially, to avoid fraud?
In regard to purchase and sale, in measure and weight.
What is that who has knowingly or unknowingly deprived others of their rightful property, in duty bound to do?
He is bound to indemnify them for the damage he has caused them.

§ 29. 4.—With Regard to Reputation and Veracity—Slander—Lie—Promise.

1. What further belongs to the possessions of man?
To the possessions of man also belongs his honor, his good name.

Why ought the honor of others to be sacred to us?

Because we desire, too, that they shall not violate ours.

2. What ought we then, to shun?

Slander!

Who is said to slander others?

Whoever designedly imputes to them trespasses and crimes they have not committed; whoever magnifies their faults, or diminishes their merits: such an one slanders

What is a slanderer under obligation to do?

He is under obligation to restore the reputation of the slandered person.

3. How ought we to speak in our conversation?

Truthfully.

Why is it our duty to be truthful in our discourse?

Because we virtually promise to the one addressed to tell the truth.

Who lies?

He who, with the design of leading others into error, speaks otherwise than as he means: such an one is lying.

Why is a lie wrong?

Because it is a kind of fraud.

4. Ought we also to avoid *white* lies (fibs)?

Yes; for they soon grow habitual, and lead insensibly to lies of selfishness and malice.

What should we do, if it be neither advisable nor our duty to speak truth?

In such a case we may keep silence.

5. What order of lies is he guilty of who in religious matters teaches otherwise than what he thinks?

Such an one becomes guilty of a *pious lie*.

What are such men called?

Religious hypocrites, Pharisees. In the Christian Church many miracles were forged in order to convert the credulous.

What did pious lies and pious frauds bring to the Church?

They brought to her immeasurable damage.

6. When are we obliged to speak the truth to others?

When they have no right to expect it. e. g., A robber has no right to expect that we discover to him the place where our money is hidden ; nor the murderer or the insane man that we show him the road the fugitive whom he persecutes has taken. No more right have the enemies of our country to expect the avowal of truth from a spy who has stolen into their camp.

7. Lastly, what does the duty of veracity command ?

It commands us to keep the *promise* we have voluntarily given to others.

In what cases is a promise not binding ?

When it violates the laws of morals or justice ; when it has been forced out of us ; when it is impossible to fulfill it, or when it could be only kept by the breach of a higher duty ; e. g., we have promised a friend a situation, but afterward we find out that he has not the knowledge which is necessary for the discharge of the duties of the office.

What precaution should we use in this regard ?

Never to give a promise which would likely afterwards to put us in collision with our duty.

What are the most important species of promise ?

Contracts.

§ 30.—Contracts.

What is a contract ?

A contract is a written or implied promise by which two or more persons bind themselves mutually to certain performances.

What is the object of most contracts ?

The object of most contracts is either property or personal service.

What does justice demand ?

That the performance and the reciprocal service shall have the same value.

What are the most important and the most common contracts ?

The loan-contract, the contract of purchase, the contract of trading-companies, the marriage-contract, the contract of service, and the State-contract.

§ 31. 1.—Loan-Contract—Usury.

1. In what condition ought we to return the borrowed article ?

In the same condition as we received it.

2. What damage have we to make good to the owner; what not?

We have to make good such damage as has arisen from our negligence in using the object loaned; but we are not responsible for the damage which has necessarily arisen from the use the proprietor has allowed to be made of it.

3. To what kind of contracts does the loan of capital belong?
To loan-contracts.

What does a creditor usually require of a debtor?
Certain interest.

Has the capitalist the right to demand interest, and why?

He has a right to do so, because his capital is profitable to the debtor, and is dead to the owner so long as it is loaned.

Into what can the charge of high interests easily degenerate?
Into usury.

§ 32. 2.—The Contract of Purchase. 3.—Trading-Companies.

1. What law is infringed by the maxim: "Buy as cheap as possible, and sell as dear as you can?"
The law of equity.

What seems to be the best rule in buying and selling?
The ruling price of any merchandise in market.

When does the seller of a ware perpetrate a fraud?
When he commends it for qualities it does not possess.

When can he not be made responsible for its defects?
When he does not warrant its superior quality.

What does he commit who counterfeits money or knowingly circulates it?
He commits a fraud.

Why?
Because money represents merchandise.

2. What is a *trading-company?*
The union of two or several persons formed for the purpose of carrying on a commercial business in common.

What is the duty of such persons?
To deal honestly with each other.

In what proportion ought the partners of the company to divide the joint gain of the business?

In the proportion of their individual interest.

§ 33. 4.—Marriage Contract.*

1. How was the wife in ancient times used and considered?

As the servant, nay, frequently, as the slave of man.

What does the Christian religion demand from the wife?

Subjection to the dominion of man.

2. What are the rights of husband and wife by nature?

They are equal.

For what reason?

Because both have the like nature, the like destination, and, in general, the like faculties. If man usually excels woman in intellect, she, on the other hand, possesses more intensive feelings.

Does the outweighing strength of man give him the privilege of ruling the wife?

No; might is not right, in such cases.

3. What is marriage?

Marriage is an alliance by which man and woman unite for a communion intended to last for life.

4. What ought to be the motive to this alliance?

Mutual love; not avidity, not voluptuousness, etc. It also ought not to be concluded inconsiderately, because it has to last through long time.

5. What duties have both consorts to fulfill?

They ought to be devoted to each other with love and unshaken fidelity, and to support each other in all changes of life.

6. What duties have they to discharge to their children?

They ought to provide well for them, to teach them to labor, to educate them carefully, and to treat them as beings who enjoy the same rights as all men. In their moral conduct they ought to be their models.

7. What are, especially, the obligations of the husband?

He is obliged to afford his family food, clothing, shelter, protection, honor, and comfort.

---

*This paragraph is inserted for such children as are more advanced in age and education.

8. What are the wife's reasonable duties?

She ought to arrange and manage prudently the household, and to try to ease the cares and troubles of the husband by kind behavior.

9. In what condition of life does man usually best fulfill the objects of life?

In matrimony.

10. Why should polygamy be reprobated?

Because it hurts generally the moral feelings of our age, violates the customs of the most civilized nations on earth, and degrades the dignity of the wife.

§ 34. 5.—Contract of Service—Indenture of Apprenticeship.

1. What do servants owe their employes?

They owe them obedience, application, faithfulness and economy.

2. How ought they to consider themselves?

They ought to consider themselves as members of the family.

How ought they to behave?

They ought to take a heartfelt interest in the prosperous and adverse fate of the family, and to discharge their obligations not from greediness of wages, but induced by benevolence towards their employers.

3. What are the duties of the employers towards their servants and employes?

They ought to do justice to them by performing strictly the conditions of their mutual contract, especially by giving them their due wages. Besides, they ought not to overcharge them with needless work.

4. What more ought they to do?

They ought to treat their servants with meekness and affability, to avoid harsh, morose manners towards them, and to grant them harmless pleasures.

Why ought employers to act in this manner?

Because servants are also human beings, like their masters, born with the same titles to life, liberty, and happiness.

5. For what ought masters not to employ their apprentices?

They ought not to employ them for by-work, but let them perform the task of their vocation.

What other duties have masters to fulfill towards them?

The same duties which employers generally have to perform toward their inferiors.

6. In what cases is it wrong to employ children in factories and workshops?

When their bodies have not yet obtained the necessary strength, and their minds have not yet received a sufficient measure of school-education.

To what do parents who hire out such children become accessory?

They become accessory to the injustice inflicted upon their children by the employers.

The most important of all contracts, the social or State contract, deserves a closer examination.

II. *Public Rights and Duties (State Rights).*

§ 35. First Principles.

1. In the Declaration of Independence of the United States of America, the following principles are proclaimed: "We hold these truths to be self-evident: That all men are created equal; that they are endowed by their Creator with certain inalienable rights; that among these are life, liberty, and the pursuit of happiness. That, to secure these rights, Governments are instituted among men, deriving their just powers from the consent of the governed."

2. Liberty, civilization and prosperity for all!

§ 36. General Definitions.

1. What is a State?

A State is a spontaneous union of men, who are living under the same laws, in equal social relations.

2. What is the object of their union?

The object is the welfare of all the members in as high a degree as possible; particularly their mutual protection.

In what way is this end to be attained?

By mutual assistance.

3. What is a State contract (social contract)?

It is the contract to which the members of a State agree explicitly or tacitly among themselves, in order to secure that end.

4. Why are social contracts necessary?

Because the voices of conscience and sympathy are often too feeble to induce man to perform his duty, e. g., to pay a debt. To the merely moral motives the fear of coercion and punishment must be joined. In the state of nature, Right cannot always be enforced. Therefore, a power must be created which man, who has to fulfill an obligation cannot resist.

Where does such a power exist?

In the State.

5. What advantages does the State afford to man?

The State is the safest foundation of Right; it promotes the welfare of all its constituents, and the general civilization of the nation.

6. What is needed in every State?

In every State a Government and Laws are needed.

7. Are Governments ever instituted by God's grace?

No; but every Government derives its power from the expressed or tacit consent of the people.

8. Of what kind can the Government of a State be?

It can be either republican, or aristocratical, or monarchical.

9. When is a Government republican (democratic)?

When the people govern themselves.

When is it an aristocracy?

When the higher castes (the nobility, or the richest families) are governing.

When is it monarchical?

When only one person rules the State.

What is a hierarchy (theocracy)?

A State in which the priests control the Government.

By what law do the sovereigns in monarchies for the most part hold their power?

By the law of hereditary succession

Into what pernicious form is the Government of a monarchy apt to degenerate?

To despotism and tyranny.

10. Why ought the people to govern themselves?

Because the welfare of all citizens demands it.

What are a people called who govern themselves?

The sovereigns (supreme rulers of the State).

11. When is the form of Government strictly democratic?

When the laws are given by the whole people; i. e., when each man casts a vote.

For what States is this kind of democracy proper?

Only for small ones.

In what manner must the people govern themselves in larger States?

By representatives.

What right ought the people to reserve to themselves in choosing their representatives, even if they fill the highest offices?

The rights to recall them whenever they do not act according to their commission; also the right to approve or to reject bills and resolutions of very high importance.

12. How many branches does the power of Government comprise?

It comprises three branches, to wit: the legislative, the executive, and the judiciary.

Do people for legislation need two chambers, and for administration a President?

One chamber suffices, and the executive power ought to be invested in a commission; for an upper chamber (a Senate) is a relic of aristocratical institutions, and the Presidency is a copy of monarchies.

What does the jurisprudence of our age teach with regard to these three branches?

It teaches that they ought to be separated, and each administered independently of the others.

13. Whose duty is it to select the State officers?

It is the duty of the people themselves.

Should they be elected for life?

They ought to be chosen only for shorter or longer terms.

14. What are the rights and functions of the legislative body?

The legislative body makes the general laws of the country; imposes the necessary taxes, declares war, makes peace, and forms alliances with other States, coins money for the use of the State, etc.

15. What is meant by the Constitution of a State?

By it those laws are meant which regulate the fundamental rights and duties of the citizens of the State.

Must the Constitution of a State be always the same? No; it ought to be amended from time to time, according to the changed condition of the State.

§ 37.—Duties of the State (Government).

1. What is the duty of the State with regard to the private rights of its citizens?

The State ought to render all the private rights of its citizens secure.

2. Especially with regard to life?

It should protect life against the attacks of domestic and foreign enemies.

3. With regard to health?

It should keep away influences obnoxious to health, and protect it by a controlling supervision of factories, provisions, and dwellings It ought also to prohibit the overwork of children for industrial purposes.

4. What other rights of its citizens ought it to secure?

Their personal and religious liberty, their property and honor, their right to assemble peaceably, and to petition the Government for a redress of grievances, the liberty of speech and of the press.

5. Has the State the right to teach religion?

It has no right to teach religion, nor to enjoin upon its members what creed they shall profess; because, by doing so, it restricts their liberty of thought (cf. § 27).

What more results from that liberty?

The State Government has no right to establish a State Church, to command what day the citizens ought to sanctify, and in what manner they ought to do so. It has no right to appoint chaplains, to establish religious festivals and fast-days, or to enjoin the judicial oath upon the Bible or in any religious form. Nor has it the right to permit the use of the Bible, or other sectarian books in the public schools. Instead of the Bible, human rights and duties ought to be taught.

6. In what manner ought justice to be administered?

It ought to be administered early, firmly, impartially, publicly, so as to help the poor as well as the rich to his right, gratuitously, at the State's expense. Juries ought to be instituted.

7. What duty has the State to discharge with regard to public education?

It ought to care for the best education of the people, mingled with wholesome labor.

What institutions should it found to this end?

The best schools, where every one, without distinction of sex, both the poor and the rich, gratuitously receives the most perfect physical and mental cultivation. Also to the higher institutes every one ought to have free admission, without distinction of descent, sex, or wealth. It ought also to provide for public libraries and museums.

Who should meet the expenses of the public instruction?

All citizens unitedly, by equable taxation.

May the tuition money of the State be divided among sects?

No; for the public schools are secular institutions.

Why ought the State to provide for the education of the citizens?

Because the people are the sovereigns, and if ignorant, and lacking civilization, are unable to govern themselves.

For what other reason ought the State to educate the citizens?

Because many crimes originate in their want of a good education.

How ought education to be conducted with regard to mental development and Progress?

It ought to keep pace with the Progress of the Age.

What is the State's duty toward parents who neglect the education of their children?

It is its duty to compel them to perform that obligation.

What should it do in regard to the arts and sciences?

It should foster and encourage their culture.

8. What duty is incumbent upon the State in regard to public morals?

It ought to superintend them, and to forbid and punish actions which corrupt them, e. g., extravagance, intoxication, games of hazzard, immoral exhibitions and publications.

Are temperance-laws needed?

No; for they are useless measures of coercion against those, against whom they are directed, and insulting restrictions of the personal liberty of those who do not need them.

9. What is its duty with regard to trade, traffic, and improvements?

It ought to advance commerce, trade, and agriculture, to build public roads, to regulate measures and weights, and to check usury.

10. For what objects should the public revenues be spent?

Only for the common welfare.

11. Is the Government permitted to grant exclusive privileges to any single class of citizens?

No! All ought to enjoy equal rights according to Law, also women, children, and colored people.

To what professions, occupations, and offices should the female sex be privileged?

To all those for which women are capable.

Why, especially, ought women to enjoy the right of public suffrage?

Because women must pay taxes, like men.

Is it just to subject the minority to the will of the majority?

No; for the laws cannot have general validity, but by the general consent, since all citizens hold the same rights.

12. With what dictates ought the laws of a country to be in accordance?

With the dictates of Reason and natural Law.

What, then, ought to be done with defective laws?

They ought to be abrogated or amended. The best legal right is often the greatest wrong, if considered in the light of natural Right, e. g., slavery, disfranchisment of woman, and, in several countries, the very disproportionate division of land.

13. How ought State officers to deport themselves?

They should try to discharge faithfully and assiduously the duties of their offices.

§ 38—Continuation—Disposition of State Land.

Since universal welfare is the object of life in a State, what is the duty of the State?

It is to take care that every one without hindrance can acquire a competence if he has ability to do so.

Whose condition ought the Government to aim to alleviate?

The condition of the poor, of the proletaries, and laborers. The rich can help themselves. Originally all things were free. Then the earth was divided in order that it could be cultivated, and that fighting for its possession might be avoided. But the partition was arranged on the tacit condition that the State would procure the ways and means for the distressed to acquire a living in keeping with man's dignity. The State is to aim at filling the chasm which lies between abundance and misery, and, therefore, to protect the weak, and to restrict the strong. Many times, also, lands were conquered and their inhabitants deprived of them by force of arms. There are countries in which there are only few landed proprietors, and the great majority of the inhabitants have no real property. Such an organization of State is a most atrocious wrong. All men still have the same right to possess the earth, because they all enjoy, by nature, equal rights.

Does not land become the property of the first occupant?

No, not without the consent of the rest of men; for it is their common property.

Does it not become his property, if he cultivates it?

By its culture he acquires, at best, the right to collect the fruit of his industry; but the soil itself does not become his property.

What follows from the nature of equal rights of all?

It follows that the State is the rightful owner of all the land.

What duty of the present landed proprietors is to be inferred from that principle?

The duty to re-cede the land they possess to the State, if the State orders it so.

Would it be just to drive them by force from the land?

No, because they have acquired it in a legal way, by purchase, inheritance, etc.

What expedients have been proposed in order to remedy the disproportion in the possession of property?

It has been proposed to distribute the land among all in equal parcels, or to procure work for the working classes by the efforts of the State, or to support them by general poor-taxes, to shelter them in work and poor houses, to assess high taxes on heritages, etc. All these expedients have been tried.

Has good success followed these experiments?

No!

What is, from the standpoint of Natural Rights, the only way to acquire landed property?

The State redeems the land of its actual possessors: they cede it to it, and for their loss they are recompensed according to the law of equity. Thereby the State becomes the real possessor of the whole territory. Any citizen who wishes to get land, then takes a piece at rent from the State for a fixed time, on certain conditions; he pays the State his rent out of the earnings of his labor, and the balance is his own.*

§ 39. Conclusion—Disposition of Heritages—Relief of the Condition of Workmen and Proletaries.

What part of lands ought the State to reserve?

Such an one as it wants for general institutions, namely for public roads, for publicbuildings, forests, etc.

Ought the tenant to be permitted to lease a part of the land he holds by rent, to others?

No; otherwise the poor would again fall a prey to the leasor.

What precaution ought the State to take in order to prevent the insecurity of possession?

It warrants the tenant and his immediate descendents the posession for as long time as they cultivate the soil; else they might be forcibly obliged to quit it.

---

*Cf. Herb. Spencer, "Social Statistics," (pp. 131-159), and Louis Buechner, "Stellung des Menschen in der Natur," (pp. 251-290), the principles of whom are the foundation of the new school of Socialism, and are represented in this section. The further proposals of reform, following after this note, in § 39, are communicated by Ch. Hinzen, and other liberal writers. But the former thinks that for such reforms still the course of many years is required, and that in our times they can only be effected by the way of revolution.

How should the State dispose of all public lands which are not brought under cultivation up to a certain time?

It should repurchase them at the original purchase price.

How should it support indigent colonists?

It should support them from the public funds under the condition of their reimbursing the State.

Against what religious organizations has the State a right to proceed?

Against such as by their tendency and power endanger its liberty.

Is the State right in granting certain companies monopolies?

No; all monopolies ought to be abolished; and the railroads, telegraphs, etc., ought to be operated by the State. Such companies or private individuals who actually own such establishments should cede them to the State, which should compensate for their loss.

To whom ought the property of the deceased return?

Generally to the State, because after his death it is without a possessor. Still, if he leaves a wife or children, and dies without a last will, the property should fall to them, because the wife gained it jointly with the husband, and the children have received their life through him. But if the succession is very considerable, these heirs ought to pay on it a convenient tax. The heirship of more remote relatives seems to be entirely devoid of right, or at best can only be admitted on condition that they pay a high tax on the heritage.

In what manner could and should the workingman's condition be improved?

They can create mutual associations, which the State should promote; and the State ought to protect them against the unjust pretensions of capitalists, by securing to them a fair compensation. The capitalist should let them have a share of his profits, in proportion to their labor, and in this way grant them the real gain of their labor. The State ought to reduce the maximum of their hours of labor in such a way that a respite for repose and self-culture remains to them.

What kind of public houses ought the State to establish for the poor?

Hospitals, poor-houses, asylums for orphans and insane, for the blind, deaf and mutes, etc.

For what other reason ought the State to secure to the citizens an opportunity to acquire their livelihood?

Because many crimes originate in their want of a competence.

How does a nation sometimes help itself, if the grievances of the Government become too burdensome?

By the way of revolution, that is, by its violent overthrow.

When are revolutions rightful?

When a nation cannot remove the tyranny of Government but by force.

Why are revolutions usually no blessing to the nation?

Because they are usually the work of blind passion, and are attempted before the people have acquired the preliminary instruction necessary to a higher degree of liberty.

What reforms are preferable to revolutions?

Peaceable ones.

Of what ought the people first to be persuaded?

Of the necessity and usefulness of a reform.

How does it arrive at this conviction?

1. By teaching the youth the principles of a better organization of the State.

2. By public orators, by the free press, in meetings where the the people receive information of the prevailing defects of the State.

3. Petitions to amend them are addressed to the Government.

In this way minds are carefully educated, and get prepared for reforms. A public opinion is created and becomes irresistible. The dissatisfaction with the prevalent defects of Government becomes general. By these proceedings finally better institutions will be effected, without bloodshed.

How can free Governments be conserved?

Only by love of liberty, and by vigilance of the nations. Where the former is wanting, the latter vanishes, too; then encroachments of the Government soon will follow, and liberty is lost.

§ 40. Duties of the Citizen—Taxation.

What are the members of a State called?

Citizens,—fellow-citizens.

What duties are the citizens of a State bound to discharge?

1. They ought to pay respect to the State officers.
2. To obey the laws of the country.
3. To pay the taxes which are necessary for the support of the Government.
4. To devote their life to industry.
5. To protect and defend their country against unjust domestic and foreign foes.
6. To concur cheerfully in all efforts for public reforms.

Why should they be industrious?

Because they cannot promote the common welfare except by industry.

Ought the property of the clergy and the religious communities to be exempt from taxation?

No: for it enjoys the protection of the state like other property.

Upon what part of possession ought the taxes to be levied?

Not upon the necessary supplies of life, but upon the abundance of possession.

What ought to be the measure of taxation?

The degree of wealth of the citizens; taxes ought to be imposed on a progressive scale.

§ 41. The Oath—War.

1. What does it signify to take an oath?

It means to attest the truth of our statement by an appeal to God as a witness.

Can an oath be a general obligation of man?

No; for all men do not believe in the existence of a personal God.

What ought to satisfy the State, if any one refuses to swear?

His assurance that, if he speaks untruth, he will submit to all the penalties of perjury decreed by public law.

Why should an oath not be frequently administered?

Because it thereby becomes trite, and ceases to be respected.

Into what does oath-taking easily degenerate if it be frequently administered?

It degenerates into perjury.

2. What is a hostile combat between nations called?

War.

Why do nations often decide their differences by war?

Because there is no legal judge constituted for nations.

Does Right always side with the stronger party?

No.

In war, is the Right always victorious?

No; often rude forces get the victory.

When are wars unjust?

If they are waged in order to conquer foreign countries, or to acquire glory.

How ought wars always to be carried on?

Humanely and mercifully.

How should they be considered?

They should be considered the severest calamity which can afflict a country.

Do they give honor to mankind?

No honor; on the contrary, much disgrace.

What is the duty of man as to war?

He ought to endeavor to so act that wars may always grow less, and at last entirely disappear from the earth.

What ought to be put in the place of the decision by the sword?

The decision by arbitration of impartial umpires, chosen by the litigant nations.

How should nations promote their mutual welfare?

By kindness and respect; by fraternity; by protecting their mutual rights; by international leagues, etc.

§ 42. Conflict of Duties.

What happens sometimes when we seek to fulfill two duties?

They contradict each other, and we must neglect one of them.

Which one must we then prefer?

The higher one.

What duties are generally higher and more sacred,—the duties of justice, or of benevolence? The duties towards our country, or our family? The duties towards the members of our family, or towards strangers?

In general, the duties of justice are preferable to those of benevolence; the duties towards our country to those towards our family; the duties towards our own family to those towards strangers.

Illustrations.—If I have got some money, must I give it away to the poor, or discharge first my debts with it? Is it right to steal the money from our neighbor with the intention to help by it a starving family in their distress? Some one has deposited some money with me; I found out that he wants it in order to support the enemies of my country: am I obliged to return it? The father of a family is a friend of science; but his children ask him for bread; may he, in this case, pass his time with his books, or ought he to work assiduously? A poor mother is sick; her daughter frequents the school; should she go there, or nurse her mother? Some one has left with you his revolver, meanwhile he turns insane, or intends to commit suicide; will you return him the weapon when he demands it? When, during the government of the thirty tyrants, in Athens, Socrates was commanded by them to bring some innocent citizen in their presence, he refused to obey them; did he do right or wrong? A similar case often happened in the United States, when the fugitive slave law was valid, by which every citizen was ordered to deliver fugitive slaves; the positive right then conflicted with the natural. During war the citizens are called to arms; must they take care of their families, or, if drafted, take arms, fight for their country, and run the risk of being killed in battle?

§ 43. Behavior Towards Animals.

Why is it immoral to ill-treat and torment animals?

Because they are also Nature's creatures, and sensible of pleasure and pain, like man.

How ought we, especially, to treat animals which we keep for the sake of our profit or pleasure?

We should feed them well, take care of them, and treat them kindly, and, in general, only for reasonable purposes subject them to servitude.

THE END.

CONTENTS.

	Page.
Preface	7—10
PART FIRST—Moral Culture	5
SECTION FIRST	11—87
Morals in Examples	11
CHAPTER FIRST	11—64
Morals (in the Stricter Sense)	11
I. DUTIES TOWARDS OURSELVES	11—33
1. Bad Habits of the Blackamoor.—*Æsop*	11
2. Bad Results of Bad Actions—Nails in the Post	12
3. Modesty—Pride—Content	12
(a)—A Modest Wit	12
(b)—The Horse and the Ass.—*Æsop*	13
(c)—The Monkey Tourist.—*J. G. Saxe*	14
(d)—The Mountain and the Squirrel.—*R. W. Emerson*	15
4. Temperance	15
(a)—The Washingtonian's Story	15
(b)—Alexander and Clitus.—*Rollin*	17
(c)—Saint Becky.—*Douglas Jerrold*	18
5. Courage—Temerity—Leap for Life.—*Morris*	19
6. Application—Inertness	20
(a)—The Panorama Boy	20
(b)—The Ant and the Grasshopper.—*Æsop*	21
(c)—The Village Blacksmith.—*Longfellow*	21
(d)—The Plowman.—*Holmes*	22
7. Parsimony—Dissipation	23
The Young Man and the Swallow.—*Æsop*	23
8. Frugality—Covetousness—Avarice	24
(a)—Quintius Cincinnatus.—*Agnes Strickland*	24
(b)—Solicitude Caused by Great Fortune	25
(c)—The Man and his Goose.—*Æsop*	25
(d)—The Oil-Merchant's Ass.—*J. G. Saxe*	25
(e)—The Little Glass Shoe.—*J. G. Saxe*	26
9. Gambling—The Gambler's Wife.—*Dr. Coats*	28
10. Education and Mental Culture	29
(a)—William Cobbett	29
(b)—Illustrations American Apprentices	30
(c)—The Nightingale and the Organ.—*J. G. Saxe*	30
11. Perseverance—Robert Bruce	31
12. Patience—Anger—The Frog and the Mouse.—*Æsop*	32
13. Vocation—The Wolf and the Stray Kid.—*Perrin*	32
II. DUTIES OF BENEVOLENCE TOWARDS OUR FELLOW CREATURES	33—64
1. Mutual Charity and Philanthropy	33
(a)—The Good Samaritan	33
(b)—The Sick Passenger	34
(c)—The Generous Neighbor	35
(d)—A Brave Boy	35
(e)—J. Howard	35
(f)—The Chieftain's Daughter.—*G. P. Morris*	36
(g)—Thomson and Quin	37
(h)—Little and Great.—*Ch. Mackay*	38
(i)—St. Phillis.—*Douglas Jerrold*	39

		Page.
2. Retribution		39
(a)—The Dove and the Ant.—*Æsop*		39
(b)—The Hawk and the Farmer.—*Æsop*		39
(c)—"We" and "You."—*J. G. Saxe*		40
3. Meekness and Forbearance		41
(a)—Chang King		41
(b)—The Turkey and the Ant.—*John Gay*		41
4. Politeness—Sham Politeness		42
(a)—Washington		42
(b)—Domestic Asides; or Truth in Parentheses.—*T. Hood*		42
5. Sacrifice of Life by Charity.—*Voltamad*		43
6. Filial Love		44
(a)—The Good Indian Son		44
(b)—Volney Beckner		44
(c)—Self-Sacrifice of a Daughter		45
(d)—The Children's Hour.—*Longfellow*		45
(e)—Filial Piety		46
7. Filial Obedience—The Wolf and the Kid.—*Æsop*		47
8. Love of Brothers and Sisters		47
(a)—The Courageous Brother		47
(b)—The Heroine, Emma Carroll		48
(c)—Stanzas Addressed by Lord Byron to His Sister		48
(d)—Isabella, the Suitor for a Condemned Brother.—*Shakespeare*		49
9. Friendship		52
(a)—Damon and Pythias		52
(b)—The Hare and Many Friends.—*John Gay*		53
10. Bad Company—The Husbandman and the Stork.—*Æsop*		54
11. Gratitude to Benefactors—Ingratitude		54
(a)—Thomas Cromwell		54
(b)—Gardener and His Dog.—*Æsop*		56
(c)—The Hart and the Vine —*Æsop*		56
(d)—The Countryman and the Snake.—*Æsop*		57
12. Tolerance—Fanaticism—Religious Constancy		57
(a)—William Penn		57
(b)—Thomas Cranmer.—*Alfred Tennyson*		58
(c)—Roger Williams —*Geo. Bancroft*		61
13. Love of Enemies—The Generous Quaker		63
CHAPTER SECOND	64—87	
RIGHTS AND DUTIES OF JUSTICE		64
I. PRIVATE RIGHTS AND DUTIES	64—74	
1. Consequences of Murder—Lady Macbeth.—*Shakespeare*		64
2. Liberty—The Yankee Girl.—*J. G. Whittier*		66
3. Honesty—Fraud—Theft—Indemnification		67
(a)—An Honest Boy		67
(b)—Mercury and the Woodman.—*Aesop*		68
(c)—The Starling		68
(d)—An Act of Indemnification		69
4. Veracity—Lying—The Oath		69
(a)—The Boy Who Would Not Tell a Lie		69
(b)—Gossip		70
(c)—Sacredness of Oath		70
5. Love		70
(a)—Love Conquers all Obstacles—Quintin Matsys		70
(b)—Lavinia and Palemon.—*James Thomson*		71
6. Master and Servant—The Old Hound.—*Aesop*		74
II. PUBLIC RIGHTS AND DUTIES	74—87	
1. Patriotism		74
(a)—General J. Reed		74

		Page.
(b)—The Last Will		75
(c)—Barbara Fritchie.—*J. G. Whittier*		75
(d)—James Lick		76
2. Heroism		78
(a)—Leonidas at Thermopylæ.—*Agnes Strickland*		78
(b)—Arnold Winkelried.—*Jaz. Montgomery*		78
(c)—Marco Bozzaris.—*F. G. Halleck*		80
(d)—General Wolfe.—*Oliver Goldsmith*		82
(e)—The Battle of Bunker Hill		82
(f)—Seventy-Six.—*W. C. Bryant*		83
(g)—Abraham Lincoln.—*W. C. Bryant*		84
(h)—Conflict of Duties—Regulus.—*Rollins*		84
3. Behavior Towards Animals		85
(a)—The Hornets' Nest.—*N. Hawthorne*		85

SECTION SECOND..87—131
DOCTRINE OF DUTIES AND RIGHTS ....87—94
INTRODUCTION...87
§ 1. Explanations—Man's Moral Faculties...........87
§ 2. Human Destination.....................................89
§ 3. Duties—Virtue and Vice—Their Consequences—Doctrine of Duties... 90
§ 4. First Principles of Ethics.............................91
§ 5. Division of Ethics......................................93
CHAPTER FIRST...94—109
ETHICS (IN THE STRICTER SENSE)......................94
I. DUTIES TOWARDS OURSELVES—(PERSONAL DUTIES)..........94—102
§ 6. First Principles..94
§ 7. General Duties Towards Ourselves..............94
    SPECIAL DUTIES TOWARDS OURSELVES...........96
§ 8. 1.—Duties With Regard to Our Life and Health.....96
§ 9. 2.—With Regard to Property.......................98
§ 10. 3.—With Regard to Mental Culture............99
§ 11. 4.—With Regard to Moral Culture.............100
§ 12. With Regard to Aesthetical Refinement......101
§ 13. Choice of a Vocation................................101
II. DUTIES TOWARDS OUR FELLOW CREATURES (DUTIES OF BENEVOLENCE).................................102—109
§ 14. First Principles...102
§ 15. General Duties...102
    SPECIAL DUTIES..104
§ 16. 1.—Duties of Children Towards Their Parents....104
§ 17. 2.—Duties Towards Brothers, Sisters, and Relations....105
§ 18. 3.—Duties Towards Companions................105
§ 19. 4.—Duties Towards Teachers.....................105
§ 20. 5 and 6.—Duties Towards Friends and Benefactors...106
§ 21. 7.—Towards Poor, Sick, Frail, and Old People....107
§ 22. 8.—Towards Religious Sects......................107
§ 23. 9.—Duties Towards Personal Enemies........108
CHAPTER SECOND...109—131
DOCTRINE OF JUSTICE (OF DUTIES AND RIGHTS, RESTING ON REASON AND NATURE)..............
§ 24. Explanation—Division of Doctrine..............109
I. PRIVATE RIGHTS AND DUTIES.........................111—119
§ 25. First Principles...111
§ 26. Rights and Duties with Regard to Life and Health—Homicide—Right of Self Defence.....111
§ 27. 2.—With Regard to Our Personal and Religious Liberty....112
§ 28. 3.—With Regard to Property—Theft—Robbery—Fraud—Indemnification.....113

§ 29.	4.—With Regard to Reputation and Veracity - Slander—Lie—Promise	113
§ 30.	Contracts	115
§ 31.	1.—Loan-Contract—Usury	115
§ 32.	2.—The Contract of Purchase. 3.—Trading Companies	116
§ 33.	4.—Marriage Contract	117
§ 34.	5.—Contract of Service—Indenture of Apprenticeship	118
II.	PUBLIC RIGHTS AND DUTIES (STATE RIGHTS)	119—131
§ 35.	First Principles	119
§ 36.	General Definitions	119
§ 37.	Duties of the State (Government)	122
§ 38.	Continuation—Disposition of State Land	125
§ 39.	Conclusion—Disposition of Heritages—Relief of the Condition of Workmen and Proletaries	126
§ 40.	Duties of the Citizen—Taxation	128
§ 41.	The Oath—War	129
§ 42.	Conflict of Duties	130
§ 43.	Behavior Towards Animals	131

Liberal Guide

—— FOR THEIR ——

*M*ORAL *C*ULTURE

—— AND ——

*R*ELIGIOUS *E*NLIGHTENMENT.

—— BY ——

PROF. H. M. KOTTINGER, A. M.

(Translated from the Revised German Edition.)

"*Fathers! Mothers! Let us live for our children!*"

FRED. FROEBEL,

Founder of the "Kindergarten."

MILWAUKEE:
TRAYSER BROS., BOOK AND JOB PRINTERS, GRAND OPERA HOUSE, G. ONEIDA STREET.
1877.

Entered according to Act of Congress, in the Year 1877,
By Prof. H. M. KOTTINGER, A. M.,
In the Office of the Librarian of Congress, at Washington, D. C.

PART SECOND.

RELIGIOUS ENLIGHTENMENT.

"We need have no fear of being too radical. Paine was splendidly in advance of his time; but he was orthodox, compared with the infidels of to-day."

ROBERT INGERSOLL, "The Gods."

SECTION FIRST.

OUTLINE OF THE HISTORY OF THE PRINCIPAL RELIGIONS.

"The world is my country, and to do good—my religion."—*Thomas Paine.*

§ 1. Introduction—Definition—Utility, and Division of the History of Religions.

What is religion? With regard to the meaning of this word there are different opinions. Originally, in the Latin language, from which it is dirived, it denotes *reflection, consciousness, tenderness of feeling,* and the Romans did not only speak of religion towards the gods, but also of the religion (to wit, of the duty) we owe to parents, friends, and to our country. Moreover, as far as man feels himself dependent on nature, religion may also be called the "sentiment and confession of our dependence on nature."— Feuerbach. The poet Shelley defines it "the perception of the relation in which we stand to the principle of the Universe." ("Notes to Queen Mab.") Generally we mean by the word "religion" the belief in God and in the doctrine of the duties we have to perform with regard to him, to ourselves, and to our fellow-creatures. But in a treatise on the history of religions (and such an one is here given) the word "religion" may be explained as the sum of the representations which men at certain times conceived of the Universe, of their nature and duties. Whereas the degree of civilization mostly depends on the character of these representations, and whereas they always grow more perfect in the course of time, the history of the religions may be defined the description of these representations, and of their influence on the advancing condition of human civilization.

The study of the history of the religions is useful; for it explains us the present condition of religion from its former times, and strengthens our sight for the future; it makes us tolerant, enlightens our intellect, warns us against errors and superstition, fills our mind with detestation of the misdeeds of fanaticism, and furnishes us a safe foundation on which we may farther build religious ideas. Especially, we learn by it to understand the difference of the diverse religious systems, to estimate their relative value, to discern their defects and hallucinations.

The religions are here discussed in the order of their sucessive origin. The history of the Christian religion is divided into six periods, in order to survey and comprehend easier its contents.

CHAPTER FIRST.

THE RELIGIONS BEFORE THE CHRISTIAN ERA, AND THE ISLAM.

§ 2. The Ancient Religions in General—Priests—Sacrifices— Prayers—Oracles.

Religion very likely sprang from the fear of dreadful phenomena and objects of nature, such as tempests, furious beasts, etc. The more human culture advanced, the more became men incredulous; but the more perfect grew also their moral doctrine.

The oldest form of religion was doubtless *fetichism* (from the Portuguese word "faticaria", witchcraft), to wit: the worship of natural objects, of which man expected that they would keep pain and suffering from him, and convey him fortune and joy. The kinds of fetichism were: the worship of animals, e. g., in Egypt, and that of stars, e. g., in Arabia. The natural, most indispensable objects for men are animals; therefore the worship of them became so general. The wonders of the sky, the radiant sun with its soft splendor in the mornings and evenings, the mild moonlight, and the bright stars in their immense hight—these objects necessarily struck the mind of the rude, natural man with awe. In the earliest imes, the priests were usually astrologers. The worship of animals is yet practiced by savage tribes; e. g., the Whida negroes worship a serpent in their temple, where it is nursed by priests: the Ashantis, in South America, worship the crocodile, to which they sacrifice chickens; the Caffres, the elephant, etc. The worshiper of a fetich receives it in his hut, talks with it, complains to it when suffering; he serves it food and drink, in order to gain its favor; he cleans and adorns it; but, if he thinks that it did not perform its duty, he cudgels it, even throws it out of the hut, and supplies its place with another. Gratitude, often, also base flattery, idolized men, particularly in Greece and Rome. On the other hand, the Deity was humanized in all religions, by attributing to it both the good qualities and the frailties, often even the vices, of man.

The *priests* conserved and enlarged the religious knowledge of the nations; but they also planted and fostered superstition, captivated the conscience, indulged to the desire of domineering, and usurped the civil authority. By obesrving the intestines of the sacrificed animals, and the flight of birds, and by *oracles*, they interpreted the future, especially in Greece and in the Roman Empire. For money they let the oracles answer according to the wishes of the questioners. The answers of the oracles were for the most part equivocal. Still these institutes contributed also to soften the habits and manners of the people, and sometimes prevented bloody wars. The most ancient States were theocracies.

Sacrifices of rural fruits, animals and men were almost everywhere established. As men imagined that their gods were irascible or selfish beings, it was natural that they tried by sacrifices to propitiate their wrath, or to gain their benevolence. They believed also that they could attain these aims by *prayers*. The better educated part of civil society had, indeed, a purer religion, but from fear of the populace, they practiced and propagated it in secret, especially in the *mysteries* (secret meetings), where a higher religious doctrine was reserved and communicated to the innitiated members.

§ 3. **Religion of the Arians—Zend-Avesta.**

Among the *Arians* and *Bactrians* (in Media and Persia) the Mage *Zoroaster* stepped forth as legislator, and religious reformer.

When they, in later times, were subjugated by the Persians, these also accepted his doctrine. His followers believed him to be the author of the *Zend-Avesta* ("the living word"), which is written in the Zend language. According to Zoroaster's doctrine (as it is contained in those books), the eternal, uncreated universe is the primitive fountain of all things, and a holy, almighty, everlasting Being. It created originally two other divine Beings, a good and a bad one, or the God of light and the God of darkness, *Ormuzd* and *Arihman*. Ormuzd created visible beings in six periods of time. Arihman opposed to the creation of Ormuzd a creation of darkness. This one was finally forced to divide the command with Arihman. The behavior of man fluctuates between these two divine beings, and he would at last succumb, if at the end of the course of the world a redeemer of mankind should not appear. Then the right gains the victory, the dead revive by resurrection, the world is destroyed by fire, the good are admitted into Heaven, and the wicked must depart into the realm of darkness.

The Arians upon heights addressed their prayers to the primitive fountain of light and virtue, and yet in our age the votaries of this religion, who live in the northwestern part of Farther India, worship the fire. The priests who once were called Mages, maintain the sacred fire; he who blows it out intentionally, is deemed to deserve death. Therefore in that country the smith's-trade is forbidden. Neither is polygamy permitted. Still the system of castes is also established there. The Zend-Avesta contains some very good moral precepts, e. g., "Man ought always to combat for virtue and truth."

§ 4. Religion of the Hindoos—Brahmanism—Buddhism.

The sacred books of the Hindoos are the four *Vedas* (the knowledge), the code of *Manu*, and the *Puranas* (a mythology). The first were written in the *Sanscrit* language, which is now dead; they emanated from the lips of Brahma. The Puranas (comprising 18 parts) are said to contain over one and a half million verses; they form a middle kind between the heroic and the didatic poetry. Primitively, the Hindoos worshipped natural objects, e. g., light, sun, lightning, etc. Their highest god (*Indra*), who sends the rain, is the god of the lightning, sky, and the air. There are yet other gods besides him, viz: the first rays of light, the aurora, etc. But already in the Vedas this religious doctrine is more spiritualized. According to them *Bram* (the primitively self-existent) is the fountain of all existence, the eternal and invisible spirit. His first revelation is *Brahma*. The world has been created by the sole word of Brahma. He created also the pure spirits, who lived in the ether. One of them seduced several others. In order to purify the latter, the visible world was created. The life on earth is but a state of trial. Man can rise by self-denial; by egotism he always sinks deeper, and must then migrate through animal bodies and plants.

In the mythological part the gods appear humanized to utter excess. From the primitive Being three gods have emanated: *Brahma* (the sun), *Vishnu* (air and water), and *Sivah* (the fire). Brahma is the creator, Vishnu the conservator, Sivah the destroyer of the world. These three compose the trinity, and are represented in one person with three heads. Brahma's wife is the goddess of wisdom. The symbol of Vishnu is the cow. His worshippers believe that, whenever a great disorder, physical or moral, disturbs the world, he decends to set it right, and thus to preserve creation. He is supposed to have assumed the form of some wonderful animal, or the human shape. Once (they say) he appeared (probably more than 900 years B C.) in human form, and was called the *Chrishna*. His mother descended from a royal family. He was cradled among herdsmen. The tyrant *Cansa*, to whom it had been predicted that one born in that family would destroy him at the time of his birth, ordered all new born males to be slain. Chrishna was fostered therefore (in Mathura) by an honest herdsman and his amiable wife. He possesed miraculous powers, by which he saved multitudes. He raised the dead, descended for that purpose to the lowest regions; he preached mysteries, washed other people's feet, descended into hell, rose again from the dead, ascended into heaven, and left his doctrines to be preached by his disciples, but committing nothing of his own to writing.*

Sivah is represented as being girded round with serpents; he has a human skull in his hand, a necklace, wrought of human

---
*Sir William Jones, Asiatic Researches

bones, and three eyes. His clothing is a tiger skin. Over his left shoulder the venomous cobra stretches up its head. The hands of his wife are red, like blood, because her thirst for blood cannot be quenched. She has four arms; in one she carries the skull of a giant; her tongue hangs from the mouth; a string of human skulls embraces her neck. Beside these three gods there are many minor ones.

The morals of these religious books are in part excellent, as e. g., the precept: "Do not insult another man, nor speak even a word by which you would grieve him, for this would hinder his progress to future bliss;" moreover the sentence: "The enemy, too, can demand of us the most exact performance of our duty;" and this remark: "If man leaves his body his friends turn round with averted faces, but virtue accompanies his soul."

Besides, the Vedas command to worship the gods by sacrifices and alms, to bathe, to atone for sins, to mortify ourselves, to fast, and to go on pilgrimages. According to these precepts, even human sacrifices are offered. The cases are not rare that mothers drown their children in the holy Ganges, and the faithful votaries crowd around the idol Dshagernauth, which is carried in public procession, and throw themselves under the wheels of the holy carriage, which is sixty feet high, in order to be crushed.

Since olden times there has also always been a class of monks (Fakirs), who have tried to sanctify themselves by cruel mortification, and to acquire the renown of holiness from a stupid rabble. Some stand during many hours on their heads; others walk in shoes which are pierced by dozens of pointed nails, hurting their feet; or they pierce their tongues, rip up their lips and nostrils, writhe living serpents around the waist, and get on the path of the procession, spreading burning coals, over which they walk with naked feet, etc.

The condition of woman is a miserable one; her dignity is little appreciated by man, and already in the days of Alexander the Great, the religious custom required that the wives of the Brahmins, after the death of the husband, should burn themselves with him. The unfortunate wife, decked with her finest clothes and jewels, approached the corpse of the husband, surrounded by her relatives; she took off her clothing, distributed her finery, walked three times around the corpse, then bid farewell to the living ones, poured oil on herself and on the defunct, whom they had thrown on the funeral pile, and threw herself over him in the blazing flames. This horrible custom is not yet entirely abolished

The caste system of the Hindoos forms, too, a part of the Brahma religion. The noblest caste consists of the priests (Brahmins), for they say that they have originated from Brahma's mouth. Their vocation is to say prayers, to read and teach. They alone are permitted to pronounce the name of Brahma. Next to the Brahmins ranks the caste of the princes and warriors; they descend from Brahma's arms; they govern the country, and manage its wars. The princes rule like despots, but are controlled by the Brahmins. To the third caste the peasants and merchants belong; it derives its origin from the belly and thighs of Brahma. Still lower is the rank of the fourth caste, the *Sudras*, to which the mechanics and day laborers belong; for they descend from Brahma's feet. They must serve the higher castes, especially the Brahmins. Their condition is never to be improved; they are not to accumulate property. Their fate was formerly even more wretched. If a Sudras molested a Brahmin, he was put to death; if he sat with him on the same carpet, he was mutilated. If he listened to the lecture of the sacred books, burning oil was poured in his ears; if he read them and learned from them, he was killed. When somebody of a higher caste killed him, that was not more severely punished than for killing a cat. The lowest class of the inhabitants is composed of the *Parias;* it comprehends the fifth part of them. They do not enjoy any rights at all; they must bury the corpses of criminals; they are not allowed to go into the houses of the other castes, nor to speak to any of them, and only possess dogs and asses as property. The castes are separated from each other by severe laws; every one is to stay in that in which he is born.

Five hundred (or six hundred) years before Christ, yet another religion, the *Buddhism* (Lamaism), was formed in India. Its founder received from its confessors the surname of *Buddha* (the wise) and *Gautamas* (the saint). He was the son of a King in

Hindoostan. When twenty-nine years old, he went into a solitary country, where he lived many years alone, and in rigid abstinence. After his return he rose as reformer of the religion of his country, and gathered many scholars. According to his doctrine there are no gods, and no immortality. All things originate and perish according to immutable and necessary laws, and are continually changing. Man can rule his fate by free will. After death every thought ceases, for its causes are suppressed, because nothing of that which before existed remains. Man's life is by death extinguished like a lamp. According to other reports, Buddha taught the transmigration of the soul; even the souls of the animals migrate from one body into another. Still, reward and punishments will not be everlasting, and everybody can be saved in Heaven by moral conduct.

In the first place Buddha required an innocent behavior of his followers. His morals are almost the same as are taught among all civilized nations. They forbid crimes, e. g., murder, fraud and theft, and command man to be true, benevolent, merciful, etc. His design was chiefly to alleviate the sad condition of the lower castes of his country. He rejected the distinction of castes; but as he was not able to break down their barriers, he tried at least to make them smoother. Therefore he proclaimed that all men are equal, that they ought to assist each other in distress, and that one day all will find rest in the lap of the primitive spirit.

According to the opinion of his followers the high priest (*Delai-Lama*), who resides in Lassa (in Thibet), is his representive, in whom his soul is incarnated. It is wandering eternally from one high priest to the other. The priests (bonzes) are commanded to live in celibacy to get their livelihood by begging, and to live together in convents. In Lassa alone there are 30,000 bonzes. Their rites much resemble those of the Catholic Church; they turn the rosary, use lights and incense in the temples, mortify their bodies, etc.

Buddha's doctrine was heartily received by the people; even Kings adhered to it; it was propagated in all parts of Further Hindoostan, and in other countries as far as China. In the course of time it was in India suppressed by the jealousy of the Brahmins;

but instead of that diffused in China and Japan, where yet it is said to count 300 millions of votaries.

§ 5. Religions of the Chinese—Kong-fu-tse.

The mind of the Chinese avoids religious enthusiasm, and is directed to real life; therefore three religions are ruling in China, and each one enjoys equal rights. The first one of them is the State-religion which Kong-fu-tse (551 B. C.) reformed; to it the well educated Chinese are adherent. The view of the Universe professed by that creed, is this : The primitive matter (the sun, the earth, etc.), and the primitive force exits from eternity ; the force is manifested in the heaven and earth. It moved and formed the primitive matter : in this way the world has its existence. There is no immortality. Man cannot expect to be recompensed after death. His duty in this life is to resign to the divine power which in nature is veiled. Confucius' morals comprehend all relations of life, and proclaim many excellent maxims, e. g., " First rule yourself; then you are fit to rule a family ; then a country."—"Wise is the man who has a profound knowledge of things, submits to reason, and follows the path of virtue and justice. He is his own impeacher, witness and judge."—" Do to another what you would he should do unto you ; and do not unto another what you would not be done unto : this law is the foundation and principle of all the rest."—" Desire not the death of thine enemy ; thou wouldst desire it in vain ; his life is in the hands of heaven."—" Acknowledge thy benefits, but never revenge injuries."

2. The religion of *primitive Reason* (Sao). It originated about 600 years B. C. Its principal tenets are : "Heaven and earth have sprung out of the chaos which emanates from an eternally creating Being, the infinite primitive Reason.—Man is the image of earth ; this is the image of heaven ; heaven—the image of Reason, and Reason is its own image. The wise man mortifies his body." Besides, the confessors of these tenets believe in miracles, exorcisms and sorcery.

3. The religion of Buddha, who is called Foe (the holy one) in China.

§ 6. Religion of the Egyptians.

The two principal dieties of the Egyptians were *Osiris* and *Isis :* the former probably meant the sun, the latter the moon, or nature in general. Isis presided over agriculture. Besides these two they worshipped many gods of inferior rank, e. g., a god of the gardens, gods of the stars, etc. The Egyptians worshipped also many animals, among them the useful bull, especially the Apis in the city of Memphis, the storklike bird ibis, which destroys serpents, the dangerous crocodile, cats, etc. People were forbidden to hurt a sacred animal. A Roman soldier, who had killed a cat by chance was attacked by the furious populace and killed, though the King himself had interceded for his life.

The Egyptians believed in the transmigration of the soul (metempsychosis); which doctrine they explained in this way: The human soul has emanated from the soul of the Universe, but has deserted the latter, and must therefore atone by migrating through diverse animal forms; finally, if it has grown better, it returns into the human body. The superstition was probably the reason that the Egyptians embalmed their corpses, which, tied round with fillets, were carefully preserved in subterraneous appartments. There these *mummies* (as they are called) remained unhurt during thousands of years.

There were also oracles in Egypt. The most ancient existed in Meroe. For the oracles particular priestesses were appointed in the temples of Osiris and Isis, where they slept, and in dreams learned the will of the deity. Even the sacred bull in Memphis promulgated oracles. In that country the system of castes prevailed too, and the priests occupied also there the highest rank. They alone were entitled to be physicians. Their religious belief was more enlightened than the common one, but they kept it secret. The priests were the judges of the dead. If they gave an unfavorable verdict with regard to the moral and religious behavior of an individual, his corpse was given up to corruption. The religion of the *Chaldeans* and *Babylonians* was similar to the Egyptian.

§ 7. Greek and Roman Religions.

The Greeks idolized all the forces of nature. So was *Jupiter* to them the god of the air and light, and also of life, and therefore they called him the father of the gods and men. *Apollo* was the god of music and poetry; *Minerva* the goddess of wisdom; *Venus* the goddess of beauty and love; *Mars* the god of war; *Juno*, Jupiter's spouse, presided over wedlock; *Vulcan* over fire; *Neptune* over the ocean; *Pluto* ruled in Tartarus. Besides there were many lesser gods and semi-gods; *Pan* was the god of shepherds; *Pomona* the goddess of fruit; *Ceres* the goddess of grains; *Flora* the goddess of flowers,—every fountain, every tree was protected by a deity, the *nymphs* and *dryads*. The *Muses* presided over song and other arts; the *Graces* dispensed charms. But all gods, even Jupiter, were subjected to the immutable *Fate*. The shades of the dead descended into the nether world, and were there judged; the good were happy in the *Elysian* fields, the wicked suffered different torments in *Tartarus*. The poets developed the mythology further, and applied it ingeniously in their works.

The Greeks had several oracles; the most celebrated was that of Apollo in Delphi, at the foot of mount Parnassus. There was a cavern which emitted a steaming vapor. He who inhaled it, fell in a rapture, in which (as they believed) he was inspired by the god, and enabled to promulgate his will, and to discover the future; The consulters must prepare by prayers, purification and sacrifices. then the priestess (Pythia) was led into the sanctuary, and seated on a large tripod, which stood above the cavern. As soon as the subterraneous vapors had permeated her, she fell into hideous convulsions, her eyes were distorted, her mouth foamed, and finally she uttered, with terrible howling, detached words, from which the priests constructed the replies, the most of which were composed in verses. This oracle ruled often the fate of whole States, and was for a long time the principal support of the Greek Governments. Frequently the bold, who divulged the frauds of the oracles, was by the priests allured into caverns and killed.

The temples of the Greeks were magnificent. The temple of Apollo in Delphi, of Jupiter in Olympia, of Diana in Ephesus, and of Minerva in Athens, were far-famed. To the latter a splendid piazza led, which was formed by five high portals, constructed of marble, and joined by two wings of edifices, and was reached by magnificent stairs. The inside was often decorated with the masterpieces of sculpture; such ones were the colossal statues of Jupiter in Olympia, and of Minerva in Athens, both formed by the great sculptor *Phidias*.

The Roman religion resembled that of the Greeks, and was established by King *Numa Pompilius*, calling it the revelation of the nymph Egeria. The Romans idolized even abstract ideas and moral qualities of man; e. g., they had a goddess of liberty, of honor, of victory, chastity, fidelity, patriotism, bravery, etc. They also considered religion as a fulcrum of the State, and therefore it was freely used as the handmaid of politics, in order to lead the superstitious people with her strings. The sacerdotal offices were State offices. Particular priests watched the flight of birds, the lightning, and the intestines of animals. The State affairs were conducted according to their interpretation. The Sibylline books, too, served the State officers as guides in doubtful emergencies. The virgins of Vesta watched the eternal fire; they were not allowed to marry during the term of their service. Human sacrifice were also sometimes offered. After the disastrous battle at Cannae (216 B. C.), several persons were burned alive in Rome.

In general, both Romans and Greeks were very superstitious, e. g., if a public meeting took place, and during it a weasel ran over the road, it was adjourned. Particular soothsayers were appointed by the authorities, in order to call the dead from Tartarus. The crime of sacrilege was punished with death; it was inflicted even for pulling a shrub in a sacred grove. Philosophy was often in close battle with religion; philosophers, who doubted the existence of the gods, were put to death; e. g., *Socrates*, who was condemned to drink the poisoned cup; Anaxagoras had to fly from Athens; and so Diagoras, for whose head a prize was offered.

§ 8. Religion of the Ancient Germans.

During the time that the ancient Germans were living in a rude condition of nature, their religious conceptions were also rude and very defective. According to the usual report, they worshipped *Wodin* (Odin), also called *Alfader* (father of all), as the Supreme Being; his son *Thor* as the god of thunder; his spouse *Freyja* as as the goddess of love and wedlock; and *Hertha*, the goddess of the earth; the *Walkyries* (goddesses of the battles) etc. They believed in a heaven (*Walhalla*), where they would drink beer and mead out of the skulls of their killed enemies, and in a hell (*Hela*). They had sacred groves, sacrifices, oracles, priests and priestesses. In those groves they kept white horses, according to the neighing of which they interpreted the future. They offered also human sacrifices They highly valued forebodings, e. g., whether at the time of a meeting the moon was full or new. For important enterprises they asked the advice of the priests. To the women also they gave credit for a prophetic look in the future.

§ 9. Judaic Religion.

Abraham (Abram), the chief of a pastoral tribe in Mesopotamia (between the Euphrates and Tigris), immigrated into Palestine about 2000 B. C. From him, whom the natives of this country called Eber, that is, "the transmigrator," his descendants derived their name *Hebrews*, from his grandson Jacob, who was surnamed Israel, the name "*Israelite*," and from *Juda*, Jacob's son, the name "*Jews*." They wandered in later time to Egypt, where the Kings afflicted them cruelly. *Moses* became their liberator. He had received an excellent education at the royal court. Especially he was initiated in the religious mysteries of the priests. He inspired his compatriots with his bold design, and happily conducted them, in spite of the resistance of the Kings, about 1500 B. C., from Egypt. They moved into the northern, free, though servile part of Arabia. Here he became the legislator of the Israelites, and founder of their religion. He conquered the country on the eastern bank of the Jordan; his successor *Joshua* subdued Palestine proper. Some historians believe the narrative of Moses to be fictitious.

The Jewish people were governed by the priests. But the insolence and the crimes of the sons of the high priests *Heli* and *Samuel*, rendered their command so odious that they finally demanded a King. Samuel gave them such an one in the person of *Saul* (1095 B. C.); but as this one refused to be a mere tool in the hand of the priest, Samuel soon after chose *David* as anti-King; then civil war began to rage. Saul lost in the war against the Philistines, the most redoutable enemies of the Jews, the decisive battle, saw his own sons fall, and despairingly inflicted death on himself. Finally (1050 B. C.), David was generally acknowledged as King. With his son Solomon the people were dissatisfied, because he vexed them with high taxes; the priests fostered this disposition, and roused an adversary to him in the person of *Jeroboam;* still he maintained his dominion. But when his son and successor, *Rehoboam* afflicted the people still more cruelly, they revolted again (975 B. C.), and ten tribes chose Jeroboam for their King; only two remained faithful to Rehabeam; they constituted the *Judaic*, the other ten the *Israelitic* kingdom. Both Kingdoms went on declining by discord, religious quarrels and visciousness, and lastly (722 and 600 B. C.), became the prey of foreign couquerors.

The ground-work of the Mosaic religion are the known ten commandments. According to them, God is the Supreme Being, who created and arranged the Universe in six days. He must not be represented by any image. His name is Jehovah, that means: the Being which has been, is and will be. He is the national god of the Jews, and their Lord; a god of vengeance, who punishes the sins of the fathers even to the fifth generation. Man ought to sacrifice everything to him, even his children, as Abraham was resigned to do. The doctrine of the immortality of human spirit was before the Babylonian captivity unknown to the Hebrews; they learned it first during it.

The Jewish religion has a great number of ceremonies and holidays. The weekly holiday was the Sabbath: there were three longer holy times, of which the Easter festival was the most important; it lasted seven days. By the moral laws the Israelites were forbidden to commit theft, murder, perjury, etc. Moses established also sanitary laws, e. g., ablutions of the body, and abstinence from pork. The first aimed at cleanliness; pork was perhaps unwholesome in that hot country.

The ancient Hebrews, too, were governed by the priests, though in the name of Jehovah, and even during the royal dominion their prevailing influence was continued. They got a tithe of all products of the country, received a share of the sacrifices, and had besides still other revenues; e. g., every first-born infant had to be redeemed from them, because the laws granted them a claim on it. The criminal laws were too severe. They ordered: "Eye for eye, tooth for tooth!" Even smaller trespasses, and the least profanation of the Sabbath was punished by death. Quite as merciless were the international laws of Moses, for by them the Israelites were commanded to exterminate entirely the Canaanites, a neighboring people. The following features of the Mosaic law were excellent. During every seventh year (the Sabbath year) the fields must remain unploughed; to the fruits which then spontaneously grew, the poor and the stranger were entitled; besides, the native slaves were manumitted, and all debts remitted. Every fiftieth year was a jubilee, in which every family recovered its former landed property.

In later times this religion was yet enlarged by many additions, e. g., by the doctrine of a devil (satan, temptor), of angels, etc. In many respects it resembles that of the Egyptians, e. g., in their country there was once a temple with the inscription: I am that which ever was, is and will be—a conception of God, which also the word "Jevovah" expresses. Their priests, too, carried, like the Jewish ones, an ephod with two images, and their temples were built like the portable tabernacle of the Israelites; like this they had their entrance towards the East, and contained also a reservoir for the ablutions of the priests, a curtain, a sanctuary, a most holy sanctuary, which always remained veiled to the looks of the people, and an ark of covenant with winged beings. Finally, with regard to the narrative part of the Mosaic books, it is certainly interwoven with many incredible legends; to these belong all the miraculous reports of the Egyptian plagues, of the circumstances which are told to have happened during the legislation upon Mount Sinai; of the creation of the world, and particularly of that of woman, etc. In general, they assert that those five books, the author of which Moses was formerly thought to be, were not composed by himself, and that the ten principal commandments never were written on two tablets.—(Cf. Bibl. narrat.)

§ 10. Mohammedan Religion—Arabian Culture.

Mohammed was born (571 A. D.) of poor parents in Mecca, a town of Arabia. He was a mumber of the noble tribe *Koreish*, and of the family *Hashim*, which formerly had to protect the principal temple (the Kaaba). He lost his parents early. When a a youth, he devoted himself to poetry; then entered the mercantile service of a rich widow, and obtained her hand by his ability and faithfulness. At a latter time he retired into solitude, and intended to establish a new religion which ought to ally the three religious parties of his country, Jews, Christians and Heathens.

He communicated his idea first to his friends, and soon gained their approbation. He then stepped forth publicly as a prophet; but the multitude paid little attention to him. The inhabitants of Mecca, earning great profits from the pilgrimage of the Arabs, declared against him. But most decidedly the Koreishites, the associates of his tribe, opposed him, because being the priests of the Kaaba, they were anxious for the loss of their authority and revenues. They conspired against his life. The family *Omejjah*, since olden times fostering adversed feelings towards his relatives, headed them. They resolved that in an appointed night one member of every family ought to thrust his sword in Mohammed's breast. His enemies surrounded his house; but *Ali*, his relative, reascued him from their hands. He fled to *Medina*, where he had got already several votaries (the 16th of July, 622 A. D.). From the day of his flight the Mohammedan nations count their years.

Now he resolved to propagate his doctrine by force of arms. According to Arabian usage he began to fight his tribe, the Koreishites, and he issued the command to make war upon all infidels. Supported by the inhabitants of Medina he gave battle to the members of his tribe and to their allies, the inhabitants of Mecca, in which he was victorious, and got a rich booty. Finally they agreed to conclude peace with him. He continued his conquests. After some years he was already so redoubtable that he dared to summon even the Grecian Emperor and other powerful Princes to embrace his religion. When, then, the inhabitants of Mecca had violated the concluded peace, he marched against them, and conquered the town (630). But he used the vanquished mildly. He purified the Kaaba of idols. Mecca acknowledged him as prophet and sovereign. In the following years he subdued almost the whole of Arabia.

His manner of life was very simple. He lived on barley, bread and dates. His couch was a carpet on the bare ground. He required no marks of honor; he did not even permit his associates to rise in his presence, when he came to see them. He would say: "I am a servant of God, like you; I eat and drink like you, and I get seated like every other man." Both he and his first successors often preached at the head of the armies. When he felt that death approached him, he set his slaves free. He died probably from administered poison. (632).

His successors conquered Egypt and other parts of Africa, Palestine, Syria and Persia, and other countries in Asia, Spain, and in more recent time (about 1400) the South-Eastern part of Europe, which now is called Turkey. Their capital first was Damask, afterwards the magnificent city of Bagdad, close to the ancient Babylon

Mohammed's doctrine, called *Islam* (creed, faith), is contained in the *Koran*, the book of religion of his followers, who call themselves *Mussulmans* or *Moslems* (the faithful ones) The principal articles of his doctrine are the following : There is only one God (Allah), and Mohammed is his prophet. God has given man his revelation by six prophets, viz: Adam, Noah, Abraham, Moses, Christ and Mohammed ; but the last is the greatest of them. The Koran promises the elect superabundant joys in the future life, and renounces the reprobate to eternal penalties. The joys are of the most sensual kind ; heaven is a beautiful garden, a paradise. Mohammed allowed his adherents polygamy, and would make them indifferent to all dangers of death by the belief in an immutable fate. Therefore they fought for their creed with courageous contempt of death. Among other duties the Koran commands principally : prayers, abstinence from crime, fasts, charity, cleanliness and ablutions of the body, pilgrimage, and above all virtues, justice. During prayers their eyes ought to be turned towards the country where Mecca and its temple are situated. During the month of Ramadan (the ninth of their year), they ought to fast rigidly. Each one ought to spend the tenth part of his fortune for alms ; also to pilgrim to Mecca, if possible, at least once in his life. The Friday of every week is ordered for public worship, which consists in prayers and sermons. It is a principal precept of the Koran to propagate its doctrine everywhere with fire and sword, and to destroy the infidels. Mohammed did not perform miracles; but his followers attribute them to him in order to confirm the faith of the blind multitude. He did not like to have any monks; nevertheless the Fakirs, Dervis, etc., have also intruded in his church. Among the Mohammedans, also, different sects arose, which made terrible religious wars against each other.

Arts and sciences for a long time found a protective abode among the Arabs. Several of their Califs (sovereigns) favored them in a high degree; some of them were themselves artists and scholars. At the time of their rule in Spain, there were alone in Andalusia seventy public libraries. The Arabs acquired great merit for geography, mathematics, astronomy, chemistry,—which science was by them created,—and for medicine. They translated the mathematical, medical and philosophical works of the Greeks. In mathematics they excelled their teachers. Their astronomical writings have become the foundation of modern astronomy. In most of the cities of their dominion there were observatories, and institutes for mathematics and astronomy. The Gothic architecture also was invented by them. In poetry they produced peculiar tales (e. g., the renowned "Thousand and One Nights"), but no dramatic works. "The Arabs may in one respect be justly considered the restorers of learning in Europe. All the knowledge, whether of physics, astronomy, philosophy, or mathematics, which flourished in Europe from the tenth century, was originally derived from them."—Mosheim, eccl. history.

CHAPTER SECOND.

CHRISTIAN RELIGION.

FIRST PERIOD (1—1024).

From the Foundation of the Christian Religion Until the Time of the Universal Government of the Popes.

§ 11. Origin of the Christian Religion—Causes of its Fast Propagation.

During the Government of the Emperor Augustus, *Jesus of Nazareth*, in Palestine, was born, who constructed a new and better religion on the foundation of the old Judaic. Of his origin and youth nothing is known with certainty; his father is said to have been a carpenter. In his full, manly age he began to teach the people publicly. His method of teaching moved his hearers deeply, as he nearly always supported his propositions by reasons, and illustrated them by parables. As he attacked the ruling abuses of the religious government, and severely censured the vices of the priests and Pharisees, who formed a powerful sect, he became the object of their hatred, and perished by the violent death of crucifixion.

After his death his confessors preached his doctrine (most with the additions of the Apostle Paul) in all parts of the Roman Empire, and founded associations of their creed. After some centuries it was spread everywhere. Emperor Constantine was converted to it, and declared it to be the religion of the State (about 300 after Christ); it then became predominant in his realm. His flatterers called him the Great, but he was indeed a monster in human form. He drowned his wife in boiling water; put to death his son; murdered the husbands of his two sisters, his father-in-law, and his nephew, a boy of twelve years of age. And this man was the first patron of Christianity ! Its confessors were called Christians, because its author, Jesus, was called Christ (the annointed, the King). Most of the German tribes embraced his religion. In Germany it was propagated by Winfried (called Boniface); in Switzerland by Gallus and Columban; in Ireland by St. Patrick. In Saxony, Emperor Charles I. established it by force of arms (771–785). He killed all who refused to be baptized. Thousands were driven to the rivers, and baptized, or drowned in the floods.

The causes of the fast prapagation of Christianity were internal and external; among those the excellence of the doctrine is to be mentioned. The Greek and Roman religion had lost their authority; the more culture and enlightenment increased, the lower was the contempt into which they sank. The Jews themselves did not more closely adhere to the Mosaic creed; sectarianism had gained ground among them, and void ceremonies had taken the place of true religion. As Jesus taught that all men are members of one family, his religion gained a great many proselytes among the poor, the humble and the slaves, who felt themselves raised higher by such principles. Besides, these people were supported by collections from the Christians, destined for the comfort of the distressed. Other external causes were the dispersion of the Jews, the religion of whom is the foundation of Christendom, and the preservation of the Christians, by which their moral force was nerved. The blood of the martyrs grew the seed of new confessors. Still sometimes the Christians themselves were to be blamed, if they incurred persecutions, either disturbing the established religious rites, or being disobedient to the laws of the country, or pressing to the tribunals of their enemies in order to be victims of their creed. Most severely were they persecuted for some time by the Emperor Gabrius; still later he was reconciled with them.

§ 12. Origin of the Evangelies—Life and Character of Jesus—His Doctrine—Paulinism.

It is doubtful by whom, when, and in which idiom the doctrine of Jesus has been written down. Jesus himself has left nothing in writing: his apostles probably did not know how to write, being illiterate men; only little by little were his precepts collected and recorded; meanwhile, probably a hundred years or more passed away. It is certain that the evangely of John was not written before the second century. It is generally believed that only three evangelies originally were composed in Greek; but they doubt now, whether Matthew wrote his in Hebrew. From the way these writings have taken origin, it may already be inferred that the truth of their contents cannot fully be proved. Besides them, in the first epochs of Christianity, many other evangelies were in vogue, which in their form and tenor vary much from those, and among themselves; finally, the church agreed to choose those four as the most authentic, and to accept them as the foundation of its doctrine, viz : the evangelies of Matthew, Mark, Luke, and John. But neither do the old copies of these correspond; scholars have collected 30,000 different versions of the divers manuscripts. To the evangelies yet other writings were joined: the epistles of the apostle Paul, of John, a history of the acts of the apostles, etc.

Neither does history relate any trustworthy particulars of the life of Jesus; his cotemporaries having been ignorant and superstitious, it is natural that they related many marvellous stories of him, in a similar way as it happened with regard to Mohammed, Numa Pompilius, and other founders of religions. His adorers desired to extol him over Moses and the prophets, consequently they gave him credit for such exploits as are more admirable than the miracles reported to have been wrought by those men. As the authors of the evangelies were not cotemporaries of Jesus, they were not eye-witnesses of his miracles, therefore their reports are not worthy to be trusted. Neither can it be assumed that on the ground of the miracles at least a nucleus of the facts lieswhich in later times have been wonderfully ornated: for the number of the pretended miracles is too great, and it may be plainly understood that the composers had the intention to create a thaumaturgic hero. Like other stories of this kind, the miracles of Jesus, therefore, belong to the province of pious myths. (Cf. Views of the Univ., § 3, and Bibl. Narr., II., 4.)

The most wonderful stories of the life of Jesus are the following : He did not descend from man, but from the Holy Ghost. His birth had been announced by a star to three wise Kings, and was celebrated by anthems of angels. When he was baptized, the Holy Ghost appeared in the form of a dove over his head. The devil tempted him in the desert. During his crucifixion the sun was eclipsed, an earthquake opened the graves, and many who were dead walked around. Jesus himself cured the sick by his sole word, by the touch of his hand, or from a great distance; he resuscitated the dead, transformed water into wine, satiated 5,000 or 6,000 persons with a few loaves of bread, arose from his grave, and ascended to Heaven.

His conduct was strictly moral and pure, in general, and even his enemies could not blame him. Still the sublimity of his character is diminished by some features of his life; e. g., he is to be blamed for having damned such men as did not believe in his doctrine; for having wandered about without a certain business, and for having suffered himself to be supported by kind-hearted women. He proposed to induce Jerusalem to accpt his doctrine by means of revolution. The demons whom he expelled from a sick man, entered at his command into a heard of swine, and drove them into the lake. By some of his miracles, his character appears ridiculous, e. g., when he is walking on a lake, or expels legions of demons.

The principal tenets of his religion are these: There is a Supreme Being, a God. He is a spirit, the loving Being, the father of men, all-perfect, all-just, all-gracious, and all-merciful. His providence embraces both the smallest and the greatest things. His essence is incomprehensible, for he lives in an inaccessible light. Man is immortal, and after this life he is forever rewarded in heaven, or punished in hell, according as he deserves. There are also a devil and demons. Ceremonies and sacrifices are not necessary.

In ethics Jesus taught these principal precepts: Love God above all, and thy fellow-creatures like thyself. Do unto others as thou wishest to be done by. He commends meekness, mercy, placability, love of enemies, trust in God, and short prayers. According to his persuasion all men are equal in the presence of God, and members of one family.

The ethics of Jesus were much disfigured by the nonsensical dogmas of the apostle Paul and his followers, namely : According to Paul the first parents committed sin in the Paradise by eating the fruit of a certain tree which they were by God forbidden to eat. Their sin has passed to their descendants like an heritage ; now, as Adam and Eve were guilty of eternal damnation, this punishment was also extended to their descendants, and all men deserve to be eternally damned. True, God is merciful, and therefore inclined to pardon the sinners ; but being also all-just, he could pardon only with the condition that his only son, Jesus Christ, rendered satisfaction for the sins of mankind on the cross. That expiation has happened ; therefore man becomes again guiltless and just before God by Christ's death. Nevertheless God has predestined some men, without their merit, to eternal bliss, and innumerable others, without their guilt, to everlasting damnation. To this frantic, abominable doctrine, the Christians of our age yet adhere !

Paul also taught that all parts of the Bible have been revealed to man by God, but he did not prove his assertion. In later times the priests built the divine authority of the biblical dictates on miracles as its foundation, miracles performed by Christ, Moses, the Apostles and others, in order to prove that they are well worthy to be believed. But the stories of the miracles themselves do not deserve to be believed ; not even the cotemporaries of Jesus believed in his miracles, according to the report of the evangelists ; much less men after 2,000 years can be expected to consider them to be genuine facts. If, then, the divine authority of the Bible gives way, we have a right to censure its contents like those of any other book, and to put human reason as judge above it.

§ 13. **State of the Church—Ecclesiastic Councils—Clergy—Monks.**

When the Christians had been acknowleged as the prevailing party of religious belief, they began soon to quarrel among themselves about obscure dogmas. So they did especially in their ecclesiastic councils (synods). From words they went sometimes on to bloody affrays, and even to wars. Since Emperor Constantin had conceded the Christian Church the same rights as the ancient State religion, the persecuted grew persecuting, e. g., as Arius, a priest of Alexandria, taught that Jesus has not existed from eternity, and that he is less than God, he was expelled in the Council of Nice from the communion with the Church, and exiled, and his writings were burned. His followers were also punished. In later times the Church declared that the Holy Ghost is also a divine person. Thus the dogma of the trinity originated, the fallacy of which may be easily demonstrated; for three times one are not one, but three.

Many ceremonies and holidays were established, pious persons idolized, images adored, miraculous stories slyly invented, and stupidly believed. The ecclesiastic laws turned despotic; true piety and moral conduct were little minded. The worship of images also caused bloody hatred, as some rejected them entirely, while others even adored them.

The clergymen obtained great privileges and riches, and soon formed a special class, the priesthood, separating from the people (the laity). They discontinued civil business, took salaries and appointments for life; to the communities only the right of confirmation was left. Many degrees of rank were established. The highest priests were styled patriarchs. These made their residences in the most important cities of the Empire, and usurped the prerogative of superintending the Bishops. The property of the clergy became free from taxes, their persons exempt from civil jurisdiction, and their residences and the churches turned asylums of criminals, sometimes, too, of the innocent; in this way they established a State in the State. The Popes soon acquired the superiority over the other Bishops, because the capital of the Empire (Rome) was their residence. After the Empire had been separated into the eastern and western part, a vehement quarrel about rank began, which finished with the victory of the Popes over the Patriarchs of Constantinople.

Finally, the institution of the *convents and monasteries* must be mentioned here also. Since olden times there lived fantastic hermits in Egypt and Hindoostan. In Palestine the Essenes had led a solitary life. Among the Christians, *Antonius* and *Paul* are said to have been the first anachorets; both lived in Egypt, in the second century. The anachorets lived generally on the banks of rivers and in deserts; but often also in caverns. One time in Egypt 76,000 of them, partly men, partly women, are said to have lived, and at the close of the fourth century the monastic population of this country equalled the entire population of its cities.

From Egypt and Syria they spread like a pest to Italy, where *Athanasius* introduced them. Some settled in the vicinity of Rome, others moved farther, even as far as the Black Sea and Palestine. Among them were also rich ladies. The first hermits lived frugally; they fed on fruits and bread, and drank only water. They indulged in an indolent, contemplative life, and passed the most of their time in prayers. Some braided mats and baskets. They despised matrimony, and were for the most part visionaries; rather often they became even insane. It is said, e. g., that *Simon Stylite* stood on a column, sixty feet high, during thirty years, in summer and winter. In Mesopotamia they crept during spring over the meadows, and ate grass, like cattle. But when monasteries were built by the funds of pious bequests, the anachorets retired there, and became monks. Since, they ceased almost wholly from work; few copied the manuscripts of the classical Greek and Roman literature. Monastic life soon grew exuberant. *Benedict of Narsia*, indeed, reformed (529) the degenerated convents in Italy, by obliging the lazy monks, besides praying, to cultivate the fields, and to instruct youth; but they were soon corrupted again. They fostered the belief in miracles, forged an infinite number of legends, advanced the relics' traffic, stupefied the multitude, and often indulged in luxury and debauches. Some mortified their bodies with voluntary torments. The holy mother Passidea of Siena hung herself like a bat up in the chimney. In order to conquer the natural aversion of man against all nauseous objects, monks devoured dead mice and rats; the brethren of St. Mary's ate even the swill in the kitchen, and licked off the limbs which the leprosy had infected. In the following periods the monks frequently preached revolt against civil power, opposed the light of intelligent instruction, and were blind tools of the Popes. According to the diversity of their monastic regulations there were hundreds of Orders, the names of which were often rather strange, e. g., the order of the Carmelites, of Black and White Spaniards, of Cistercians, Carthusians, etc. The Dominicans were the most redoubtable Judges of the Inquisition Tribunals. The most learned monks belonged to the Orders of Benedict and of the Jesuits. The former Order is said to have furnished the Catholic Church 24 Popes, 200 Cardinals, 7,000 Archbishops, 25,000 Bishops, 4,000 Saints, 20 Emperors, 100 Kings and Queens. It possessed 37,000 convents. As to Jesuits, see § 32.

SECOND PERIOD (1024—1300).

From the Universal Government of the Popes Unto the End of the Crusades.

§ 14. Germany—Henry IV. and Gregory VII.

Emperor Henry IV. (1056—1106) is in history especially known by his struggles against Pope Gregory VII. Being already German King, when only six years old, he was torn from the hands of his mother by the ambitious Archbishop of Cologne. Afterwards he came to the luxurious Court of the Archbishop of Bremen. The priests gave him a bad education. The latter especially fostered the boy's propensity for pleasures, and permitted him to live in the company of immoral young men. Declared already of age when but fifteen years old, he used the Saxons in a rude and unjust manner. They applied to Pope Gregory for redress. The Pope menacing him with anathemas, summoned him to come to Rome, as if he had been his judge. In return, Henry convoked some German Bishops, who should pronounce sentence against the Pope; they did so, and declared that Gregory had forfeited the Papal See. The Pope promulgated the anathema against the Bishops, and also against Henry, declared him to have forfeited his royal dignity, and dispensed the Germans with the oath of allegiance due to Henry. Most of the German Princes, then, declared to the King that, as long as he remained excommunicated, they would not acknowledge him as their King, and that, if he were not absolved of the anathema within a year, they would proceed to another election.

In this critical moment Henry at last resolved to go to Rome He had much trouble to raise the money necessary for the journey. Nobody but his faithful wife, whom he had often grieved, his little son, and one common servant, accompanied him. As his enemies had obstructed all passes through the Alps, he had to travel on detours, in the winter season, over the mountains, which were covered with snow and ice. He achieved the voyage under many dangers. As he arrived in Italy, forthwith many Bishops and Princes gathered around him, because they were dissatisfied with the Pontiff, and offered him their assistance; but Henry had become so dejected that he did not dare to accept their proposals.

Gregory, who had already started for Germany, in order to manage there Henry's trial, learning of his arrival, looked fast for a shelter with his friend Matilde, Countess of Toscane, and went in her castle Canossa. Here Henry had to stay (1077) between the second and third wall of the castle, in penitentials and barefooted, during three days, from morning until evening, not allowed to take the least food, and he had to beseech Gregory to dispense with the anathema. Finally the Pope granted the dispense through the intercession of Matilde and other powerful friends; but he must abstain from government until the German sovereigns should decide that he could continue to be their King. These had elected indeed a new King, *Rodolf of Suabia*.

But the people did not forsake Henry; the citizens of the towns and the peasants flocked to him, and he resisted bravely his adversary with their aid. The legates of the cunning Pope meanwhile assured both parties of the favor of their master. But as Henry lost a battle, the Pope inflicted again the anathema on him, and sent Rodolf a crown. But in a second battle Rodolf received a fatal wound, of which he died.

Henry now went again to Italy, no more as a penitent, but at the head of an army, in order to chastise his enemy. He besieged Rome, and appointed an anti-Pope. In the spring of the next year he conquered the city, and was anointed as Emperor by the latter. Gregory still defended himself in the angels' citadel.

The Duke of Puglia, though, released him, and conducted him safely to Salerno; but here, in a foreign place, he felt forsaken, and precipitated from the summit of his power. Before his death he again excommunicated Henry. One of his successors repeated the anathema. Beside, the Emperor had to struggle against other adversaries, to which even his sons joined. At last the helpless man died (1106). But the implacable priests grudged also the defunct his rest; twice he was buried, and twice pulled out of the grave, because loaded with the curse of anathema, until the Pope revoked it; then Henry's son buried the corpse once more.

§ 15. Frederick I.—Arnold of Brescia—Frederick II.—The Albigenses.

At that time an Italian priest, *Arnold of Brescia*, an ingenious and high-principled man, conceived the intention to re-establish the primitive simplicity of the Church. According to it, the clergy ought not to possess civil power, but only to apply themselves to their spiritual vocation. He wanted also the secular power of the Popes to be abolished; beside, he would deliver Italy from the government of the German Emperors. His gigantic design elicited enthusiasm in the whole country, except from the clergy; the Popes excommunicated him; Arnold fled to the quiet valleys of Switzerland, where he obtained a safe asylum. Meanwhile the Romans held a meeting, renounced allegiance to the Pope, and declared themselves free. Arnold returned to Rome (1145), accompanied by large bands he had engaged in Switzerland. The Romans expelled the Pope, and imitating ancient Rome, elected a Senate, Consuls, and Tribunes of the people. But Emperor Frederick I. came with an army to Italy, subdued the the revolted towns, forced his entrance into Rome, and vanquished the inhabitants of the city. Arnold had again taken to flight, and kept himself hidden. The Pope summoned the Emperor to get the heretic delivered to him. Frederick liked to obey him so much better, because he hated Arnold too as the friend of the people. His spies soon ferreted him out. In a dark night Arnold was dragged to Rome, and immediately burnt (1155). His memory was highly venerated by the Romans.

Frederick II., too, found the Popes to be his adversaries. As he deferred a crusade he had promised to make he was excommunicated by Gregory IX., and the anathema was repeated, as he, though outlawed, finally started on it. While he was combatting the Turks in Palestine, the Pope devastated his Italian States. Therefore Frederick turned his arms against him (1230), routed his soldiers, and compelled him by force to retract the promulgated anathema.

As Frederick would deprive the Lombards of their liberties, the Pope hurled the threefold anathema against him. The Emperor invaded the Papal dominions, conquered them almost all, and prevented a Council, which was contrived for his ruin, by taking the Bishops who traveled there, prisoners. To such heavy blows the almost centennary Pope succumbed. But an other quite as redoubtable champion, Innocent IV., soon replaced him. Not being secure in Rome, he fled to Lyons in France, and held there the mentioned synod. He reiterated the anathema (1245), dispensed Frederick's subjects with the oath of allegiance, declared all his dominions forfeited, and summoned the Germans to elect another King. Soon two Kings rose against Frederick. These kept his arms busy in Germany, while the Lombards in Italy continued to combat with great efforts. He died during this war, and the Lombards finally obtained their freedom (1250).

At that time in *France* the harmless sect of *Albigenses* arose, called so from the town of Alby. From their leader, Peter Wald, who was a merchant, they were also named *Waldenses*. They rejected the baptism, the Catholic doctrine of the Lord's Supper, the Popes, Bishops, indulgences and the purgatory; they censured the vices of the clergy, and took a peaceable, charitable course of life. Pope Innocent III. established an Inquisition Tribunal, and commanded to preach a crusade against them, as one of the inquisitors was murdered (1207). The Count of Toulouse, who was suspected to have instigated the foul deed, was forced to participate in the crusade, and to fight his own subjects. Whole towns and villages were destroyed, and their inhabitants extirpated by fire, sword and rope. Alone in the town of Beriers 20,000 persons, without any regard to age or sex, were killed, and 7,000 of them burned in a church.

§ 16. Crusades (1096—1300)—The First Capture of Jerusalem.

Already since Emperor Constantine many Christians made pilgrimages to the grave of Jesus, and to the graves and monuments of the Apostles and other Saints of the Primitive Church; for they imagined that, partly by the merits of those Saints, partly on account of the great hardships they had to suffer during the long journey, they could more easily obtain the grant of their prayers, and especially the pardon of their sins. As long as Palestine was a dominion of the Arabs, the pilgrims could there mostly perform the acts of their devotion unmolested. But when the Seldschouks (a Turkish tribe) possessed that country, they were often robbed, ill-treated, and even killed. These persecutions first suggested to the mind of Gregory VII. the idea of conquering Palestine, and he only wanted a longer life for the execution of his project. That was reserved for *Urban II.* He found an excellent tool for it in Peter of Amiens. This fanatic hermit who had long lived in Palestine, delivered to the Pope a letter from the Patriarch of Jerusalem, in which the distress of the Christians was represented, and the Occident implored for help. Bare-footed, on ass-back, and with a crucifix in his hand, he passed through Italy, France and Germany, and in the name of Jesus, who, as he asserted, had appeared to him in the vestibule of the temple, he summoned the Christians to deliver the holy countries from the infidels. The Pope himself discussed in the Councils at Piacenza and Clermont the merit to help the Oriental Christians, most impressively. It was resolved to make war upon the enemies of their creed. Crying: "God wills it!" the assembled crowds fastened a red cross on their shoulders, whereof they got the name "Crusaders."

First, *Peter the Hermit* and *Walter the Penniless*, a poor knight, started with some hundred thousands, and, murdering and pillaging, passed through Germany, where they killed especially the Jews, and moved through Hungary to Greece. The most of them were dispatched during their march by the inhabitants of these countries. The rest were quickly shipped by the Greek Emperor to Asia Minor, where they also perished miserably; only Peter saved himself with a small troop, and fled back to Constantinople

Then the well organized main army, counting 600,000 men, began its march, led by the valiant *Godfrey of Bouillon*. They reached Asia safely; but here want, danger and combat commenced also for them. The Crusaders were in an unknown country, and had to deal with warlike, courageous enemies; nay, the Greeks themselves, by whom they were hated, being confessors of Popery, became their traitors, and often led them astray on purpose. The siege of the towns was protractive; hunger and disease destroyed thousands. So it happened that the Crusaders did not arrive in Syria before two years. Here they besieged Antioch for nine months. Famine was raging. Many, and Peter himself, took to flight; but the latter was overtaken and brought back to the camp.

Finally, the army reached Jerusalem; but it had dwindled down to 60,000 men. There it had to struggle again with hunger; besides, water was very scarce, for the enemies had obstructed all fountains far and near. Moreover, the country being destitute of woods, blockading machines were wanting, and the Seldschouks defended the city with the courage of desperadoes. Nevertheless, after five weeks, it was taken by treachery (14th of July, 1099). Godfrey was among the first who scaled the walls The victors committed a horrible slaughter of the enemies. Crying again: "God wills it!" they massacred every one; not even the babes were spared. Down the stairs of the mosque drizzled the blood of 10,000 butchered Saracens. The Jews had to share the same fate; they were driven into the synagogue and there burned. With the fury of cannibals, the bellies of many were cut open in order to see whether they had not devoured any coin. In this way 40,000 or according to other reports 70,000 persons were killed in one day. The Crusaders then passed through the blood-stained streets to the sepulchre of Jesus, who had enjoined meekness upon his followers, and entuned anthems of praise to his honor. They elected Godfrey King of Jerusalem; but he refused to accept this honor in a place where the founder of his religion had walked in humility; he called himself modestly the protector of the holy sepulchre.

§ 17. Continued—The Three Next Following Crusades—Emir Saladin.

The war against the Mohammedans was continued; several principal crusades were yet waged against them. Emperor Conrad III., and Louis VII., King of France, were the leaders in the second. Saint Bernard had instigated them to it, predicting its happy success; but of 200,000 crusaders, almost all perished. Bernard was smart enough to attribute the sinister issue of their enterprise to their sins.

The third crusade was caused by Rainold, a knight of Antioch, namely : A Mohammedan caravan pilgrimed to Mecca. With it was also the mother of the celebrated *Saladin*, Emir of Egypt, who ruled this country, and had also conquered Tripolis, Tunis and Syria. Rainold surprised the pilgrims, plundered them, and killed the companions of Saladin's mother. The Emir demanded satisfaction for that hostile deed from Guido, King of Jerusalem ; as it was refused, he waged war on him, defeated his army totally at Tiberias (1187), and took him prisoner, with many other noblemen. But he released the King generously from captivity, when he had promised by oath not to take up arms against him ; only Rainold received the death blow. Jerusalem was besieged and surrendered ; Saladin did not stain his victory by wanton cruelty. Nobody was killed ; the captives were permitted for a ransom to go free with their property ; and those who were unable to raise it were dismissed without pay. Finally he distributed almost the whole sum of the collected ransom among those who had no money to pay their fare.

Saladin's generosity did not touch the feelings of the Christian sovereigns ; the most powerful of them made preparations for a a new campaign. First, Emperor Frederick I. set out with 100,000 warriors (1189). He vanquished, indeed, the Seldschouks at Iconium, in Asia Minor, in a bloody battle ; but as he was crossing the river Saleph, on horseback, he was drowned in the rapid billows. His army, too, perished miserably by disease.

One year later, Richard Lion-hearted (Cœur de Lion), King of England, *Philip August*, King of France, and *Leopold*, Duke of Austria, set out marching. But national hatred disunited them.

Their sole joint exploit was the conquest of Acre (Ptolemais) in Syria. Richard ordered Leopold's flag to be torn from the house he had taken possession of, and to be trampled in the mire. Provoked by this insolence, Leopold and Philip left the army of the crusaders and returned home. The besieged had capitulated by promising a ransom; when Saladin did not pay it in the preconcerted time, Richard commanded the prisoners to be cruelly slaughtered. Meanwhile, neither was he able to conquer Jerusalem; he obtained for the Christians only the right to visit the city unopposed. Then he, too, started on his return. To his great personal valor he was indebted for the surname "Lion-Hearted." At his return he was still unfortunate enough to be taken prisoner by Duke Leopold, who delivered him to the Emperor. He must suffer a long time in the dungeon, and redeem his freedom with an enormous sum of money.

Soon after Richard's departure the noble-minded Saladin died (1193). Before his death he distributed alms among Christians and Mussulmans, without any distinction of their religion. He was so poor when he died that the expenses of the funeral had to be paid with a borrowed sum of money.

§ 18. Concluded—The Rest of the Crusades—Frederick II.—Louis IX.—Effects of the Crusades.

The next important Crusade was undertaken by Emperor *Frederick II*. He had vowed it when he was crowned. His troops were to this end assembled in Italy, but the most of them succumbed to an epidemic disease, which also attacked the Emperor. Therefore he was obliged to defer the promised Crusade. However, he was excommunicated by Gregory IX., and the anathema was repeated, as he really set out after one year (1228), without having been absolved of it. Scarcely had he landed in Syria when the priests got ashore, too, and here also published the Papal curse. Thereby dissensions arose which divided the army. Frederick therefore concluded a truce with Sultan Kamel (1229), by virtue of which the latter ceded Jerusalem, Bethlehem, Nazareth, and the tract which leads to these towns from the sea. Now the Emperor entered Jerusalem joyfully, and put himself the crown on his head, as no priest dared to do it for him. Immediately the Patriarch here also promulgated the interdict. Frederick got the priests who sided with that, whipped and driven away; then he returned to Europe, in order to chastise the Pope also. Fifteen years after this Jerusalem was again lost.

Louis IX., King of France, yet endeavored to support the tottering cause of the Christians. He had received the surname of the Saint for his piety, which conformed to the taste of his age, and was, therefore, much praised. He marched the highest noblemen of France, and many thousand soldiers to Egypt. First he was favored by fortune; he conquered the fortified town of Damiette, but as he advanced farther he was so entangled by the many canals and branches of the Nile that he was obliged to surrender his whole army (1248), to return to Damiette, and give a ransom of 800,000 pieces in gold to be paid for the prisoners. Fortunately the Sultan was killed by his enemies, who set Louis free because his courage induced them to respect him. He returned home, and found that during his absence his dominion had been laid waste by internal enemies. Notwithstanding the unfortunate termination of his Crusade, he enterprised a second, against Tunis (1270), in order to fight the Saracens from that side; but he lost by the pest his army and life. Twenty years later also Ptolemais (Acre), the last place the Christians yet possessed in the Orient, was torn from their dominion.

Between these greater Crusades many smaller happened. Even women and children undertook several. Such an one was ventured by 30,000 boys (1213). Priests were their leaders. They had flattered the children by the illusion that God would work a miracle, in order to help them over the Mediterranean Sea; that he would separate its waters and lead them with dry feet through it, as he once had led the Israelites through the Red Sea. Most of the children miserably perished during the march; the rest were sold in Egypt into bondage.

Europe lost by the Crusades about seven million men, and Palestine was nevertheless gone. Most of the Christians engaged in the Crusades from fanaticism, excited by the priests, especially by the Popes. Many others were allured by other vile motives; for the Popes promised the Crusaders the release of their debts, and the indulgence of all, even the darkest sins and crimes. However, these wars had also good effects. By them Arabian culture was diffused through Europe, the knowledge of nations and countries augmented, the power of the hierarchy concussed, the chain of feudalism in many places broken, and the sense of freedom awakened. Many serfs received liberty, as their lords took the cross, either alone or accompanied by them. Commerce, especially, was by the Crusades advanced. Entire fleets sailed from Venice, Genoa, Pisa, and other maratime towns of Italy, to those distant countries, carrying their armies, arms and provisions, and on their return brought the merchandise of Persia and Hindoostan to Europe. By such a commerce they acquired great riches and power. Beside, the Crusades diminished the number of the noble families, because many noblemen died by them.

§ 19. The State of the Church—Anathema—Interdict.

True, in Europe the Slaves, Hungarians and Russians, and in Asia the Tartarian tribes were converted to Christianity; but its doctrine and spirit remained unknown to them, for they yet stood on the lowest degrees of civilization. They were driven to the rivers, and aspersed with water; then they were baptized and called Christians. Their Princes who had accepted the Christian faith before them, commanded them to follow their example, and they thoughtlessly obeyed them.

The Roman Bishops and the Patriarchs of Constantinople mutually nourished hatred and jealousy; both strove after the supremacy of the Church. By degrees they gave vent to manifest hostilities. They hurled the anathema upon each other; finally they cut off all communication. The Roman Church separated from the Greek, and the Pope became the head of the former.

In Rome and the other Churches of Italy, the Latin language was primitively employed in the divine service, because it was the native language of the country; by and by it was also adopted by other countries, and finally its use ordered for the whole Occidental Church. The chaffering with relics and indulgences, and the number of Church festivals increased. During the Crusades whole ships were freighted in Palestine with holy earth, as they called it, and this earth was sold to the Christians of Europe. Every Church wanted to get the relic of a Saint. Feet, teeth, heads of such Saints were purchased at high rates. Most of the relics were spurious, frequently taken from the bodies of criminals, or artificially counterfeited. In the Cathedral of St Jago, in Spain, a head was exhibited which was told to be that of St. James, and after his decapitation, to have swum to Spain. With the infidels and heretics, as they called them, they dealt most cruelly. The Jews, too, were often very severely persecuted.

The most dreadful weapons of the clergy were the *anathema*, the *interdict*, and the *Inquisition Tribunal*.

The *anathema* deprived a man of the enjoyment of all ecclesiastic, civil and natural rights. He was excluded from the Communion with the Church, was not allowed to assist in the divine service, nor to have intercourse with other Christians. He was unfit to make contracts; the laws did neither protect his property nor person; none were obliged to keep their word to him. His children could dispense with their duty of respect and obedience. Even his life was at the mercy of every murderer; every one had a right to kill him. His life was not safe neither in the company of his friends nor his family; nay, it was held to be a meritorious act to kill such a man.

By the *interdict* the divine service was suspended in entire countries. Then no church-bell sounded; the altars were unclothed, even the church doors locked, the marriages contracted on the graves, all public amusements interdicted, even greetings forbidden. The hair and beard were to be left unshorn, the use of meat was entirely prohibited, and the dead were usually not buried in consecrated grounds, but either interred in some other place, or thrown away to feed dogs and birds of prey. These punishments usually were inflicted on Princes, who would not comply with the caprices and ambitious designs of the Bishops and Popes.

§ 20. Continued—The Inquisition Tribunal.

The Inquisition Tribunal, this infamous pillory of Popery, was instituted by Gregory IX. against the Albigenses (1229), and soon after directed against all heretics. He committed it to the Order of the Dominicans. The objects of this Tribunal were not only heresies, but also pretended services, and even philosophic, political and mathematic doctrines. So e. g., Galileo was put in its dungeon, because he had taught the theorem that the earth revolves around the sun.

The Courts of the Tribunal were horrid castles, where the prisoners were tortured in subterranean chambers, in order to extort from them the confessions which they refused to make spontaneously. At the first degree of torture the tormentors raised them high in the air, and then suddenly let them fall again to the ground. At the second degree their mouth was forcibly opened, some cloth put on its opening, and through it a great quantity of water was poured into their throat. Thereby in the unfortunate victims the sensation of choking arose. At the third degree their feet were slowly roasted over a coal-fire.

The penalties of the sentenced were confiscation of property, service on the galleys, life-long imprisonment and combustion. Many of the rich were judged guilty only for the reason that their impeachers and Judges longed for their treasures. The combustion was in Spain called Auto da Fe (judicial decree of faith). On the way to the execution the condemned wore the Sanbenito, a peculiar dress, on which they were represented burning in the flames, and surrounded by devils; moreover a high cap, painted over also with demons; finally they had a rope around the neck, and carried a burning candle in the hand. In this attire they were paraded in the streets, and had to pass by a stage on which the King and his Court-Officers and Court-Ladies were seated. For such an execution was for the barbarians of those ages a kind of play in which their hearts and senses delighted. At last the sentenced victims were brought to the place of execution, where funeral piles were raised. There they were the last time summoned to forswear their faith, and if they persevered in it, put on the wood-piles. At a given signal these were kindled, and the unhappy victims slowly burned. Their torments sometimes lasted many hours; sometimes their skin burst, and through the scalds the intestines gushed forth. Generally they were burnt alive. It was considered to be a particular grace if they first were strangled, and then thrown on the wood-stack. If the executed were authors, their writings were burnt at the same time.

This infernal tribunal was established in most of the countries of Europe, and even in Asia and America. Especially it subsisted in Spain and Portugal, in France and Italy. In America many Indians were burned, if they would not be converted to Christianity. They were shown the gospel, and required to believe in its contents, though they could not read it; if they refused to obey, they were to expire in the flames. No rank, no sex, no age was protected against the power of the Tribunal; even Kings and Bishops were subjected to it.

Most of the victims of the Inquisition were sacrificed in the Spanish Dominions during the Governments of Ferdinand, the Catholic, and of Philip II. *Isabella*, Ferdinand's wife, had promised to her confessor to exterminate all heretics, if the royal crown would fall to her share. She became Queen. Now all Jews and Moors, who then formed a great part of the inhabitants in Spain, had to consent to be baptized, or to leave the country; but as many of them who submitted to baptism, secretly remained attached to their former creed, she induced her husband to establish the Inquisition Tribunal. In this country 10,000 men were burned alive in the course of eighteen years. Even more dreadful was the rage of Philip II., who persecuted the Protestants in the Netherlands (see § 29). The last combustion happened 1782 in Seville. They have computed that the number of all individuals who since the institution of the Inquisition have been burned in the different countries of the earth, amounts to nine millons.

§ 21. Concluded—The Clergy—The Popes—Gregory VII.— Innocent III.

During this period the clergy was the most powerful caste in State; but its members indulged in ambition, luxury and indolence. Even the Bishops set out on feuds, or were used to hunting and military exercises. Frequently priests returning from hunting went accompanied by their hounds, immediately to church, in order to say mass. The Monks grew wild and savage; many clergymen did not even know how to read. The Popes, in particular, [were greedy for more dominions, ambitious, cruel and perfidious. They shunned no fraud, if it served to increase their authority, e. g., they frequently appealed to the *canon law*, a collection, partly of fictitious or adulterated laws of the oldest Synods and Roman Bishops, and partly of later Papal edicts. They introduced it as the statute-book of the Church. By it they were declared to be the sovereigns of the Church, the Bishops being only their representatives.

With *Gregory VII.* (1073—1085), the universal sovereignty of the Popes begins. He demanded of the Bishops an oath, like that of allegiance, and declared most countries to be fiefs of the Roman See. He asserted that the Papal power resembles the sun, the Royal the moon; as the moon gets her light from the sun, in the same manner Emperors and Kings do not exist but by the Pope; consequently those are obliged to obey him. He robbed the sovereigns of the right to nominate the prelates of the Church, and to invest them with tracts of land, and usurped it for himself. Moreover he instituted celibacy (the unmarried state of life) of priests, forbidding them matrimony, and separating them forcibly from their wives and children. Namely in the former ages of the Church the priests were not forbidden to marry, and even in Gregory's age many of them had wives. Therefore they opposed the introduction of celibacy, and even caused revolts against the Pope; however, he carried his prohibition through by dint of force.

Next to Gregory, *Innocent III.* (1198—1216) was the most imperious and most powerful Pope. During the war between Otto of Brunswick and Philip of Suabia, he contrived to augment considerably the Papal dominions; he deprived the laymen of the chalice of the Holy Supper; he censured them severely for reading the Bible, introduced the auricular confession by law, and set the interdict at work. Proof of his cruelty is the persecution of the Albigenses.

THIRD PERIOD (1300—1518).

From the End of the Crusades Unto the Reformation of the Church.

§ 22. War of the Hussites—Philip IV. of France.

Under the reign of Emperor Sigismond IV., in Constance, the great Synod was held, by which *John Huss* and *Jerome of Prague* were burnt. From their ashes one of the most dreadful religious wars flashed up (1419—1433). Their adherents, the Hussites in Bohemia and Moravia, already exasperated, because they were forbidden to confess the doctrine of their teacher, and to use the chalice at the Lord's Supper, and now enraged by his fearful execution, united close to the town Kniss, upon a mountain which they called Tabor, where they also founded a town of the same name, and celebrated the divine service. Their General was the nobleman of Trocznowa, called *Ziska*, that means, the one-eyed. The Pope summoned all Christendom to wage a crusade against them, and Emperor Sigismond came (1422) to Prague with an immense army; but *Ziska* repelled him. A second army was also vanquished, and the Emperor had to flee from Bohemia. After Ziska's death the two *Prokop* became the Generals of the Hussites. They vanquished still several Imperial armies, and spread the flames of war over Germany. Everywhere terror preceded them. Finally, the Council in Basil invited them to negotiations. Procop the Great made his appearance there at the head of a large embassade. The Synod granted to the moderate party of the Hussites the chalice and the free sermon. They would have obtained still more important rights if they had lived in concord instead of quarreling with each other.

Philip IV., King of France, with the surname of the Beautiful, was a scourge of the Popes. Boniface VIII. forbade him to assess the clergy, and as the King yet carried his will into execution, sent a bull (decree) wherein he declared himself to be the Supreme Judge of the King, France being a Papal fief. Philip ordered the Papal letter to be burned at an assembly of the States. Then the

Pope excommunicated him, and dispensed his subjects with their oath of allegiance, the King held (1303) another assembly of the States, which protested against all Papal decrees. In order to chastise the Pope yet more severely, he intended to have him seized secretly, and conducted to France. Boniface was suddenly attacked in Anagni, put on the back of a miserable nag, which had neither bridle nor saddle, and imprisoned. The people, indeed, delivered him and carried him to Rome; but he was so much enraged by the suffered insult that he smashed his own head on the wall of his own room. Philip then got Clement V., by birth a Frenchman, elected Pope, because he hoped that he being a native, would be suppler; in order that he might the more easily rule him, he bound him by the condition that he should take up his residence in France. From that time *Avignon* was the seat of the Popes during seventy years (1307—1377).

Through covetousness Philip attained also the abolishment of the Order of the Templars. This Order had been founded during the Crusades, and was originally destined to protect the pilgrims in Palestine against the attacks of their enemies. Upon the same day all Knights of the Temple in France were seized, then, under the pretext of having committed secret crimes and vices, put to the rack, and forced to make untrue confessions. Fifty-nine of them, and James Molay their Grand-Master, too, were by a slow fire burnt (1310). In the hour of death they retracted their confessions; Molay himself had never declared himself to be guilty. The King confiscated the large dominions of the Order, and divided the booty with the Pope, who abolished the Order of the Templars also in the other countries.

§ 23. State of the Church—Wycliffe—John Huss—The Popes.

Public morals were in this period barbarous and corrupted; cruelty and debauchery generally prevailed. To this evil were also joined the belief in witches and ghosts, exorcisms, persecutions of the infidels and heretics. The Jews, e. g., were generally ill-treated, even by the magistrates; their testimony against Christians was null and void; they were not entitled to acquire landed property; their children were precluded from the public schools; in larger towns they were confined to special districts, and by capital punishment forbidden to educate a Christian child in their faith, or to marry a Christian maid.

John Wycliffe, professor of theology in England, was excommunicated and suspended, because he censured the Popes and the Monastic Orders, and admitted the Bible alone as the rule of Christian faith. He translated the latter into the language of his country, and continued, till he died (1385), to teach with candid courage. Some of his disciples were burned, others exiled. The latter propagated his doctrine in Germany and Bohemia.

In the latter country, soon after, *John Huss*, professor of theology in Prague, was teaching with Wicleff's spirit, whose books he was assiduously reading. His writings and sermons were anathematized. Still, even the anathema of the Pope did not diminish the authority which he enjoyed with the people. He burned the Papal bull of indulgence amidst great tumult. Large crowds accompanied him, and listened to the sermons he delivered in the open air.

He was summoned to the Synod of *Constance*, at which Emperor Sigismond, Pope John XXIII., and many other Princes, Bishops, Abbots and Doctors were present. He was ordered to recant his doctrine. He attempted to defend himself; but the priests did not allow him to speak, preventing him by clamor; they thrust him into a marshy dungeon, in which he languished during seven months, and fell sick. As he would not retract, he was sentenced to the stake (1415). He appealed in vain to the safe conduct he had received from the Emperor, and to the promise of security given to him by the Pope; the Synod declared that people are not bound to keep their word to heretics. First his writings were burned, then he himself, and his ashes dispersed in the Rhine. One year later his friend *Jerome of Prague* suffered the same fate.

In order to extort money from the credulous, the Popes employed many different means: they disposed of the prebends by auction, sold the indulgences, dispensed with the ecclesiastic laws, and imposed contributions for fighting Turks, the Peter's pence and other taxes. For money they were ready to sell the remission of any crime; this was extended even to the defunct. After the introduction of the inquisition the execution of the heretics was one of their ordinary functions. Their thirst for more dominions involved them in wars continually. For a time two Popes reigned, one in Rome, the other in Avignon ; finally, even three were ruling (1409). In order to end the schism of the Church, and to reform both its head and members, that great Synod of Constance was held (1414—1418). The three Popes were deposed, and a new one, Martin V., elected ; but he was not more energetic than the others, and dismissed the assembly with his benediction. Since that time the Popes pursued their scandalous life, oppressed the National Churches, and charged the nations with taxes for the benefit of their own families and relations.

FOURTH PERIOD (1518—1648).

From the Reformation Unto the Westphalian Peace.

§ 24. Causes of the Reformation of the Church—Martin Luther.

In the preceding period the condition of the Christian Church had been so wretched that the outcry for its reform universally resounded. But this was neither heeded by the Popes, nor by the prelates of the Church generally, and the great Synods of Constance and Basle passed without success; therefore the laymen themselves must set to the work of reformation

In *Germany* there were some additional reasons for it. The sovereigns of this Empire depended much upon Rome. Even the Emperors were obliged to obey the Popes, because they were crowned by them. The German prelates and churches possessed the larger and finer part of the public property, and were exempt from all civil charges and duties. The corruption and tyranny of the clergy was unbounded. The assurance of impunity encouraged them to perpetrate the gravest crimes. They indulged in the grossest luxury. The Popes extorted from Germany immense sums under the titles of dispensations, indulgences, taxes for the Turkish wars, etc. They reserved half of the benefices for themselves, and let them out to the highest bidders, who sold them again to others. By their notorious viciousness they had already lost a good deal of their authority and power. Finally, the printing press diffused the rays of enlightenment wider and wider, and public opinion gained more and more importance.

But the next cause which excited the religious revolution, was the scandalous traffic of indulgences of Leo X. In Germany, especially, this Pope hoped to acquire by them the sums he wanted to satisfy his love of splendor and his luxury. He asserted that the money paid over to him would make amends for the lack of morality, and deliver the guilty ones from their civil and divine penalties. For a trifling sum the remission of all, even the grossest sins, could be purchased, and Heaven was thrown open to every criminal. Of the Papal agents the Archbishop of Metz, and the Dominican *John Tezel* carried on this traffic the most successfully. "Now," cried Tezel, and his fellow-preachers, "now Heaven is open; *when* will he enter who does not come in by such a cheap bargain? What mind must he have who does not hurry to release his father from the torments of purgatory? As soon as the shrove-money jingles in the chest, the soul jumps out of purgatory."

Every intelligent man was disgusted by this scandal; the most so was Dr. *Martin Luther*, an Augustine friar, and professor of theology at Wittenberg. He was born in Eiselben (1483), where his father was a poor miner. He was destined by him to study jurisprudence. One day he took a walk with a friend, who was killed by lightning at his side. The youth grew melancholy, and joined the Order of the Augustine Monks. Here he had to perform the lowest work, to open and shut the church doors, pass with the beggar-boy through the town, etc. His melancholy increased; nothing but music was able to divert him. Still he was assiduously studying, and was graduated as Doctor of Philosophy. He liked best to study the Bible. From this gloomy state of mind which wasted his mental and physical forces, the Prior of the Convent, Dr. Staupitz, delivered him, by proposing to *Frederick the Wise*, Elector-sovereign of Saxe, to appoint him Professor in the University of Wittenberg. Here Luther entered into a sphere of activity, which was better suited to his erudition (1508). Soon after he became also town preacher. During a journey on which he went to Rome (1510), by order of his convent, he became better acquainted with the infamous life of the Popes, and with the immorality of their Court.

After having in vain complained in a missive he had addressed to the Archbishop of Metz, of the mischief of the indulgences, he affixed on the church of the castle of Wittenberg those famous ninety-five theses, by which he declared the indulgences to have been merely invented by the Popes with the design to make money. The theses were translated into the German, and spread abroad in innumerable copies. Luther was summoned to Rome, and only with difficulty could his sovereign procure him a trial in Augsburg. Luther appeared with a safe conduct, which Frederick had provided, in the presence of the Papal legate (1818). This dignitary demanded unconditional recantation, and threatened him with anathema. Luther quickly departed, for the legate made preparations to take him prisoner. A second attempt which another legate made in order to induce him to recant, had no better success.

Afterwards the Papal excommunication bull directed against Luther arrived from Rome (1520), but without great effect. In Leipsic the students nearly killed its bearer. Dr. EcK. Luther assembled all the teachers of the University of Wittenberg outside of the town; the students raised a wood-pile, a teacher kindled it, and Luther threw, amidst general exultation, the bull, the canon law, and Eck's writings in the fire.

§ 25. Diet of Worms—Confession of Augsburg—War of Smalkalden—Religious Peace of Augsburg.

Meanwhile the lately-elected Emperor, Charles V., came to Germany, in order to hold a Diet in Worms, and Luther was summoned to be present at it (1521). Though suffering from the effects of a fever, he resolved to set out immediately. A friend warned him against Worms; but he answered: "I shall go, even if as many devils are in town as tiles on the roofs." However, his sovereign did not consent to his journey until the Emperor had promised him a safe conduct, and a secure return. Luther's journey resembled a triumphal procession; whatever town he passed through, there crowds of people met him, and hailed him as their deliverer. The Papal legate, on the contrary, though traveling in the train of the Emperor, was only scoffed at and derided; hardly anybody would receive him. Worms re-echoed Luther's praise, and abounded with apologies for him, and with menaces against his enemies. A great many noblemen swore to assist him.

Luther stepped forth in the Diet; intimidated by the aspect of the large, resplendent assembly, he asked them to grant him one day for consideration; but on the second day he defended his doctrine with resoluteness and courage, declined absolutely to retract as they ordered him to do, and concluded by saying: "Now, because they demand a plain, simple answer from me, I will give one which has neither horns nor teeth. I do neither believe the Pope, nor his synods; for both have often erred, and contradicted themselves. Therefore, I cannot and shall not recant, unless they refute me by testimonies of the Holy Writ, or by evident reasons; for it is not advisable to do anything against conscience. Here I stand, I cannot do otherwise! God help me! If this be human work, it will fall to ruins by itself; but if it be from God, you will never destroy it."

Luther's numerous friends were delighted by this bold answer. He was indeed excommunicated; but his sovereign Frederick had already taken precaution to protect the Reformer. On his return, accordingly, Luther was suddenly stopped in a forest by masked riders, and safely carried by them to the fortified castle *Wartburg*, near to Eisenach.

In the profound concealment in which he lived here, he composed new writings, especially the excellent translation of the New Testament. But hearing that in Wittenberg turbulent crowds were violently throwing out the images from the churches, that they were destroying the altars, and perpetrating other mischief, he suddenly appeared there, and restored order (1522).

Meanwhile the anathema, inflicted on him, was forgotten, and the work of reformation speedily advanced. Many convents were abolished, and a large part of their revenues set aside for the ministry of the gospel, for the instruction of the youth, and for poor-institutions. The priests were permitted to marry. Mass and confession were abrogated. Luther himself put off the habit of his Order, and married (1525) *Catherine Bora*, who had left the convent with other nuns. His faithful friend and associate in the reformatory task was the meek and learned *Philip Melanchton*.

When some Catholic Princes concluded an alliance for the protection of their creed, the Lutheran States did the same for the defense of their belief (1526). At the Diet of Speier (1529) some restrictions on their faith were decreed; but they protested solemnly against them; whence they received the name *Protestants*. At the Diet of Augsburg (1530) they presented a memorial, containing their religious confession: therefore they were called *the relatives of the Augsburg Confession*. The Catholic States of the Empire rejected it, and summoned the heretics (as they called them) to return into the fold of the orthodox Church. Indignantly the Protestants left the Diet, whereupon their belief was declared to be heresy, and its propagation forbidden under the severest penalties. Therefore all the Protestant Princes confederated at Smalkalden, in order to defend their religious liberty, if necessary, with open force. Neither was the Council, which the Pope held in Triente, able to restore peace; the Protestants did not even attend it, but refused to submit to its decisions. Finally, Charles prepared war against them. They also took up arms. Luther, who in vain had recommended peace, died shortly, before the war broke out (1546).

Both parties were fighting during several years with alternate fortune; at last the Protestants became victors, and at the Diet of *Augsburg* a treaty was effected, which granted them the free practice of their religion. Still, if in future, States and prelates should convert to the Protestant Church, their prebends ought to be reserved to the Catholic Church. This article of the ecclesiastic reservation, which the Emperor had arbitrarily added, became, in later time, the cause of indescribable sufferings for all Germany.

§ 26. The Thirty-Years War—Restitution—Edict.

Emperor *Rodolf II.* had accorded to the Bohemian Protestants a charter by which he had granted them religious liberty, and especially the right to build churches and school houses. According to this right the evangelic inhabitants of the towns Klostergrab and Brannan built churches, but by order of Emperor *Matthias*, who meanwhile had succeeded Rodolf, one church was demolished, the other locked up. The States of the country addressed a petition to him, but with no success. Therefore they called the nation to arms, expelled the Jesuits, and took possession of the Government of their country (1618). Moreover the Bohemians even besieged the new Emperor, *Ferdinand II.*, in Vienna. But he unawares got aid, formed an alliance with *Maximitian*, electoral Prince of Bavaria, and vanquished the Bohemians. Educated by cunning Jesuits, he had vowed long ago the extirpation of the Protestants ; now the hapless country must feel his full revenge. Twenty-seven leaders of the rebellion, and besides an uncounted number of common citizens were cruelly executed, their property confiscated, the Protestant preachers and school teachers ill-treated and exiled, the Catholic religion, and with it the Order of Jesuits re-established, over 30,000 families driven into exile, and free religious exercise suspended. His Generals *Tilly* and *Wallenstein* vanquished all his adversaries, and now it depended upon him to terminate the the pernicious war, which for ten years had devastated Germany ; but he, believing that now the moment had arrived to strike the decisive blow on the Protestant Church, issued the ill-famed *Edict of Restitution*, and by it prolonged the terrors of war for twenty years. Appealing to the treaty of Augsburg (§ 25), he ordered the Protestants to restore all the ecclesiastic possessions they had confiscated since the conclusion of that treaty. To these belonged not less than two Archishoprics and twelve Bishoprics, besides all canonicates of Northern Germany, and a countless number of Abbeys and convents. An universal outcry of horror passed through the entire Protestant Germany ; but too weak to resist longer the implacable enemy, she could only be saved by foreign succor ; this was unexpectedly brought by *Gustavus Adolphus*, King of Sweden.

§ 27. Concluded—Gustavus Adolphus—Battles of Leipsic and Luetzen—Westphalian Peace.

Gustavus Adolphus turned his arms against Ferdinand, induced by the most important reasons. He saw his country, and his faith, to which he was devoted with enthusiasm, threatened by the conquests the Emperor had already made, and was still increasing. He felt himself also competent to the great enterprise. He was the first General of his age, and his troops were the best. He maintained strict discipline, and punished every excess in camp. At the morning and evening prayers every regiment was to form a circle around its preacher, and to perform its acts of devotion in open air. He shared every fatigue with the soldiers, and was personally valiant. Such a leader was followed by the army into all dangers.

Gustavus Adolphus landed with only 15,000 men, but they were chosen warriors, and the Emperor himself soon augmented their number by dismissing 18,000 men of his army, the most of whom enlisted with the King. At the same time Ferdinand discharged Wallenstein, his ablest General, on request of the commander's personal enemies. The King chased the Imperials from Pommerania and Mecklenburgh, gave the latter country back to her Princes, and allied with them. He invited also the electoral Prince of Saxony to take part in the treaty; but the latter, through fear, hesitated to make up his mind. Meanwhile, General Tilly took Magdeburgh by assault, and perpetrated an awful massacre among the inhabitants (1631); 30,000 of them lost their lives. No age, no sex was spared. Infants were thrown into the flames, and babes speared on the bosoms of their mothers. The entire city was consumed by fire. The electoral Prince, and the rest of the Protestant States did not tarry any longer to participate in the league with Adolphus.

The allies immediately tried their strength against the redoubtable Tilly, on "the large plain," near Leipsic (1631). This General charged the Saxons impetuously, and put them to flight; only a division of Swedes, which the King had added to them, stood firmly. Meanwhile, Gustavus himself repelled the wild attacks of the Imperialists with his Swedes. Seven times Poppenheim attacked him, and he must always give way. Finally the King mounted the hills, on which the hostile artillery stood, took it, and directed it against the foe himself; thus Tilly's defeat was decided.

He took to flight; his army was annihilated. Ferdinand did not any more despise the Snow King, as he ironically called Gustavus.

The King rapidly continued his victorious course, passed through all Germany, defeated the Imperial troops everywhere, forced the crossing over the Leck, where Tilly fell on the field of battle, and celebrated his entrance into Munich. In the meantime the Saxons had conquered Bohemia.

Ferdinand had now no army, nor a General. In his difficulty he applied entreatingly to Wallenstein, the offended subject, who indeed created for him a new army of 40,000 men in three months, but he consented to take its command only on the condition of dic-tatory power.

At *Luetzen*, in the environs of Leipsic, Gustavus Adolphus attacked him. The Swedes rush on the Imperial troops with the watchword, "God with us," and soon beat the wing against which the King himself is fighting. The other wing wavers. The King hastens to its aid. Being near-sighted, he is carried too near to the foe; an Imperial Sergeant perceives him, and calls to a musketeer: "Discharge on him; he must be a distinguished man." That moment the ball shatters the left arm of the King. He orders his companion to lead him out of the crowd, and on the way receives a second shot through the back. "I have enough, brother," he says to him, "save only yourself," drops from the horse, and dies.

The news of the King's death inflames his troops, instead of dispiriting them, to new rage. The Duke *Bernard of Weimar* leads on with the King's spirit; they twice cross again the hostile ditches; whole regiments expire on the place where they stand fighting; Wallenstein's left wing is entirely routed; fire seizes the Imperial powder wagons: Count Poppenheim, Wallenstein's bravest General, is killed. At last night puts an end to the combat, Wallenstein begins his retreat, and the Swedes keep the battle ground More than 9,000 dead of both armies covered it. Gustavus' corpse, disfigured by blood and wounds, robbed of the clothes and the adornment, was drawn forth from under a mountain of slain. The gray land-mark, where it was found, is since that battle called the Swedes-stone.

War continued ; the Protestants fought with various fortune ; in the battle at Noerdlingen they suffered another heavy blow (1634), losing there 12,000 men. Many of their conquests were retaken from them, and the electoral Prince, and other Protestant sovreigns concluded ignominiously a separate peace with the Emperor. France, then, was ready to assist the Protestants in their distressed condition, declaring war against Austria. He paid Bernard's troops their wages. This excellent General gained several victories. After his death French Generals commanded his troops. The Swedes themselves went on bravely fighting ; led by the great Generals, *Banner, Horn, Torstensohn, Wrangel,* all pupils of Gustavus Adolphus, they soon again obtained the superiority, and maintained it almost continually till the end of the war.

In the meantime Ferdinand II. had died, and his son *Ferdinand III.* finally consented that a general congress of peace of the belligerent States ought to be convened (1640). The negotiations were protracted, and continued in the midst of the tumult of arms, until the Swedes invaded the hereditary States of the Emperor, drove him to flight, and conquered a part of the city of Prague (the Kleinseite). Then peace finally was concluded in *Muenster* and *Osnabrueck* (1648). According to it the three principal religious parties, Catholics, Lutherans and Reformers, ought to enjoy equal rights, the Protestants to retain the ecclesiastic property they had possessed before the year 1624, Sweden to obtain the Province of Pommerania, and France that of Elsace.

The first effects of this lengthy war were dreadful. Germany lost by it many millions of inhabitants; whole countries were utterly desolated, many towns ruined, and the rays of civilization for a long time extinguished. Still, the menacing preponderance of the Spanish-Austrian dynasty was by it destroyed, the power of the Papacy broken, and the tyranny of the Church annihilated. Free investigation, especially in religious matters, was secured, an open path beaten to the sciences, and the road to civil liberty prepared.

§ 28. Switzerland—Zwingli—Calvin.

Contemporary with Luther, *Ulricus Zwingli* rose as a Reformer, in Switzerland. He was a child educated by his uncle, who was a clergyman. In Vienna he studied philosophy. He then applied himself to theology, and took the orders of a priest. First he was pastor in Glarus (1506), where he eagerly pursued his higher mental culture. The Pope would have granted him a pension, but he refused it. From Glarus he was called (1517) as a pastorate to the village of Einsiedeln, which was frequently visited by pilgrims who there worshiped the image of the Virgin Mary. In his sermons he boldly censured the abuses of the Christian Church, especially the nuisance of the indulgences, the worship of the relics, and the pilgrimages. He also called upon the Bishop of Constance to abolish these abuses; but with no success. Finally he was called by the Government of the Canton of Zurich to the city of Zurich (1518), and here his higher efficiency commenced.

At that time the seller of indulgences, *Bernhardin Samson*, came to Switzerland and gathered much money. Zwingli caused that in Zurich his traffic was prohibited. In spite of the invectives of his adversaries, especially among the friars, he continued to censure the prevailing abuses of the Church, and defended his doctrine in two public disputations with so good success that the Government encouraged him to preach further the evangel. The Reformation gradually succeeded. The images were removed from the churches, processions and pilgrimages abrogated, the convents abolished, matrimony allowed to the priests, the mass discarded, and a simple celebration of the Lord's Supper instituted, at which, according to Zwingli's doctrine, bread and wine only as figurative signs of the body and blood of Jesus were distributed.

In other Cantons similar reforms were accomplished. In *Geneva* they were effected by the urgency of *John Calvin*. He was, indeed, very active and zealous in the discharge of his official duties, but also obstinate and sullen, nay, sometimes cruel. For he caused the learned *Michael Servetius*, when traveling through the territory of Geneva, to be taken prisoner, because he in a Latin book had vented more liberal views on the Trinity than others. Calvin denounced him as heretic teacher who deserved capital punishment, and Servetius was burned.

In Switzerland, too, the Reformation was resisted, especially in the interior Cantons. They marched their troops into the field.

The Reformed Cantons were disunited; Zurich alone opposed the the Catholics at Cappel with a feeble corps, which commenced the attack (1531). Later the main corps arrived; the troops were tired; but Zwingli, who as chaplain accompanied them, admonished them to fight, crying: "I, at least, will join these honest men, and die with them, or help to save them." They obeyed his advice, but were beaten with a loss of six hundred men; the rest took to flight. Zwingli, who was one of the last on the battle field, was first hit with a stone, then wounded with a spear. As he refused to invoke the Saints, he was killed, and his corpse quartered and burned. The Reformers had to submit to a disadvantageous peace, and in many places the Catholic ritual was re-established.

§ 29. Spain—Revolution of the Netherlands—Philip II.

In the Netherlands, which country at that time belonged to Spain, the Protestants also suffered cruel persecution. Charles V. issued several edicts by which it was ordered that they should be beheaded, burned or buried alive. Whoever bought, sold, or even copied a heretic-book for his own use, was punished with death. During his reign from fifty to one hundred thousand Protestants were there killed. In his testament he recommended to his son and sucessor, *Philip II.*, to extirpate, without any exception, all heretics, and to maintain the Inquisition, this institution being the fittest means to that end. The son readily complied with his counsel. He established this Tribunal, and thereby caused revolts which presented him a welcome pretext for destroying the heretics, as he called the inhabitants; for he declared that he would rather not govern at all than to rule heretics. Conformable to his orders, the Duchess *Margaret* his stadt-holder in the Netherlands employed the force of arms. She conquered the mal-contents after a short resistance, and behaved cruelly towards the subdued; by her orders the Protestant Churches were destroyed, gibbets raised of their rafters, and on them hundreds in every town suspended. Now Duke *Alva* arrived at the head of a well-organized army, and took Margaret's place. He had received unlimited power from the King. He took the chiefs of the nobility, the Earls *Egmont* and *Horn*, prisoners, and executed them. An uncounted number of victims followed them; even the sick were dragged from the hospitals to the gallows. In Harlem the heroic citizens, two by two, were thrown into the sea. He boasted having executed, during the six years of his administration, eighteen thousand men with the executioner's axe, on funeral piles, etc. A larger number still was killed by him on the battle-field. No rank nor age nor sex was spared; for the King had declared the whole nation to be guilty of revolt and heresy. But in the most cases the Protestants had to suffer the fatal lot. The goods of the killed and proscribed were confiscated; they brought the King annually at least twelve million dollars profit.

After all, a heavy tax overturned Alva's terrorism. Besides the hundredth part of the whole property, he commanded the inhabitants to pay the twentieth of their immovable, and the tenth of the movable goods, as often as they were sold. The nation rose and declared (1572) *William of Orange* stadt-holder. Though the southern provinces, in which the Catholic creed prevailed, separated from the northern, William united the latter in a confederation, which declared itself independent from Spain (1581), and elected William its chief. Soon after the Prince was shot by an assassin, who would earn the prize Philip had promised to pay for William's head. But his son *Maurice* followed after him as stadt-holder; both he and his brother *Henry* resisted the King bravely, and at last Spain was compelled to acknowledge the independence of the Netherlands in the Westphalic Peace (1648).

§ 30. France—War against the Huguenots—The Saint Bartholomew—Henry IV.—Edict of Nantes—England—Episcopal Church—Henry VIII.

In France the number of the Reformers was very considerable; even among the nobility and at the Court many of them were found. They were called *Huguenots*, which name was probably derived from the word "Eidgenossen" (confederates), as the Swiss, among whom the Reformed Church had the most members, were usually called so. But King Francis I. persecuted them cruelly, he even caused several of them to be burned, during a solemn procession. Under his son, Henry II., executions by fire frequently occurred. Under the sons of the latter these persecutions turned into open war. The Reformers, indeed, had bad success in several campaigns; still their religious liberty was always increased and finally peace was made. Even a marriage was to be concluded between Prince *Henry of Navarre*, who confessed the reformed creed, and the sister of King Charles IX. But probably the vigilance of the Reformers was thereby only to be lulled to rest. The noblest of them were allured to Paris, and lodged in the neighborhood of Admiral *Coligni*, who was the leader of the Reformers. The nuptials were celebrated in the ill-famed night of Bartholomew (Aug. 24th, 1572). At a signal, given by the King, all Huguenots in Paris, together with the Admiral, were murdered. The Royal Guard, the city militia, and many inhabitants emulated each other in fury and cruelty. The Catholics wore white crosses as badges on their hats; the windows of their dwellings were illuminated. In the royal castle the blood was drizzling in all corners. The murderers penetrated to the very bed-chamber of the new-married Queen; she fled to her sister, and saw at the door a nobleman stabbed close to her; Charles himself fired at the fugitives. The next day he walked with his courtiers through the streets, looked at the decaying corpses, and, as they, disgusted, turned away from Coligny's corpse, he jokingly said: "A dead enemy always smells nicely." His mother, too, passed with her court-ladies through the streets, and rejoiced at the hideous sight.

The slaughtering in Paris lasted one week; 5,000 men lost their lives. To the Provinces also, Charles sent his orders for slaughter, and only a few Governors refused to execute them. In all, at least 40,000 French Reformers were killed. Henry of Navarre must forswear his creed; as he hesitated to do so, Charles threatened to kill him; after this he turned Catholic. The Pope celebrated the news of the Saint Bartholomew like a holy-day, and got a medal stamped in memory of it. Charles and his mother sent him the bloody head of the generous Admiral Coligny; he received it laughing; by his order the act of his murder was represented in a picture and the ignominious words written below: " The Pope approves and praises the murder of Coligny."

But the Reformers nevertheless remained unsubdued; they continued the combat courageously, till Henry became King of France; he then granted them by *the Edict of Nantes* equal rights with the Catholics (1598).

In England *Henry VIII.* (1509—1547) founded the *English* or *Episcopal Church*, the tenets of which are between the Catholic and Protestant one. He carried his reforms into execution by capital penalty, which he inflicted, without discriminating any creed, on Catholics, Lutherans, and Calvinists. He put even women and maidens, hardly being of age, to the flames, e. g. *Anna Askue*, a lady distinguished by youth and beauty, who had slightly doubted the real presence of Jesus in the Holy Supper. When Mary, Henry's daughter, and wife of Philip II., King of Spain, became Queen of England, she ordered the mass to be said again, and subjected the country to the Pope. Within three years 270 Protestants were put to death in the flames. After her, *Elizabeth*, also a daughter of Henry VIII., and Mary's sister, reigned in England (1558—1603); she reinstated the Episcopal Church, and since, England has confessed its doctrine.

In other countries, too, besides Germany, Luther's doctrine was introduced: in Sweden by *Gustavus Wasa*, and in Prussia by *Albert of Brandenburg*. The Reformed religion, according to the tenets of Zwingli and Calvin, from Switzerland, passed to *France* and the other countries along the Rhine, to *Holland* and *Scotland*.

§ 31. Outline of the Ecclesiastic Reforms—Their Effects—Distinctive Doctrines of the Several Churches.

Reformation created these improvements in the Christian Church:

1. The belief in the infallibility of the Pope and of the universal Councils was dismissed, and the Bible as the only source of Christian creed accepted. Therefore its use was also permitted to the people,

2. The Pope was not now generally acknowledged as the head of the Christian Church. The secular power of the Pope and of the Clergy in general was denied, and every sovereign claimed to have a right to exercise it himself in his territory.

3. The rites and ceremonies were partly derogated, partly simplified; in particular, were abolished: the auricular confession, the mass and its accompanying instrumental music, the traffic of indulgences, and the pilgrimages. For the divine service plain songs were introduced which had to be performed by the people, and were only accompanied by the organ. The sermon ought to be the principal part of the service. The most holy days and the fast-days were also abolished, the images of the Saints were removed from the churches, and matrimony conceded to the priests.

4. The convents of monks and nuns were abolished and their revenues bestowed upon the care of the sick, and upon the instruction of youth.

The effects that the Reformation of the Church produced, were very beneficial. The consciences of men were freed from the arbitrary dictates of the clergy; every one ought to have a right to scrutinize for himself the truth in the Bible. The great treasures of the convents were employed for the public welfare. People were no longer defrauded of their money by indulgences, masses, confessions and pilgrimages. As most of the priests entered into matrimony, and themselves educated children, their example exerted also a salutary influence upon their parishes. In general, the Reformation advanced progress in the sciences and the arts. Profusion and luxury were also limited, and a more frugal way of life took their place.

On the other side, the Reformers attributed to the Bible too much authority, declaring its dictates absolutely decisive; thereby the liberty of conscience was again limited, nay, soon entirely bound by their catechisms, and formulas of faith. For as the new sects grew more powerful, their leaders ranged those books of Confession over reason and Bible, and defined, like the Catholic Church, as a first principle: "the Church instructs, reason must keep silence."

In the above stated articles, all denominations of the Reformation together agree; in some others their creeds and rites differ from each other, namely: The Lutherans and the English Church are superintended by Bishops, but the clergymen of the Reformers are ruled by Synods, the members of which are partly ministers, partly laymen. All ministers of the Reformation are mutually equal in rank and dignity. The Lutherans believe that Christ's body and blood are present in the bread and wine of the Lord's Supper; the sectarians of Zwingli think bread and wine to be only the signs of his body and blood. The Reformers in France, Holland and Scotland, where they are called *Presbyterians*, believe that God has destined some men from eternity to everlasting felicity, others (even innocent children!) to everlasting damnation. The Zwinglians do not believe in this doctrine.

§ 32. State of the Church—Expulsion of the Unitarians—The Popes—Order of the Jesuits.

Soon differences arose between the new denominations of the Church themselves. Luther already bitterly opposed Zwingli's view regarding the Lord's Supper, and the Langrave of Hessia arranged in vain a religious conference of both between them; by Luther's obstinacy every attempt at an amicable compromise was frustrated. He did not keep the promise of mutual friendship with which they had parted; he wrote with bitterness against Zwingli. These internal quarrels even caused bloodshed in some places; e. g., in Holland the Presbyterians, who also were fighting for political liberty, were violently persecuted, many imprisoned, others banished or executed.

In the southern part of Switzerland, *Socinus*, a pious priest, had uttered the persuasion that there is only one God, and that Jesus is not his equal in essence, but that his nature was human. He got many adherents, who called themselves *Socinians* or *Unitarians*. They were cruelly persecuted by their Catholic governors, and finally expelled. The Papal legate ordered even to tear from them their children; but in this he was opposed by the Government. In the middle of winter they were forced to pass, deprived of all their property, with their wives and children, over the Alps, which were covered with ice and snow. They wandered to Zurich, and implored the inhabitants, who had already been converted to the Reformed religion, to afford them a quiet home; even here, too, they were turned away, being considered to be atheists. They finally found an asylum in the forests of Poland, and in North America.

The state of the Catholic Church grew worse and worse, and the Council of Trent did not remedy it. The Synod lasted eight years in all. It was evident that its decrees only tended to enlarge the Papal power, and to humble the Protestants, against whom it incessantly hurled its anathemas.

The life of the Popes also continued to be the same as before. *Alexander VI.* (1492—1503) was the most cruel of all Popes, and an outcast of humanity. He, his son *Cæsar*, and his daughter, *Lucrece Borgia*, dispatched their enemies by poison and poniard. He aided this ambitious son to enlarge his dominion in Italy. Finally he himself perished by the poison he had prepared for another. He instituted the censorship of books. *Leo X.* was the notorious adversary of Reformation. *Paul III.* anathematized the heretics, and sent troops against them. *Jules III.* appointed a keeper of monkeys as a Cardinal, because he was his favorite. *Paul IV.* was ambitious, and enlarged the register of prohibited books. *Sixtus V.*, though intelligent, was hard and despotic. *Gregory XIII.* celebrated the St. Bartholomew.

A new institute of the Catholic Church in this period is the *Order of the Society of Jesus* (of the Jesuits). *Ignatius of Loyola*, a Spanish nobleman, did, when a young man, military service in the army of Ferdinand the Catholic; he was wounded during a siege, and fell sick. Being so confined to bed, he excited his mind, which was already disposed for fanaticism, even more by reading odd legends. Then he instituted the Society of Jesus (1540), the members of which, besides the three usual monastic vows, obliged themselves to obey unconditionally the Pope, especially in matters of heresy and in fidelity. Their principal object was to combat the Protestant doctrine and to suppress mental liberty. The General of their Order resided in Rome. They entered public life in a thousand different forms; they made their appearance as teachers of the youth, as penitentiaries, tenders of the sick, inquisitors of faith, missionaries, confessors, ministers of States, and even as trades-men. Among laymen, too, they created fraternities to which even Princes and their sons joined. They tried chiefly to captivate rich young men; the fortunes of such victims became the prey of their

Society. Their Order spread rapidly. It was admitted in all Catholic countries; it entered even Hindoostan, China and Japan. The number of its members was very considerable. In the eighteenth century it counted at one time twenty-two thousand members. In the Council of Trent it carried the issue. In Asia it established the Inquisition Tribunal. In Germany its principal seats were Munich and Vienna. Bavaria was called its Paradise. It fostered the belief in miracles, arranged painful exercises of penance for the stupid populace, and permitted the rich and powerful everything they longed for. By and by the education of the Catholic youth was seized by the Jesuits, whereby they obtained the greatest influence in civil society. They crept into the confidence of the sovereigns, became their confessors and counselors, and soon also the governors of the State affairs. Though the praise of great scholarship cannot be withheld from single members of their Order, still their performances remained far behind the demands of their Age. They were enemies of enlightenment, of political and religious liberty. Their moral code permitted the use of all means, even regicide, in order to obtain good ends. They possessed immense riches which they acquired by the most diverse ways, even by commercial business.

FIFTH PERIOD (1648—1789.)

From the Westphalian Peace to the French Revolution.

§ 33. Germany—Frederick II. and Joseph II.—Persecution of the Huguenots—England.

Emperor Leopold I. was an enemy of political and religious freedom. As he ceded to the Turks some frontier-fortresses of Hungary, which passed for the bulwarks of this country, many Hungarians got hereby irritated, and conspired against him; the plot was discovered, and the culprits were punished. Therewith not content, he let the whole Hungarian nation, especially its

Protestant part, feel his vengeance. The Reformed Christians were forced to conform to the Catholic Church, the refractories of them killed, their most zealous ministers sent to the gallows, their school-teachers deposed, etc. In the Archbishopric of *Salzburg*, too, the Protestants were persecuted by the Bishop, and all of them, twenty thousand persons, were forced to emigrate.

On the contrary *Frederick II.*, King of Prussia, and Emperor *Joseph II.* granted in their States perfect religious liberty. The former declared: "In my States every man has a right to contend for his salvation according to his own fashion." *Joseph II.* (1780—1790) protected also the Israelites against the severity of barbarian laws. He made the Catholic Church independent from the Roman See, and abolished a great number of Convents, the possessions of which he devoted to the curacy and to the instruction of youth. Pope *Pious VI.* showed an unprecedented condescension; he came himself to Vienna, in order to remonstrate; but the Emperor persevered in his enactments.

In *France*, *Louis XIV.*, instigated by the Jesuits, and his wife, cruelly persecuted the Reformed Christians. They were excluded from the public offices, and robbed of their children; the sick who refused to become Catholics lost their property, and were condemned to the gallows if they recovered, but thrown in the flaying-place if they died. Military troops made these cruel measures more efficient. At last the edict of Nantes was expressly annulled, and all Reformers summoned to confess the Catholic religion; but 500,000 of them emigrated in spite of prohibition and penalties, and carried, to the great damage of France, treasures, industry and arts to England, Holland and Germany. The cruel measures were repeated, and directed against the Reformers in the province of Languedoc, and its inhabitants oppressed with taxes; despair drove them to a revolt, which three marshals of war were hardly able to suppress (1703—1704). Ten thousand Reformed Christians shed their blood on the scaffold.

Charles I., the Catholic King of *England*, appointed thirteen Bishops in *Scotland*, which confessed the Reformed Religion (1633), introduced a new book of common prayers, ordered the ministers to wear cassocks, etc. These innovations, which betrayed the spirit of the Catholic Church, displeased the people. As in Edinburgh the new prayers at the service were read the first time, the people present rose, and flung Bibles and chairs in the face of the clergymen. The nation concluded a league, resolving to resist the King; all his innovations were to be abolished, the Bishops to be dismissed, and the ministers again, as before, superintended by a General Assembly. The King attempted to maintain his will with an army of 20,000 men. The Scotchmen also armed, and vanquished him. The spirit of resistance seized also the English Parliament, in which the adversaries of the Catholic and Episcopal Church, the *Puritans*, got the majority. Charles lost by his inconstancy and falsehood, his throne and life; he was decapitated (1649). His son *James II.* ruled in Scotland still more cruelly. As he belonged to the Catholic Church, he would force the Scotchmen to forsake their creed, and appointed Bishops, suspended 350 Presbyterian ministers, and expelled them, together with their families. Winter set in; the people were in despair. A part resisted the King's arbitrary power, but they were vanquished, hung, speared, or slowly burned. The usual kind of torture was the iron boot. The feet of the victims were put in it, and then wedges driven between till the bones broke, and the marrow oozed out. At these scenes of torture James used to be present, in order to delight in them with demoniac malice. His hangmen drove the inhabitants like chased game together in one place; there they put the children, aged from six to ten years, in one group, and fired at them at short range (though the pistols were not charged), in order to frighten them; men and women were mutilated, stigmatized, shipped, and landed in unwholsome regions. A son was executed, because he refused to inform the tormentors of the hiding-place of his father; and a wife was killed, because she had abetted the flight of her husband. In England, too, the King assailed the National Church. Guided by the Jesuits, he abolished religious freedom, appointed Catholic teachers in the colleges, turned out Protestant ministers, and committed the public offices to Catholics, in opposition to the laws of the country. In Ireland, also he gave orders to persecute and to exterminate the Protestants. The nation then appealed for help to his son-in-law, *William III.*,

Stadtholder in Holland. He landed with an army in England (1688); the tyrant was frightened, and fled to France, where Louis XIV. received him. William was chosen King, and the Catholic religion forever excluded from the throne of England.

§ 34. State of the Church—William Penn—Scots—Puritans.

Religious toleration was in Europe still very imperfect; proof of which were the persecutions the Protestants in Hungary, Salzburg, France and England had to endure (§ 33). Single individuals were also persecuted, if their views disagreed with the creed of the ruling religious parties. When *J. J. Rousseau* published his far-famed book, "Emile," it excited the hatred of the Catholic and Protestant clergy; the book was burnt in Paris, torn in pieces by the hangman in Geneva, and he himself banished from this city, though he was its citizen. For some time he lived in the Canton of Bern, but was ordered by its Government to leave this asylum also; then Frederick II. offered him a shelter in the Canton of Neufchatel, which at that time belonged to the Kingdom of Prussia; but neither there could he stay long in peace, because the populace hated and treated him ill, he being an infidel; he must retire to England.

Northern America was kinder to religious liberty. *William Penn* founder of the City of Brotherly Love (Philadelphia), declared in his "charter of liberties," that nobody should be persecuted or molested for the sake of his religious opinions. In the charter of *Rhode Island*, liberty of conscience was also granted. Unitarians from Poland, Huguenots from France, Catholics and Puritans from England, flocked to America.

Yet even here some instances of persecution occurred. When, in New England Quakers settled among the Puritans, violent religious quarrels arose between the two sects; the Quakers were banished, and if they returned to the colony, flogged, imprisoned and executed. After some time fanaticism subsided, and capital punishment was abolished. Presumptive witches, too, were often accused of sorcery, and several were burned at the stake.

In the Protestant Church the sects of *Puritans, Quakers, Pietists* and *Herrenhuters* had their origin, which, beside many sound principles, also confess some eccentric opinions. True, the Puritans were distinguished by a blameless life, but they hated every innocent pleasure. Being Calvinists, they clung to the doctrine of predestination, salvation and eternal damnation. As they became in England, after the execution of Charles I, the ruling sect, they interdicted the customary public festivals, shut up the theatres, forbade dancing, and celebrated the Sabbath with Pharisaical rigor. The ministers of the Episcopal Church lost their benefices and livelihood. People soon got tired of the fanatics, and then it was *their* turn to be persecuted. Three hundred of their preachers were put in prison, or exiled. Many Puritans fled to Holland; but as they also were not much pleased in *this* country, they emigrated to *Massachusetts*, and settled in Plymouth (1620). Soon many other associates of their faith arrived, and gradually occupied the whole territory of New England. The name "Puritans" was given them as a nickname by the Established Church of England.

The *Quakers* also probably received their name in derision from the vehement gestures with which they prayed and preached. They first appeared in England, and many went to America, because they were despised and abused in their native country. The generous *William Penn*, who had joined their association, and shared their sufferings, was their leader. The Government owed him a considerable sum of money, and instead of cash payment, ceded him a tract of land in America. He called it *Pennsylvania*, and founded there a colony of his religious brethren. The Quakers are also called *Friends*. They believe that man in his resolutions and actions must be guided by the inner light or glimpse of divine reason, and extirpate the sensual propensities by every means. They sit silently in their churches, until the inner light urges one of them to speak. Women are also entitled to preach. They have no holy-days, nor ceremonies nor prayers, no singing in church, no baptism. They refuse the oath, and formerly they did also no military service. They are "thouing" every man, and bare the head in nobody's presence. They are known to be very honest in their life and dealings. Their manners of life are plain and simple.

The *Herrenhuters*, a German sect, resemble the Quakers in their principles and mode of life. The sect of *Pietists* also originated in Germany. Their founder was the learned and pious *Spener*. They held conventicles, in which exalted feelings prevailed, misleading them to abuse their body too severely, and sometimes also to commit excesses and crimes. They are often intolerant against other sects.

§ 35. Beginning of Rationalism—Voltaire—J. J. Rousseau—Lessing—Dr. Paullus—Abolition of the Order of Jesuits.

About the middle of the eighteenth century the epoch of *Rationalism* broke forth as liberal authors commenced to interpret the Bible in such a manner that its contents would harmonize with the dictates of reason; this was the age of *Rationalism*. The *Deists* and other ingenious scholars wrote against superstition. The former attacked every revealed religion, in particular the Christian and its sects, denying the supernatural origin of Revelation, and preserving only the belief in God (Deus). *Voltaire* and *Rousseau* are the most celebrated among the Deists. The former wielded the weapons of wit and irony with great success; he had free admisson even to the Courts of Princes, e. g., of Frederick II., and gained in the high ranks of all countries many admirers and followers. He was a decided enemy of the Catholic Church. On the contrary, it was warmth of feeling by which *Rousseau* promoted religious enlightenment. In his book "*Emile*" he proves with charming eloquence that neither the Jewish nor the Mohammedan nor the Christian Revelation deserves to be called divine, for they all are composed in languages which the people do not understand; the miracles upon which their believers found their divine origin are not truly proved; if the question is that of facts, we must not be credulous, etc. From this view Rousseau infers that children ought to be educated in no historical religion at all, till they are more advanced in age; they ought to get knowledge of the different religions, and then to have liberty to choose any one of them, as they please.

In Germany, also, the belief in miracles was contested by excellent scholars. To these, e. g., that annonymous writer belongs, who assailed the miracles of Jesus, proving that they lacked a historical basis. *Ephraim Lessing* published the book of this scholar by the title, "The Fragments of Wolfenbuttel;" it caused a great sensation in Germany. In England, *Thomas Woolston* and others also wrote against the miracles. The Bishops instituted a prosecution against Woolston; he was tried before the Chief Justice (1729), imprisoned, and condemned to pay a fine. Lessing himself illustrated in his fine drama, "Nathan der Weise," the principle that we should not confess any special creed, and be tolerant towards every religion.

The leader of the German Rationalists was *Dr. Paulius*, Professor of Theology in Heidelberg. He explained the miracles of Jesus in a natural way, trying to put the Bible by this method in accordance with the human intellect. The miracle of the few loaves and fishes may illustrate it. The New Testament relates that Jesus fed 5,000 to 6,000 persons with a few loaves and fishes. As common sense hesitates to believe in such a narrative, Dr. Paullus explained the apparent contradiction in the following way: Among the crowds there were also many rich persons who had more provisions in store than they wanted for themselves. Exhorted by Jesus, they divided them with the needy ones; so they all got their fill. We can see that by this explanation is more put in the text than it really contains. Though this method imposed constraint upon the explanation of the Bible, it was much applauded, and applied everywhere, in the Catholic and Protestant sermons.

A hard blow struck the Papacy in this period in *the abolition of the Order of Jesuits*. As their general procurator in France transmitted a large sum for a debt to a trading house in Marseille, and the money was captured by the Englishmen, that house demanded the payment from the entire order in France; as it was refused, a lawsuit was commenced against it, which brought on an examination of its inner organization. *Choiseul*, Minister of Louis XV., found that the Society was endangering the State; it was therefore abolished (1764).

The Spanish Jesuits had founded a State in Paraguay and Uruguay, which they governed under Spain's sovereignty. As at that time Spain intended to cede some districts of that State to

Portugal, the natives, led by the Jesuits, opposed the Government, and commenced war. Beside, the Jesuits in Portugal were said to have participated in a secret conspiracy against King Joseph I. Therefore *Pombal*, the energetic Minister of the King, required the Pope to abolish the Order in Portugal, and as he did not consent to do it, the Minister abolished it himself, and dispatched the Fathers to Rome. Their goods were confiscated. The war in Paraguay caused also their suspension in Spain (1767). In one day their colleges were here closed, their treasures seized, and they themselves carried to Rome. *Pope Clemens XIV.* (Ganganelli) at last abolished the Order in all countries (1773); only in Prussia and Russia it was still tolerated.

SIXTH PERIOD (1789—1877).

From the French Revolution to the Present Age.

§ 36. **Effects of the French Revolution on Religion and Church—Epoch of the Restoration.**

After the great Revolution in France (1789) the Constitution, created by the *National Assembly*, beside other rights, granted the country general freedom of religion. The dominions of the clergy, forming the largest and finest part of the territory, were declared to be State-property, confiscated and sold, the sums which were collected from the sale spent to pay the public debts, and the clergymen, since, like other officers, are paid from the public treasury. After the model of the French Constitution the form of Government of most other States in Europe was by degrees improved, and now the right of free religious confession is almost everywhere acknowledged and exercised.

But when Napoleon I. had been dethroned (1815), and the Bourbons reinstated by the sovereigns of Europe, the reaction against religious liberty also began in most countries; the dignitaries of the Church went on hand in hand with the aristocratic Princes. First religious freedom in France was assailed. The inhabitants who in the western and southern part were known to be Protestants, were persecuted; the infuriated rabble attacked and murdered them, and committed worse misdeeds than the epoch of the Revolution had seen. The priests fomented the fanatic spirit. They subjected again the instruction of the youth to their superintendency. Missionaries passed through the country, and infatuated the blind multitude. New secret orders sprang up, and the Jesuits returned, assuming the name "Fathers of the Faith."

In Switzerland, Spain, Naples and the Papal dominions, also, their Order was re-established; in the three last-mentioned countries, besides, the Inquisition and the convents were restored. In Switzerland the preservation of the yet extant convents was warranted by "the Holy Alliance." The monarchs of Russia, Austria and Prussia had contracted this alliance, as they pretended, to the end, to rule their people according to the precepts of the New Testament; but they really intended to oppress the rising popular mind. In Austria, Italy, Spain, Germany, and wherever the nations rose for the defense of their rights, the movement was stifled in the blood of the participants. In Germany the ministers of Rationalism were displaced from the pulpits, the liberty of teaching in the Universities, and the liberty of the press were limited, and the common schools again subdued to the coercion of faith; the clergy occupied again their former position. This was the religious state of the epoch of Restoration, as they call it (1815—1830).

§ 37. Revolutions of 1830—Historical Criticism—Modern View of the Universe—Dr. Strauss—Reaction.

With the days of July 1830, in which France reconquered its liberty, by driving its despot from the throne, for religious progress also dawned a finer time, the time of historical criticism. Such scholars, as *Bruno Bauer*, *Zeller*, *Schwegler*, showed the contradiction of the Bible and reason, proved that Christianity has developed like every other religion, investigated and censured the contents of the Christian documents by the same principles which are applied to other historical writings. The philosopher *Louis Feuerbach* proved in his book "The Essence of Christianity" (das Wesen des Christenthums) that all ideas of God, represented by the old view of the Universe are only shaped to the forms of the human mind. Liberal natural philosophers e. g., *Moleshot, Charles Vogt, Louis Buechner*, destroyed the old intuition of nature by teaching that force and matter, mind and body, God and the Universe are not two opposite entities, subsisting out of and beside each other. *Dr. Frederick Strauss*, a young scholar, composed his book "*Life of Jesus*," in which he demonstrated that very few particulars of the life of this man are known, and that the miracles which he is said to have performed belong to realm of pious myths. The book caused the highest sensation in Germany, was translated into foreign languages, and read with immense admiration. Many adversaries, indeed, rose against Strauss, defending the old ecclesiastic belief; but he refuted them all successfully. He was called to the University of Zurich to teach theology there.

Meanwhile the Conservative party had regained its strength; it opposed in the Canton of Zurich the arrival of Strauss; he was to be pensioned, and a fanatic mob, led by a shrewd parson, overthrew the Liberal Government by revolt. The Catholic Cantons were still bolder; they formed a secession league, in order to take care of the interests of their Church (as they pretended), and followed blindfold the dictates of their leaders, the Jesuits and the Papal legate. In vain the Reformed Cantons admonished them to dissolve their league; they had to be compelled to do it by force of arms. Then the Jesuits were banished forever from Switzerland (1847).

§ 38. **The Revolutions of 1848—German Catholics—Religion of Humanity—Free German Congregations— Reaction—Renan.**

Similar attempts as in Switzerland were made, too, in Germany. *Arnoldi*, Bishop of Triers, hung out the pretended close-coat of Christ, in the Cathedral, as the object of public worship, and, like the indulgence-chafferer Tezel in former time, allured large crowds of pilgrims. *John Ronge*, a simple priest, wrote then the celebrated open letter to the Bishop, which kindled the minds of Catholics like an electric spark, and was everywhere communicated Many Catholics renounced Popery, and founded independent congregations, calling themselves *German Catholics*. Unfortunately, they stopped half way; they retained the Bible as the foundation of their faith, and created a new priest-hood, new sacraments, and a new restraining Church government. The most of these associations decayed again.

In the Protestant Church, especially in Prussia, the clerical and secular rulers cried again : " Return to the old creed ! " For they saw that Rationalism was a two edged sword. But the people would not listen to the cry. The society of " the Friends of Light " was formed; their number was very large; they met in the fields, forests, and at the railroad junctions ; everywhere they considered the interests of Protestant liberty. They confessed still the doctrine of Rationalism. But by the writings of the historical critics it must needs become evident to them that they could not longer adhere to it, for the Bible holds an incorrect view of the Universe, consequently it contradicts human reason ; they had to choose between the former and the latter. Then the writing of *G. Adolf Wislizenus* appeared: " Writ or Spirit ? " He answered this question himself with the words: " The Bible is not the highest authority to us ; *that* is the *spirit* which lives in us." This writing was the inducement to establish *free religious congregations*. With it the period of the religion of Reason and free *Humanity* begins. For, as the Christian expects truth and happiness from Christ, so the man addicted to the religion of free humanity acquires these boons by the use of his reason and by self-energy.

Wislizenus built the first free congregation in Halle ; *Edward Balzer* that of Nordhausen ; *A. T. Wislizenus* another in Halberstadt. These men, beside *Frederic Schueneman-Pott, Sachse*, and others, became the leaders of the new party ; *Uhlich*, too, approached them more and more. In Prussian Saxony alone more than 40 congregations arose. They united in general meetings (1847 and 1849), and formed a friendly union with the German Catholics. Periodical papers were issued by Schueneman-Pott, Edward Balzer, Wislicenus, Uhlich, etc.; and the favor of the people for the new cause was increasing.

To these victories of humanity the *revolutions* of 1848 contributed much, by which the humanitarian rights were increased in *France, Germany, Prussia, and Austria*. But only a short time the State power and religious liberty followed the same path; the former soon gained again the ascendency, and reaction recommenced its dark work. In Austria, Bavaria, Hessen-Cassel, the free congregations were suppressed by force, in other countries, especially in Prussia, superintended by the police; their ministers were imprisoned, sent to asylums for the insane or exiled, their schools shut up, their property confiscated, their adherents who carried on a trade, starved by hunger. Their dead were hardly permitted to be buried. The press was put to silence.

This sad condition lasted eight years; with *William's* accession to the Prussian throne it partly disappeared. In consequence of the amnesty granted by him, several agitators of religious freedom, who lived abroad, returned to Germany; several new communities were organized, others revived. Their number has since increased over one hundred. They concluded a new union, and convene annually provincial Synods, and once in three years a General Assembly. The first President of this was Edward Balzer; after his resignation Uhlich took his place. In Austria, too, religious liberty has been somewhat enlarged.

In *France, Renan*, an intelligent priest, wrote also the life of Jesus. He professes in general the views of Dr. Strauss, but is less liberal. His work got an extensive circulation, because it is composed in a comprehensible, tasteful style.

In *England*, Bishop *Colenzo* has proved in a learned book, that the five books which thus far had been attributed to Moses, were not written by him. The English Church raised a loud clamor of discontent, and suspended the Bishop from his office. *Darwin, Huxley* and *Tyndal, H. Spencer* and *Mills, Harriet Martineau* and *Marian Evans, Buckle, Grote, Lecky*, with a hundred more of the finest intellects of England, are the authors of works hostile to the Christian religion. The rapid progress of infidelity in this country is even admitted, and lamented by the advocates of Christianity.

In *Italy*, too, finally, free exercise of religion was accorded;

now several Protestant churches there exist in a flourishing condition; one of them even in Rome. Since all Italian States are united by a central Government, the Pope has also lost his dominions (1871). A Council held in Rome, declared him infallible (1870); but many of the Bishops who were present at it, and several German Governments, e. g., that of Wurtembergh, protested against the declaration. In *Switzerland*, at last the Jews, too, were emancipated, and are to enjoy in future the same rights as other citizens.

§ 39. America—Sectarianism—Religious Liberty—Thomas Paine.

America is truly called the land of sects. To the old sects of Europe, which all are represented here, from time to time new ones were added, e. g., the Congregationalists (a revised edition of the Presbyterians), the Universalists, the Methodists, Baptists, Shakers, Spiritualists, Mormons, etc. Many of these sects originated in Europe. The Unitarians and the Universalists are most liberal. The latter once held that all sin and punishment terminate with this life. They now, generally, teach that they will extend beyond this world, but will eventually be conquered by the power of righteousness.

The Unitarians believe the Scriptures inspired only in proportion to the truth they teach. They generally hold that all great and good writings are more or less inspired. They do not believe in a Satan. Unitarianism is a transitional stage of thought between "Orthodoxy" and Rationalism.

The sect of the Methodists is a relative of the Episcopalians, and originated the last century in England. Its founders were John Wesley and his brother. The name of Methodists was given to them and their followers on account of the regularity of the manner of their lives. Methodism spread from there, since 100 years, widely in America, and forms presently here the largest body of Protestant churches. The Methodists count at least five million members, with thirteen thousand preachers. They are divided into two sections, the Northern and Southern. The views of the former are more liberal, e. g., they advocated the abolition of slavery.

The Spiritualists believe in the existence of a world of spirits, and that an human intercourse with them is possible and common. Their number in America is said to amount to several millions They hold public meetings, have many periodicals, etc. They have done more, perhaps, to destroy belief in a personal God, a personal Devil, and a local hell, than any other form of Liberalism

The Shakers got their name from the practice of wild, freakish gestures. Now-a-days this is rarely done. They join dances and music to the divine service.

The Mormons, who have also a fifth evangely, hardly deserve the predicate of a religious society; for, as polygamy by their creed is a legal institution, they have not even risen over that degree of civilization which the Mosaic religion and the Islam already have attained. They owe their last evangely to their prophet, Joseph Smith, who asserted to have received it by a miracle from Heaven. They call themselves the last saints of earth.

Religious liberty is in America, both by the central Constitution and by the special Constitutions of most of the States, in a higher degree granted than in any other country on earth. The former declares: "Congress shall make no law respecting an establishment of religion, or prohibiting the free exercise thereof." Here the Church is almost completely separated from the State; the people elect and pay themselves their ministers. Beside, the religious instruction of youth is by law precluded from the public schools. Still some States have encroached on the liberty of con science, e. g , by severe Sabbath laws. The clergy (almost without any difference of the sects), occupies still the old standpoint of faith, and is averse to every reform. They took little interest in the abolishment of slavery, and believed it to be the duty of every citizen to deliver fugitive slaves to their masters. Many clergymen called slavery a divine institution; many of them were themselves slave-holders. In the report of the pro-slavery meeting in Charleston, 1835, it is stated: "The clergy of all denominations attended in a body, lending their sanction to the proceedings." Neither does the clergy, in general, favor the emancipation of woman. The American press has vigorously promoted the progress of free thought in this period. *Thomas Paine* fought as courageously for religious as civil liberty, in his admirable book: "The Age of Reason," he submitted the Bible to a severe criticism; he denied its divine origin. The first part of his book was written 1793, when he was a member of the National Convent of France. Being a political adversary of Robespierre, this brought it about that Paine was confined to prison in Paris, and he would have lost his life by the guillotine, but that he fell sick in the jail, and Robespierre was soon after executed himself (1794). After the death of the tyrant, Paine was set free, and again admitted to the convent. The second part of the book appeared in 1795. It was first published in France. It roused many enemies against him, but procured him also many admirers; the anniversary of his birthday is celebrated in many places of the country. The Paine's Hall in Boston was erected to his honor. "A few more years, a few more rays of light, and mankind will venerate the memory of him who said, 'the world is my country, and to do good my religion.'"

§ 40. Continued—The Liberal Press—Liberal Orators—Trancendentalism in New England.

Robert Dale Owen founded (1828), in partnership with Miss *Frances Wright*, an English lady, the *Free Enquirer*, a weekly journal devoted to socialistic ideas, and to opposition to the supernatural origin and claims of Christianity After the breaking out of the rebellion he was a warm champion of the policy of emancipation. He has published: Discussion with Origen Bachelor on the Personality of God; The Authenticity of the Bible, etc. He did, fifty years ago, a great work for Liberalism.

Frances Wright(Frothingham) in her book, "A Few Days in Athens," defends the Epicurean philosophy, and gives liberal views on immortality and a personal God. She published also a course of "popular lectures" on Free Inquiry, Religion and Morals, delivered in New York, and other large cities of America, and "popular tracts" in partnership with R. D. Owen and others. She was the Pioneer Woman in the cause of Women's Rights.

William Lloyd Garrison, the pioneer and leader of the modern anti-slavery movement in America, was committed to jail, but liberated, his fine being paid by Arthur Tappan, a merchant of New York. He delivered many lectures in which he first declared its immediate abolition in the name of God and humanity. He made special efforts to enlist the sympathy and co-operation of the clergy and the churches of different denominations, repudiating all creeds, and alleged revelations that reject the fundamental truth of the equal and inalienable rights of every man. His efforts had little success. In 1831 he commenced to issue the *Liberator* in Boston, taking for his motto: "My country is the world; my country-men are all mankind." Isaac Knapp was his partner. Their resources were so restricted that they had to make the printing office their domicile, and to bed themselves on its floor. Garrison was frequently threatened with asassination, and the Legislature of Georgia offered five thousand dollars to any person which should arrest, and bring him to trial in that State. He organized with other friends the Anti-Slavery Society of New England, and continued the Liberator, until the close of the year 1865, when the abolition of slavery was proclaimed in the Constitution of the United States.

Other Liberal periodicals are the *Correspondent*, published as far back as 1820, the *Beacon*, by Gilbert Vale, *the Regenerator*, by P. S. Murray, the *Investigator*, the *Index*, edited by F. E. Abbot, the *Truth Seeker*, by D. M. Bennett, the *Pioneer* (a German paper), by Ch. Heinzen, etc. The *Investigator* was founded by Samuel Kneeland (1832); to this paper the *Infidel Relief Society* was joined, which still is extant. Kneeland was put in prison, and tried before the Supreme Court of Boston on a charge of blasphemy. In memory of this event that Society has ordered an anniversary.

The most learned and liberal of the American theologians of his age was Theodore Parker (†1860); he promoted much the cause of free religion and humanity by his sermons and numerous writings. He was first an Unitarian minister, but soon widely differed from the views of conservative Unitarians, and became the leader of a school which rejected as unhistorical many portions of the Scripture, and renounced all belief in the supernatural. At the present time liberal pulpit orators and lecturers are: F. Abbott, Rowland Connor, O. B. Frothingham, B. F. Underwood, M. J. Savage, W. H. Spencer, Robert Ingersoll, the famous author of "The Gods," and many others.

An important factor in American Liberalism was *Transcendentalism* (idealism), as it is called. Though brief in duration it left a deep trace on ideas and institutions. Its name denotes the doctrine of fundamental innate conceptions, or ideas which transcend experience. The authors of this philosophy asserted that there are such innate conceptions in the human mind, namely, the idea of God, and his moral attributes, of moral law, of absolute right and goodness, of immortality, etc. They attributed to the mind an intuitive faculty to gaze at those ideas with an inward sense, a spiritual eye, by which their existence becomes as evident as material objects to the physical eye. The first promulgators of Transcendentalism were German philosophers (Kant, Fichte and others), and their doctrines were imported to New England about fifty years ago.

It advocated free thought in religion, had no sympathy with dogmatism, and fostered skepticism by causing a reaction against Puritan orthodoxy. It inaugurated both the theory and practice of sound dietetics, created reforms in education, and inspired philantropists. The moral enthusiasm of the last generation which broke out with such prodigious power in the holy war against Slavery, which uttered such earnest protest against the wrongs inflicted on women, and against capital punishment, owed much of its glow and force to Idealism. Men and women are healthier in bodies, happier in their social and domestic relations, more kind and humane in their sympathies, than they would be if its disciples had not lived.

It found expression in several magazines and newspapers, especially in the *Dial* (1840—46), a treasury of literary wealth which contains even texts from the Hindoo religion, Confucius, and Chaldean oracles. To publish and read such scriptures showed an enlightened and courageous mind, and a disposition to do justice to all expressions of religious sentiment. Its foremost advocates were Theodore Parker, R. W. Emerson, and Margaret Fuller, authoress of "Woman in the Nineteenth Century," a work which contains all that is worth saying on the woman question, and has been the storehouse of argument and illustration from that day to this. Among other prominent disciples were Bronson, Alcott, W. H. Channing. Henry Thoreau, G. Ripley, Charles Sumner, Bancroft the historian, the poets Bryant and Whittier, Nathaniel Hawthorne, Mrs. Lydia Maria Child, and Julia Ward Howe, with many lesser lights in literature.

Transcendentalism deified the human mind. According to the Evolution theory there are no innate ideas, and the claim of intuitive knowledge of any order whatsoever, is untenable on scientific grounds. (Views of the Universe, § 11, etc.) Still "the disciples of this doctrine were earnest men and women, no doubt ; better educated men and women did not live in America. Their generation produced no warmer hearts, no purer spirits, no more ardent consciences, no more devoted wills."—O. B Frothingham, "Transcendentalism in New England."

§ 41. Continued—Liberal Associations—The Anti-Slavery Society —Free Religious Associations—The National Liberal League.

Among the liberal American *associations* which, in this Period, opposed to the orthodox teachings of the Churches, the *anti-slavery society* was the strongest and most efficacious. It was organized in 1833. Its constitution asserted: Whereas slavery is contrary to the principles of natural justice, and of the Christian religion, we do hereby agree to form ourselves into a society, and declare that the object of this society is the entire abolition of slavery in the United States. It immediately adopted and published a "Declaration of Sentiments," in which they declared that to invade personal liberty is to usurp the prerogative of Jehovah, that therefore all slave-laws were, before God, utterly null and void. The society sent agents, who remonstrated against slavery, circulated anti-slavery tracts and periodicals, enlisted the pulpits and the press in the cause of freedom, and aimed at a purification of the Churches from all participation in the guilt of slavery. Arthur Tappan, Lindley Coates, W. Lloyd Garrison, and Wendell

Phillips successively presided over this society. Numerous antislavery societies were soon organized throughout the North. The members of the society were frequently the victims of the violence of the mobs, who disturbed their meetings, assailed their persons, destroyed their property, and imperilled their lives. Rev. Elijah P. Lovejoy, editor of the Observer, in which he occasionally censured the institute of slavery, was in Alton (Ill.), killed by a mob (1837). Pennsylvania Hall, erected in Philadelphia for anti-slavery meetings, was burnt to the ground by a furious mob (1838). The purpose of the society was at last accomplished. When by the amendment of the United States Constitution slavery was abolished, it disbanded its members (1870).

In recent time (since 1868) associations were organized by liberal Americans, the chief object of which is to promote the practical interests in pure religion; they call themselves *free religious associations*. In those the various religious opinions and faiths meet and mingle on perfectly equal terms; their members are free to avow themselves Christians or non-Christians, or Anti-Christians, Atheists, Materialists, Spiritualists, etc. They hold regular annual meetings and have allied with the German free religious associations.

In the United States, too, the reactionary party of the Christian Church takes much pains to frustrate religious liberty, and to prevent the religious progress of the age. It calls itself " *The National Reform Association*," has created a journal for its special organ, and conceived the purpose to secure such an amendment to the Constitution as will acknowledge Almighty God as the author of the nation's existence, Jesus Christ as its ruler, and the Bible as the foundation of its laws. A Judge of the United States Supreme Court is its President, its members are many of the leading divines in the land, and of other men high in authority.

In order to counteract their unconstitutional aim, a Congress of Liberals met in Philadelphia, when there the Centennial Festival of the Union was celebrated (1876), and organized the *National Liberal League*. It was the most important body of men and women ever convened on the American continent. One hundred and sixty-seven delegates enrolled their names as members of the

League. The Germans of America, especially their "Free Congregations," co-operated with them. An Executive Committee, and other officers were elected. *Francis E. Abbott* was chosen President of the League. It framed a Constitution, and an Address to the people of the United States. According to these documents its general object is to accomplish the total separation of Church and State, to the end that equal rights in religion, genuine morality in politics, and freedom, virtue and brotherhood in all human life may be established, protected and perpetuated. As means to the accomplishment of this general object, the specific objects of the League are: To urge the adoption of such "*a Religious Freedom Amendment* to the United States Constitution as shall effect the complete secularization of the Government in all its departments and institutions, State and National; to advocate the equitable taxation of church property; the total discontinuance of religious instruction and worship in the public schools; the repeal of all laws enforcing the observance of Sunday as the Sabbath; the abolition of State-paid chaplaincies; the substitution of simple affirmation, under the pains and penalties of perjury, for the judicial oath; the non-appointment of religious fast, festivals and holidays by public authority," etc.

In order to realize these objects, the League resolved to promote the formation and multiplication of local auxiliary Liberal Leagues throughout the country. The Executive Committee shall be composed of one member from each State and Territory of the Union.

42. Concluded—German Free Congregations—Their Organization and League.

At the time when the free congregations in Germany suffered from persecution, many of their adherents were driven from their homes; some went to England, others to Holland or Switzerland; the most emigrated to North America. To them joined thousands of political fugitives, who, after the revolutions of the year 1848 had been expelled, or were tired of their native country, and carried their better knowledge to their new fatherland.

The first free German congregation was founded by Edward Schroeter, in July, 1850, in New York, and some months after this, the second, in St. Louis, on motion of Frank Smith, Parliamentary member of Loevenberg; it still exists there, under the leadership of Charles Luedeking. The third one, and its organ, the "*Humanist*," was likewise called into existence by Schroeter (1851), in Milwaukee, after he had organized such associations in Boston Hartford, etc. By his efforts similar ones rapidly spread from Milwaukee over the State of Wisconsin; but they did not subsist long, because they lacked able, enthusiastic leaders. Only the congregation of Sauk City, which for its origin is also indebted to Mr. Schroeter, subsisted, because he kept up the banner of free humanity with a strong arm in all tempests of the time. In Philadelphia a free association was founded by Edward Graf (1852), whose place Frederic Schuenemann-Pott took (1854), who during sixteen years developed much energy as an orator and author. By and by new congregations were founded, viz: In Milwaukee (1867), San Francisco (by Schuenemann-Pott), Peru and Granville (LaSalle Co., Ill.), Kilburn Road, Painsville, Mayville, Plymouth, Bostic Valley and Mosel (all in Wisconsin); in New Ulm, Young America and Minneapolis (in Minnesota), in Washington, D. C., etc.

The only object which unites the members of these associations are the deliveries which regularly take place in their meetings. Their themes are derived from the sphere of the natural sciences, of the modern views of the Universe, of the Ethics, the universal History, etc. In most places the orations are accompanied by exquisite songs. Several societies possess their own halls, which are built, though in a plain style, yet with good taste. Prayers and all ceremonies are precluded from their meetings. The mutual care of the cultivation of the whole life supplies the want of a divine service. In their Sunday Schools the principles of morals, the results of the scientific views of the Universe, the history of the religions, etc., are communicated. Periodicals, e. g., Blætter fuer frei religiœses Leben, edited by Schuenemann-Pott (discontinued 1877), the "Freidenker" in Milwaukee, etc., diffuse their views also in wider spheres. The objects of the free congregations are also ably discussed by the eminent thinker, *Ch. Heinzen*, in his book: "Six letters addressed to a pious man, with a preface directed to a Jesuit," as in others of his writings.

These congregations organized a *general league* (1859), the executive of which administrates its current affairs. Every third year the league holds a Diet, at which the delegates of the single associations consult the general concerns. A periodical paper is the organ of its resolutions and acts.

The constitution of the league, which was revided 1876, contains only this article : "The league declares the highest leading principle, which every member is obliged to acknowledge, to be the free self-determination according to the advancing Reason and Science in all relations of life."

The following general principles, also, were adopted by the last Diet :

1. The books of *Nature* and *History* are the sole fountains from which Reason derives every necessary and useful knowledge, all moral and political laws.

2. Terrestrial general happiness (happiness of body, intellect and mind) is our highest good.

3. Universal liberty, universal culture, and universal welfare are the path for the highest good.

To the aims of the free German congregations those of the North American Turners'-League are congenial ; for, besides other tendencies of the league it avows also the task to check sectarianism, to promote enlightment and humanity, and to take an interest in religious progress.

In conclusion, this sketch of the progress of religious Liberalism in the United States may be finished by the following statements of two of its most powerful leaders : " Free religious movement led on by cultivated and earnest minds, like Frothingham, Abbott and Higginson, is gaining strength rapidly, and shows how dissatisfied the people are with the creeds of the churches. Materialism is the belief of no small number in this country. The American literature is comparatively liberal. Indeed, its infidel tendencies are the lament of the pulpit and religious press. The great majority of professional men are undoubtedly Free-thinkers. The public advocates of Free Thought now speak in the best halls and to larger audiences in the West than the clergy can get to hear their sermons, and the liberal cause is gaining strength every day."—B. F. Underwood, "the influence of Christianity on civilization." "The Americans are disgusted by theological questions. Christian dogmas are discredited; the churches contain more unbelievers than believers, more Non-Christians and Anti-Christians, than Christians. Preaching is giving place to lecturing; the pulpit has been taken down; science alone is permitted to speak with authority; literature, journalism, politics, trade, attract young men that once sought ministry. The destructive Period has about passed by; the constructive Period has begun: to build up the religion of Reason and Humanity."—O. B. Frothingham.

THE END.

SECTION SECOND.

BIBLICAL NARRATIVES AND THEIR CRITICISM.

"You first teach children that a certain book is true—that it was written by God himself—that should they die without believing the book, they will be forever damned. The consequence is that long before they read that book, they believe it to be true."—*Robert Ingersoll, "The Gods."*

CHAPTER FIRST.

NARRATIVES FROM THE OLD TESTAMENT.

1. The Author of the Mosaic Documents.

Those five books which, in former times, were attributed to Moses, cannot be his work; for:

1. Jehovah warns the Israelites against idolatry (3 Mos., 18, 28), saying: "Lest the land spit out you, too, as it has spit out the people who were before you." By these words the Canaanites are signified, who have been exterminated by the Israelites, when they occupied Canaan. Now, the Israelites did not conquer this country until after the death of Moses; therefore history contradicts the above quoted passage, which, then, cannot have been written by Moses.

2. The author reports that Sarah, Abraham's wife, died in the town of Arba, and adds: "That is Hebron." The name "Hebron" was given to the town of Arba in a much later time, when the Israelites had already conquered the country.

3. In the fifth book, Moses, standing upon the mount Nebo, looks over the whole country (?), over Gilead as far as Dan, over the whole Naphthali, and Ephraim, and Manasse, and the country of Juda. But these countries did not receive those names until the tribes who bore them had conquered those lands; which conquest also not occurred until after the death of Moses.

4. In the fifth book, Moses himself relates where and in what manner he has died, and has been buried, namely: "And Moses ascended the mount Nebo, in the country of Moab, and *died* there. And Jehovah buried him in the valley, and nobody knows where his grave is till to this day." Can a dead man relate the events of his own life?

5. The idiom in which these books are written, is almost the same as that which was used by the Jews in the time of the Babylonian captivity; from Moses until that epoch, almost one thousand years have elapsed; in such a large space of time a language suffers many considerable changes; therefore the idiom of the books of Moses cannot be that which in his time was used by the Israelites.

6. These books have been written with Hebrew characters; but Moses had in Egypt only learnt the use of hieroglyphics; the art of writing with letters was invented in much later times. Now, if these books have not been composed by Moses himself, but many centuries after his death, the narrations contained therein, even by this reason, incur much suspicion.

2. The History of the Creation—Adam and Eve.

The creation of the world is related in the first chapter of the books of Moses, in the following manner: "In the beginning God (the Elohim, the gods) created the heaven and the earth. The earth was desert and void, and darkness upon the face of the deep (of the ocean); the spirit of God (the wind) moved upon the face of the waters, and God said: 'It shall be light!' And it *was* light." The second day God created the celestial vault; the third he separated the water from the earth; the dry land and the sea appeared. Moreover God bade grass to sprout, and trees to grow. The fourth day he created the sun, the moon and the stars; the fifth, the fish and birds; the sixth the other animals and the man; "he created one male and one female man." The seventh day he rested himself from all his works, and sanctified it.

By the author of the history of creation the earth is deemed to be the centre of the universe, and the world proper; the sun and the other celestial bodies are considered by him only as an addition to the earth, "great and small lights," created in order to illuminate it. He puts the great and small light with the stars, like fixed points on the celestial vault, which he imagines to be solid. Such a puerile notion is not adapted to the doctrine of astronomy, which teaches us that some celestial bodies equal the size of the earth, other surpass it by far, e. g., the diameter of the sun is 112 times greater than that of the earth, and if it were a hollow globe, the earth could within turn around its centre, and would yet be so far distant from the hull of the sun as the moon from the earth. One million of terrestrial globes could be made out of the sun. (Cf. Views of the Univ., § 4.) The sun determines by its irresistible attractive power the orbit in which the earth must move; it is to the earth the fountain of light and heat; it adorns her flowers with their gorgeous colors; it is the source of all life and growth on earth. The author, also, contradicts himself, for he tells us that it has become light already on the first day, consequently before the sun was created. What man of good sense can believe that there was a first, second, and third day, and that every one of these days had a night, while there were not yet a sun, nor a moon, nor stars?

The Creator performs his work in a human, though more perfect manner; he is humanized. We know, again, from the scientific view of the universe, that the earth has not been transformed and organized in six days, for geology proves that probably millions of years have elapsed before our planet has attained its present state of evolution. The single periods of terrestrial formation were by no means the duration of only one day; but it can easily be seen why the author gets the whole work of creation done in six days; he wanted to point out the seventh day as the Sabbath, to-wit, as the day which ought to be sacred to the Jews.

Man is represented as the final aim of the whole creation, and nature as his servant. With regard to his creation, in the second chapter another narrative follows, which directly contradicts the former. While the first report says that first the plants, then the animals, finally two men, and both at the same time, were created; in the second tale first the man, then the plants and animals, and after them the wife were created; consequently man and wife were not created on the same day. Namely, after the creation of man, Jehovah first creates the animals according to their several classes and species, and introduces them to Adam. As this does not find any helpmate among them, Jehovah let him fall in a profound sleep, takes during it a rib out of Adam's body, closes the place with flesh again, and makes from the rib the wife. How absurd is this fiction! But the author would explain by it that the woman is not the equal of man, but destinated already by her origin to be dependent on him. The inhabitants of Greenland even narrate that the wife has been formed from man's thumb. Both reports of the creation evidently have been written by two different authors. The names of the primitive parents are also fictitious; for the word "Adam" in Hebrew denotes only "man," to-wit: the progenitor of mankind, and "Eve" the mother of the living.

3. The Garden in Eden.

Jehovah planted in the paradise, called Eden (deliciousness), a garden towards the East, therein was a stream, from which four others arose, flowing in the direction of the four quarters of heaven. Jehovah put Adam, and later Eve, too, in it; there they were to reside. Jehovah got several fine fruit-trees growing in the garden; in its centre were the tree of life, and the tree of the knowledge of good and evil. Jehovah ordered Adam and his wife to cultivate the garden, and permitted them to eat every fruit but that of the tree of knowledge of good and evil, threatening them that they had to die if they trespassed his command.

But the serpent told them that Jehovah had forbidden them the fruit, only because he knew that, after they had eaten it, their eyes would be opened and they, like himself, would also know what is good and evil. The wife felt a great desire for the forbidden fruit; she ate and gave also a share to the husband, who also ate. Then their eyes were opened, they saw that they were naked, sewed fig leaves together, and made themselves aprons. Jehovah inflicts hard punishments upon them all. The serpent shall (so he said) henceforth be cursed above all animals, creep upon the belly, live with man in enmity, and always eat dust. The wife shall suffer many hardships on account of her children, and be ruled by her husband. Adam shall cultivate the soil in the sweat of his face, and return to earth and dust. And lest they also might eat from the tree of life, and live eternally, he expelled them from Eden, and placed in the East the Cherubim, and a flaming sword, which turned every way, in order to watch the access of the tree of life.

This myth contains a poetic explanation of the origin of the evil in the world. The author finds it in man's transition from the state of childlike ignorance into the life of culture. He derived his legend from the religious books of the Arians and Hindoos. The latter have in their mythology also four universal torrents, flowing from the mountain of their gods : that was certainly situated in the highland of Tibet, from which streams in all directions come down, the Oxus and Jaxartes in the West, the Indus, Ganges and Bramaputra in the South, the Yangtsekiang and Hoangho in the East. In the Zend Avesta it is told that the God of Light (Ormuzd) has also planted a beautiful garden ; there neither quarrels rule, nor frauds, neither begging, nor poverty, nor disease, but men enjoy the happiest life. The God of Darkness (Arihman) also created in the world of sin a large serpent, which is called *his* serpent; he is even called himself the serpent, and he is full of death, to wit : the cause death and every evil.

The meaning of the myth is this : The Old Testament calls the ignorance of the good and evil the state of infancy. Knowledge begins only with the progress of age. The author compares that state with the life of culture ; he imagines the former to be abundant of happiness, this full of misery for both, the man and the woman ; the first men lost that happy state, when they ate the forbidden fruit, for they obtained thereby the knowledge of the good and evil. Trees are made representatives of knowledge and immortality, because their fruits have a refreshing vigor ; in the hot Orient people long for them even more than in cold countries. Especially children like fruit. In the Avesta, too, a tree of immortality is mentioned.

The Cherubim were probably originally thunder clouds, and their fulminating swords the lightnings. For Jehovah is the god of thunder who rides on Cherubim (Psalm 18). In later times they attributed them a shape composed from man, bull, eagle and lion, and still now-a-days bulls and lions with human heads are found among the ruins of Ninive. The Cherubim reminds us of the Egyptian sphinxes (lions with human heads), who were placed at the entries of the temples, as if to guard them.

Jehovah appears in this myth as an envious being, which grudged man immortality, and therefore ordered the Cherubim to guard the Paradise. The features of this Jehovah, according to the legend, are very human, e. g., when he altogether searches and calls Adam, he does not know where he is hidden ; he takes a rib from man's belly; takes an evening walk in the cool garden, is conversing with Adam, makes for him and Eve coats of skins, etc. It is probable that this fiction took origin at the time of the captivity of the Israelites; at the epoch of Moses they had not yet any intercourse with the Orient.

4. The Great Deluge.

As God sees that people had turned wicked, he resolves to destroy them by an universal inundation; only to Noah and his family he is merciful. He orders Noah to build a large vessel, 300 cubits long, 50 wide and 30 high, to put in it all species of animals of the earth, and to go on its board himself with his family. Then the deluge begins, for it rains forty days and nights; the water covers even the highest mountains, and towers 15 cubits above them; one year, after having commenced to rain, the earth is again dry. All men and animals perish; finally the ark subsides on the mount Ararat, and Noah sends first a raven, then a pigeon out, in order to see whether the floods had passed away. First they return; then they stay away. At the end of one year he leaves the ship with his family, and the saved animals, and the earth is populated anew.

Never such a huge quantity of water could be on earth that it covered the highest summits of mountains, of which some are known to be over 28,000 feet high; where could it have passed after the inundation? According to the author's opinion, to the reservoirs of the fountains of ocean; for he supposes that the ocean receives its water in the same manner as rivers and brooks, from subterranean fountains: an erroneous supposition! How did Noah know that all countries of the earth had been inundated? And how does the author know that the water has overtopped the highest mountains by 15 cubits? The ark was perhaps three times as large as now-a-days our great sea-ships, so that its hold was not by far spacious enough to shelter all animals and their food. How could Noah there assemble all animals, as they were dispersed all over the earth? Neither could all be fed on hay, as e. g., the carnivorous quadrupeds and the rapacious birds. This myth also has two reporters. According to the one Noah admitted but one couple of every genus of animals, and according to the other seven couples of the clean animals, but only one of the unclean. One of these reports must be wrong. The ark has hardly settled on the Ararat, for this name was much later attributed to that mountain.

The whole story of the deluge probably originated in Chaldea or Hindoostan, where the large rivers also often cause desolating inundations. The Chaldeans and Hindoos have similar myths. The god Kronos reveals to the tenth King of the Chaldeans that he would destroy the mankind by a great deluge. He commands him to bury the extant documents, to build a ship, to enter it with his relatives and with animals, etc. The King built the ship, 9,000 feet long, and 1,200 feet wide, consequently about eighty times larger than Noah's ark. He sends out birds, as the floods decrease, for the third time; the ship stands firm upon a mountain of Armenia. According to the myth of the Hindoos, Brahma who arranges the deluge as a wet purgatory for the sinful man, bids Mann to build a ship, and to go on board with seven wise men, and with every kind of animals and seeds. The flood covers the entire earth; Brahma himself steers the ship, and it finally rests upon the highest summit of the Himalaya mountains. Therefore it is very likely that the Israelites have received their flood-myth either from the Hindoos or from the Chaldeans, when they were living in the countries of captivity. In this story, too, Jehovah shows himself in a very human form, shutting even the door of the ark behind Noah with his own hands.

5. Abraham.

Ur, in Chaldea, is reported to be the primitive home of *Abraham;* therefore he emigrated with his father and nephew Lot, to Canaan. He is wandering through it with his numerous herds and servants, builds altars in several places, and is dealt with by the neighboring chieftains partly in a friendly, and partly in a hostile way. He migrated even to Egypt (according to the reporter), and after his return he passed again through Canaan in all directions. The pasture grounds are here represented as if being common property of the whole mankind. It looks as if all tribes had esteemed it an honor to receive the stranger in their homes. Is it probable that no tribe has handled the intruder and his three hundred servants in a hostile manner? It is the apparent intention of the author to let already Abraham take possession of the land for his nation and his God, that the title of possession of the Israelites might appear more valid. Therefore he lets Jehovah say to Abraham: " Rise and pass through the land in all directions, for it is thy seed to which I will give it." Abraham, then, seems also to be only a poetic figure, which also his primitive name, " Abram," to wit, the high father, indicates; for only in the sequel of the narrative (1 Mos., 17, 4) the form " Abraham" takes its place. The two other primigenitors, Isaac and Jacob, are likely also nothing but mythical characters.

The most important scene in Abraham's life is the offering of his son. He rose (according to the 22d chapter) early in the morning, girdled his ass, took two servants and his son Isaac, chopped wood for the sacrifice, and proceeded to the place Jehovah had showed to him (to Moriah). The third day, as they arrived there, he ordered the servants to remain behind, took the sacrificial wood, put it on Isaac's shoulder, took the fire and the knife in hand, and so they were proceeding. The boy said: " Father, there is fire and wood, but where is the sheep for sacrifice?" Abraham replied: " God will provide it." When they had arrived he built an altar, arranged the wood, and crying: " The sacrifice art thou, my son!" He tied the boy, put him on the altar over the wood, seized the knife, and lifted it up, ready to kill his son. In this moment an angel called to him from heaven to spare the boy, because it was only the intention of Jehovah to try him. Abraham saw a ram, whose horns were entangled in the thicket; he seized and sacrificed the animal instead of the boy. The principal meaning of this myth (for it is nothing more than that) consists in the aim to advocate the abrogation of the sacrifice of the first born sons, and in general, of the sacrifices of infants; for the use of human sacrifices was common among the Israelites, and lasted till they were abducted in captivity. In one form it was yet commanded even by the Mosaic law. In which character appears here the Jewish Jehovah, who could expect such sacrifices from his adorers, and how barbarous must the fathers of that period have been, who, like Abraham, were ready to sacrifice their children, or really offered them!

A similar narration is found in the Greek mythology. The Greeks are assembled in Aulis, in order to march to Troja; but for a long time the head winds prevented them to set out. The priest Kalchas then announces that the irritated goddess Diana has sent the calm, and that she demands Iphigenia, daughter of King Agamemnon, to be sacrificed to her. The father delivers his daughter, and the priest is already raising the knife, as the virgin is removed by the goddess in a cloud, and on her place a hind appears, whom the Greeks forthwith offer as a sacrifice. The abolition of human sacrifices was a most important progress in civilization.

6. The Egyptian Plagues, and the Emigration of the Israelites.

The Bible relates that Moses had received the order of Jehovah to conduct the Isrealites from Egypt, and that *Pharao* (the King), could only by the severest plagues be moved to grant them the exodus. The plagues were these:

1. Moses raising his staff over the Nile, changes the entire water of the country to blood; all fish, therefore, die therein. The Egyptian magicians imitate the miracle of Moses immediately, though all the water was before this changed to blood, and animal life in it was extinct.

2. After seven days the whole country is covered with frogs, which penetrate even all houses and beds. The sorcerers imitate also this miracle, although it is difficult to understand where any room for their frogs remained.

3. Aaron, the brother of Moses, turns all the dust of the earth into gnats, which torment people and animals.

4. Crowds of flies spread over the entire country, and desolate it.

5. Jehovah sends a pest by which all animals of the Egyptians die, but none of those of the Israelites.

6. Moses scatters ashes from the furnace in the air; then blisters afflict men and animals, even the sorcerers. Here the reporter forgets that the animals have already perished by pestilence.

7. Hail destroys all products, and kills animals and men; but in the country of Gosen, where the Israelites lived, not a single hailstone falls. The author forgets again that he had made all the animals already twice to die, and that before this the flies have desolated the whole country

8. So many locusts invade Egypt that they obscure the air, and devour all

the products that the hail had left. But the flies had already desolated the entire land, and the hail had destroyed all products, consequently nothing more was left for the locusts.

9. Egypt is during three days entirely covered with darkness, while it is broad daylight in Gosen. The author does not know that the earth revolves in twenty-four hours around its axis, and therefore day and night equally must alternate everywhere.

10. Lastly, in one night, all the first-born creatures die.

The author still relates that Jehovah had ordered the Israelites, immediately before their departure from Egypt, to borrow golden and silver vessels from their Egyptian friends, neighbors and inmates, and to rob them in this way. This order stains the sanctity and justice of the national God of the Jews with dark spots. For the rest, it is right for us to ask, how such a defraudation was possible, as the Israelites lived far distant from the Egyptians, and were so much hated by them that they hardly would have lent them their treasures.

At last Pharao permits the Israelites to leave, but soon again he changes his mind, hastens after them with his army, and overtakes them as they cross the Red Sea. It heaps up its floods like two walls, to the right and left hand, and they pass it with dry feet; the Egyptians follow them; at Jehovah's command the billows are precipitated over them, and all are drowned. The author imagines the bottom of the sea to be like an even street, without mud and stones, rocks and monsters of the deep. The whole story aims, evidently, to represent Jehovah as the powerful national God of the Israelites, and was dictated to the writer by hatred against their enemies. Its single incidents are so improbable that likely no truth at all is at the bottom of them. To be sure, Moses has never operated these miracles; and presently they even doubt whether Moses ever has lived. The history of the exodus of the Israelites from Egypt is the national epoch of this nation.

7. Legislation on Mount Sinai—The Two Tablettes.

The grandest spectacle the Mosaic documents relate, is Jehovah's legislation; its stage was the mount *Sinai;* in the fifth book the mount Horeb is named instead of it; both are tops of the mountains which cover the southern part of Arabia. Sinai, or Horeb, then, is the real mount of gods of the Israelites, like the Olymp of the Greek gods, and like similar mountains of the Arians and Hindoos. The author narrates: " Moses led the people forth from the camp in the presence of God, and they drew near to the bottom of the mount." (A place opposite to the mountain, large enough for a whole people is there not to be found, for these mountains are quite full of rocks and cliffs.) " And the whole mount was smoking, because Jehovah had descended upon it in fire, and its smoke rose, and the whole mount quaked greatly, and there was a sound of trumpets, exceeding loud. Moses was speaking, and Jehovah answered him in the thunder. And Jehovah descended on the mountain, and called Moses to the top, and Moses mounted." (Jehovah appears in clouds and fire, in a cloud of tempest, in the midst of thunder and lightning; he is the god of thunder.) "And all the people saw (!) the thunderclaps, the flame, the sound (!) of the trumpets, and the reeking mount. And Moses entered the cloud, and passed on the mount forty days and forty nights with Jehovah; he did not eat bread, nor drink water (?). And Jehovah spoke to Moses from face to face, as a friend speaks to his friend." (Moses, then, has seen Jehovah's face; but seven verses farther down he asks him to let him see his majesty, and Jehovah answers: "You may see my back, but you dare not see my face." And Jehovah passed by him, and showed him his back.) On the mount Jehovah contracts a covenant with the Israelites, saying to them: "You shall be unto me a priesthood, and a holy people." The league is solemnly consecrated; namely, Moses builds an altar at the bottom of the mountain, and bids the young men of the people to put burnt-offerings upon it, sprinkling it with the blood of the sacrifices. The people vow obedience to the laws of Jehovah.

Hereafter the author reports (2 Mos. 24, 7) that Moses has written down all the words of Jehovah, and read them to the people. But according to another passage, Jehovah gives him the law upon two tables of stone, written with his own finger (2 Mos. 31, 18, and 32, 16). Later, as Moses again descended the mountain, he sees the Jews dancing around a golden calf, adoring it; he flies into a passion, and smashes the tables on the rocks; Jehovah orders him to make two new ones, and says that he himself will copy on them the same words which had been written on the former. But in contradiction to this, it is stated farther down (2 Mos. 34, 27): "Moses was with Jehovah, and wrote on the tables the words of the covenant, the ten words." On the one hand, then, Jehovah will write them himself, on the new tables, and on the other, Moses is said to have done it. It is also not stated which the ten words are, and on which place of the book they are written; therefore the doubt remains which the true content of the tables may have been. Besides this, the ten commandments, as they call them, would not have had space enough on two tables of stone which one man would be able to carry. The tablets are mentioned as late as in the books of the Kings and in the Chronicles, which both were written during or after the captivity; the older books, even the writings of the prophets, do not commemorate them; therefore they certainly did never exist, neither the book, in which Moses is said to have penned down the whole law "According to the custom of the earliest times to write the laws on tables, and to put them up publicly, the author has created the tables himself, and put them in the hand of his legislator." *

8. The Tabernacle.

At the Sinai Moses raised also the Tabernacle (according to 2 Mos. 25, etc.) which ought to be Jehovah's residence. It is described in detail. It was 30

---

* G. A. Wislicenus, "the Bible."

cubits long, 9 wide, and 10 high. A curtain parted it in two sections, called "the Holy," and "the Holy of the Holies." From the outside it was surrounded by a court, which was formed by curtains of fine linen, and was 100 cubits long, and 50 wide. In the Holy of the Holies the ark of the covenant stood, over which two golden Cherubs spread their wings. On those Jehovah was said to throne, in a similar way as he also rode in the sky upon the Cherubim (the thunder clouds); from there he promulgated his oracles. In the ark the two tables are said to have lain. The author does not consider the objection obvious to his statement, how the people, which is said to have wandered during forty years in the desert, has been able to carry along such a large tent, its court, 70 wooden columns, of which some were 10 cubits long, many gold-covered boards of the same length, a sacrificial altar, and a great many carpets and tools. Such holy arks are used by many people, especially by Nomades. The objects of veneration, in particular the idols, were conserved in them, and carried along in their migrations. This was probably also the custom of the Israelites.

A dreadful power is attributed to the ark of covenant. Even the Levites, though they were to carry it, were forbidden to seize it, or to look at it, and besides the High Priest nobody, under pain of death, was allowed to behold the Holy of the Holies. Once the ark was taken by the Philistines, but as it caused death and calamity among them, they brought it back to the confines of the Israelites. The inhabitants of the frontier-town beheld it joyfully, and the Levites lifted it down from the wagon. "But Jehovah killed 70 men of the inhabitants; 50,000." (1 Sam.) The number "50,000" was probably added by a writer in a later time, though it can not be comprehended, how in a little town so many inhabitants could live. When David would bring the ark to Jerusalem (2 Sam. 6), and the team tried to break loose, a man (called Usa), with the best intention to save the ark from falling, stretched out his arm, and seized it; but he also was killed by Jehovah. "It is impossible that the law has originated in the desert, and that Moses has given it. A great many institutions, which are of use only to a settled people, and only with such a one could originate and continue to exist, as e. g., agrarian laws, municipal institutions, the royal law, the numerous priesthood, the large pompous sanctuary, testify irrefragably to the contrary. Therefore the content of the law offers a new testimony that the books of Moses are neither authentic, nor have been written in so early a time." *

9. Conquest of Canaan—Joshua—Samson.

When Moses had died, Joshua conquered Canaan. (Jos. 1—12 ch.) First the people crossed the Jordan. The crossing was again effected by a miracle which the ark operated, because Jehovah was throning upon it. The priests carry it before the people, and step with it in the water. "The water now stopped, and rose like a dam; and the water flowing down in the Dead Sea, disappeared."

---

* A. Wiscilenus, "the Bible." 1 vol. p. 273.

The first town which was to be conquered, was Jericho, the town of palm-trees lying on the road to Jerusalem. During six days the army, headed by the ark of the covenant, and seven priests with trumpets, passes once a day around the town; the seventh day the procession is repeated seven times; at last the priests blow the trumpets, the people set up cries, the walls fall in ruins, and the town is taken. A terrible massacre followed; all inhabitants, not even women, children and old men excepted, were killed, with all animals, and the houses burnt; for Jehovah commanded it. Then it was the turn of Ai; the inhabitants of this town were also killed by order of Jehovah, and their dwellings burned. Successively Joshua vanquished thirty-one Kings; they and all their subjects lost their lives. Once Jehovah assisted him by stopping the movement of the sun (ch. 10). Joshua cried during the battle: "Sun, stand thou still upon Gibeon, and thou, moon, in the valley of Ajalon!" The sun then stopped in the midst of the sky almost one day, and the moon stayed too, until all the enemies were destroyed. Such a solstice is impossible, because it would suspend nature's laws, which are eternal, unchangeable, admitting no exceptions. (Cf. views of the Univ., § 3.) In this manner, at Jehovah's command, all inhabitants of Canaan were extirpated, their abodes burned, and then the country was divided among the tribes of the Israelites. What atrocious actions are attributed to Jehovah in this book! In honor to humanity the truth of this whole story may be doubted. National hatred against the aboriginals of the country has dictated it to the author. There are several contradictions in the book; e. g., it states (21, 43): "Jehovah gave Israel the land entirely; he delivered all their enemies into their hands." On the other hand, Jehovah tells to Joshua (13, 1): "You have grown old, far gone in years, and much land remains to be conquered;" and moreover the book remarks (17, 12): "These towns could not be conquered, and the Canaanites remained in this country." Finally, it first tells that Joshua has conquered the entire country at the head of the whole people, and after that the conquest is left to the single tribes (1, 12—4, 12, —17, 14, etc.).

The book of the Judges contains also the poem of Samson (ch. 13—16), the greatest adventurer of whom the Old Testament narrates. Samson, first, tears a lion in pieces, as easily "as a kid." As he goes, some time hereafter, to his bride, who was a Philistine girl, in order to celebrate his nuptials with her, he finds in the decaying lion a swarm of bees, and honey. At the wedding feast he proposes a riddle to thirty Philistines, and agrees with them to give every one a holiday garment if they could solve it, but that they must give him such a one in the opposite case. The riddle referred to that lion, and was this: "From the glutton food was gained, and sweetness from the strong one." As the young men could not expound it, they induced the young wife to elicit the explanation from Samson by caresses and menaces, and on the seventh day they rendered this reply: "What is sweeter than honey, and what is stronger than the lion?" The irritated Samson kills then thirty Philistines, and gives the young men their festival dresses. As his father-in-law gives the young wife in matrimony to one of them, Samson, desirous of revenge, catches three hundred foxes, ties two and two of their tails together, with fire-brands between them, lets these animals run into the fields of the Philistines, and thereby sets them on fire. They insist on his delivery. The Israelites deliver him, bound with two new ropes. But he tears them like threads, and kills, with the jaw-bone of an ass, one thousand of them. He implores Jehovah, as he much suffers from thirst; the cavity of the jaw-bone opens, water pours out, and Samson drinks his fill. Another time he takes his night's rest in a town of the Philistines; they will take him prisoner, and watch the door; but he unhinges its foldings and carries them on the summit of the bordering mountain. They promise to the Philistine Delila a large sum of money if she would elicit from Samson the secret of his strength. First he pretended to lose it, if he were tied with seven new sinews. Delila tied him with such ones but Samson broke them like threads. Then he told her that he would grow weak, if seven braids of his long hair were nailed on the wall; but as she called the Philistines, he pulled also the nail out. Tired by her reproaches and caresses, he at last discovered her that the secret of his strength was in his long hair. Being consecrated to Jehovah, he had never before got it cut; he would be as feeble as other men, were it cut. When he again was sleeping in her house, she allowed his braids to be cut, and called the hidden Philistines. They seize him, put out his eyes, and forced him to grind as a slave in the mill. After some time, as they celebrated a festival in honor of their god Dagon, they brought Samson in the temple, and ordered him to make sport, and to dance. But he takes hold of both columns, between which he stands, and which supported the roof, and pulls them down. He was killed by the ruins of the temple, with all the people who were present, and three thousand more who stood upon the roof of the temple. Samson is the fictitious ideal of the Israelitic young men fighting at the borders the young Philistines, of the bullies of the frontier villages; he is the Jewish Hercules.

10. The Prophets Elias and Elisha.

In the history of the Ancient Testament the prophets occupy an important position. Moses already was called a prophet. When David was King, the Prophet *Nathan* once comes forth as his adviser and judge. But it is the period after the schism of the realm, in which the efficiency of the prophets is most conspicuous. The occasion of their appearance were the moral corruption of their cotemporaries, and idolatry. They saw that this public state of the nation must soon be followed by the dissolution of the realm, and they recommended morality and the service due to Jehovah as the only means of safety. They hoped that the people would embrace these means, and that in this way Israel would become the supreme of all nations on earth, and that they all would serve Jehovah. Undaunted, they made bitter reproaches to both the people and the vicious Kings of Israel and Judah. They believed in their divine mission;

therefore they believed the impulse of their religious and patriotic feelings to be divine inspiration, and announced their thoughts as Jehovah's dictates. The people attributed them the gift of miracles, and of a prophetic knowledge of the future. In general their thoughts were also right; but they erred also if they predicted particular circumstances. Their prophetic gift is not to be wondered at; it can be explained in a natural way by the circumstances of that time. So, e. g., the separation of the ten tribes, which a prophet is said to have predicted at Salomon's time, could be foreboded then. Isaiah (the greatest and most respectable of all prophets) saw himself the kingdom of Israel attacked and conquered by the Assyrians, saw also Judea threatened by the enemies, and Jerusalem, where his residence was, assieged; was it, then, marvellous if he foresaw and prophesied the approaching ruin? Now-a-days the prophetic gift is also rife; some politicians and state-men enjoy it even in a higher degree than those seers of the Old Testament. As for the rest, at those times there were also false, egotistic prophets, who carried on prophesying as a lucrative business.

The greatest miracle-workers among the prophets were Elias and Elisha. The former announced to King Ahab that no more rain would fall in his realm, till Jehovah would be pleased to send it again. During the time of drought, a raven brought the prophet daily, bread and meat. Finally, after two years, in consequence of his prayers, Jehovah accorded again rain. But how could plants, animals and men subsist, during this time, without rain?

One of the most famous Biblical legends is the butchering of the Baal priests by Elias. They performed the service in the temple of the god of the sun, whose name in Israel was Baal (Mithras in Persia, and Osiris in Egypt), and were appointed by Queen Jesabel. Elias proposes to the people that the prophets of Baal first ought to offer a sacrifice, and that then he, too, would sacrifice to Jehovah, and the god who would answer with fire ought to be their god. The people approve the proposal. The prophets of Baal, then, are crying for fire to their god from the morning until night; but in vain. Now Elias rebuilds the destroyed altar of Jehovah, digs a large ditch around it, puts wood and the dissected bull upon the altar, bids to pour many buckets of water on it, and to fill also the ditch with water; then he implores Jehovah; fire fell immediately from the sky, and consumed not only the sacrificed meat, and the wood, but also the stones, and earth, and licked up the water in the ditch. Now the people believed in Jehovah, seized upon the Baal priests by order of Elias, and this butchered them all.

In spite of this miracle the Queen did not turn to the belief in Jehovah, but assailed the prophet's life. Finally he rides during a tempest on a fiery chariot to which fiery horses were put, to heaven.

Elisha, his disciple, operates even more miracles than he. He curses in Jehovah's name the boys who stoned him on the road, and nicknamed him baldhead; two bears then emerge from the woods, and tear forty-two of them to pieces. He satiates one hundred men with twenty cakes of bread, of which yet some part is left, etc. From these narratives it is evident that the author intends to represent the efficacy of the two prophets in a superhuman splendor. It may be that there are some truths at the bottom of them, but it is also possible that both prophets are entirely fictitious persons; for the books of the Kings, in which their exploits are related, were not composed until nearly 300 years after Elisha's death. The name Elias signifies: " My God is Jehovah," and Elisha: " God's aid." These names are quite adapted to their deeds.

CHAPTER SECOND.

NARRATIVES FROM THE NEW TESTAMENT.

1. The Birth of Jesus.

The birth of Jesus is reported by Matthew and Luke, but in two different ways. According to Matthew, Jesus was born during the reign of King Herod, in Bethlehem, where his parents lived. About the time of his birth Mages came from the Orient to Jerusalem, saying: " Where is the new-born King of the Jews? For we have seen his star, and have come to do homage to him." By this news Herod and the whole city of Jerusalem are terror-struck; he assembles the high priests and scribes, and understands by their statement that Christ ought to be born in Bethlehem. Then he inquires in a conversation of the Mages for the time, when the star has appeared, and concerts with them that, if they would find the child, they should report it to him, in order that he also could do homage to him. But it was his secret design to dispatch the dangerous child. They find the child, as the star stopped above the house of his birth, pay him their homage, and make him presents; but warned in a dream by a divine direction, they do not return to Herod, but travel on another road back to their home. As Herod saw that he was deceived, he ordered all children to be killed, who were aged two years or less, and lived in Bethlehem and its environs. But Joseph, Mary's husband, obedient to a divine order, had already fled with the mother and child to Egypt, and did not return to Palestine until after Herod's death; then he took his residence with his family in Nazareth.

A similar story is related in the Old Testament (4 Mos. 22—24). There also a wise man of the Orient, named Bileam, travels to Palestine; he, too, sees the star of an Israelitic King, professes also his veneration to this King, returns then to his home, etc. Matthew has imitated this story and enlarged it with some features. It is seen, how incorrect his notions of the nature, magnitude and motion of the stars were, as he lets a star precede the Mages, stop and move as he pleases, etc. At those times the prejudice was yet common that great, high-famed men were born under the influence of stars, which ruled their fate. The massacre of the Bethlehemitic children is also a mere fiction, and drawn from the ancient Mosaic legend that Pharao had ordered all Israelitic children to be killed, and that only Moses was saved in a wonderful way. Though the Roman historians depict the character of Herod as cruel, still they know nothing of snch an unprecedented blood-shed.

Luke relates the birth of Jesus in this way : When Quirinus was Governor of Syria and Palestine, the Roman Emperor Augustus decreed that the whole world ought to be taxed. Every one went to his native town to be taxed. Joseph also went from Nazareth, his residence, with Mary to David's town, called Bethlehem, because he descended from David's house and family, in order to get taxed himself and his wife. Mary brought there forth in the inn her first son, wrapped him in swaddling clothes, and laid him in a manger, because in the inn there was no room for them. An angel announced the child's birth to the shepherds in the field ; they came and venerated it. Hymns of praise were sung by angels in the air, etc. Hereafter the parents brought the child to Jerusalem, and represented it in the temple ; and after having performed all rites of the Jewish law, they returned to their town Nazareth in Galilee.

This account does not deserve more credit than the former. By the Roman Emperors, indeed, Palestine, like the other provinces of their dominion, was taxed, but for the sake of the census nobody had to travel from home to his native place ; the descent might be important to the Jews, but it was not so to the Romans, who only cared for the taxes. Besides, Luke subjects Mary to the census also, though it was confined to men. Nay, it is proved by history that such a taxation could not take place at the time of the birth of Jesus, because Palestine then was not subjected to the Romans. Matthew distinctly reports that Jesus was born during the reign of Herod ; and Luke also puts his birth in the period of the government of this King. The taxation mentioned by Luke, happened not till ten to twelve years after the birth of Jesus, when Palestine had become a Roman province. Finally, the statement of Luke that the census was extended over the whole world (to say, over the whole Roman Empire), is also incorrect ; the Roman taxations never comprised the entire Empire, but only single provinces. The angels also play a considerable part in Luke's report. The belief in angels developed among the Jews since their captivity rapidly, and was most flourishing in the epoch in which the evangelies were written.

This birth story turns yet more incredible, if both evangelists are confronted. The circumstances of their stories are quite different, some portions even contradict and annul each other. According to Matthew the parents of Jesus originally lived in Bethlehem, and did not move to Nazareth until several years after their flight to Egypt; according to Luke they always lived in Nazareth, and were only for a short time (at the time of the child's birth) in Bethlehem. Matthew states that Jesus was born in his parents' home ; Luke, that he was brought forth in the inn, and that a manger was his cradle. Matthew let the whole family first flee to Egypt, and from that land come to Nazareth; at Luke they return to their usual residence immediately after the performance of the legal rites. Both evangelists let homage be done to the new-born infant, the one by wise men, the other by shepherds and angels, in order to illustrate more brightly the high dignity of the King's and God's son.

2. The Baptism of Jesus.

John, whom all evangelists called the precursor of Jesus, founded a peculiar sect, and baptized in the river Jordan those who vowed to improve the morals of their life, and to do penance. Jesus, too, wanted to be baptized. The reason of it can hardly be surmised; for, if he was entirely sinless (as the evangelists report), why did he need the baptism? Matthew narrates: "When Jesus was baptized, and stepped out of the water, he saw the spirit of God descending, and come upon him." Jesus, then, himself, and he alone, saw the Holy Ghost; how could it be that John and other people who were present, did not perceive him? This descension of the Holy Ghost was also very needless; for, according to the evangelists, Jesus was without that a child of the Holy Ghost; why was this particularly troubled to come down from his celestial residence? Three evangelists state simply that this Ghost descended *like* a dove; but in Luke there are even the words: "He descended in *body form*, like a dove." The dove was to the Jews the symbol of innocence. Jesus himself admonished his disciples: "Be as prudent as serpents, and as simple as doves." In general, in the Orient the dove is deemed to be holy. In the Bible it denotes God's spirit. So Isaiah says in a similar way (ch. 42): "See my elected one in whom my soul takes delight. *I put my spirit upon him;* he shall promulgate the right to the nations." For the rest celestial voices were an article of creed in which people of ancient times usually believed, they happened also frequently among Greeks and Romans.

3. The Temptation of Jesus.

After the baptism of Jesus, his temptation immediately followed. Matthew says: "Jesus was then conducted by the spirit into the desert, in order to be tempted by the devil. After having fasted forty days and nights, he was hungry. The tempter then approached him, and said: 'If thou art a son of God, command that these stones be made bread.' But he answered: 'It is written: Man does not only live on bread, but on every word, which proceeds from the mouth of God.' Then the devil takes him up into the holy city, sets him on the pinnacle of the temple, and says to him: 'If thou art the Son of God, cast thyself down; for it is written: He will give charge to his angels concerning thee, and they will bear thee up in their hands, lest thou dash thy foot against a stone.' Jesus said to him: 'Again it is written: Thou shalt not tempt the Lord, thy God.' Again the devil takes him up into a very high mountain, and shows him all the kingdoms of the world, and their glory, and says to him: 'I will give thee all this, if thou fall down and worship me.' Then Jesus says to him: 'Begone, Satan! for it is written: Thou shalt alone adore God, thy Lord, and serve him alone.' Then the devil left him; and behold angels approached, and ministered unto him."

Here in the New Testament we meet the devil the first time. The Israelites had received him at the time of the Babylonian captivity from the Zend religion; he is the Ahriman of the Zend Avesta. Besides, he is also called Satan (the adversary) and diabolos (the accuser), wherefrom the term devil has originated. Moses, the Israelites, and the prophet Elias, before Christ, dwelt in the desert, Elias during forty days; the Israelites and Elias were there in want of food; those were fed with celestial manna, Elias by a raven. Moses, too, fasted on the mount of Sinai during forty days and nights. Therefore Jesus also, like his models, was to wander and to fast in the desert. But it can be justly asked, how the devil could possess so much power with regard to the Son of God, to carry him along with himself; how it could be done to carry him (of course through the air) to Jerusalem, to put him upon the pointed pinnacle of the temple, from there to conduct him upon a mountain, and to show him all countries of the earth. Did Matthew not know that even on the highest mountain only a small part of the earth can be observed, because it has the shape of a sphere? The Jews and Greeks imagined the earth to be a level disk. And finally, was the devil entitled to give away all the kingdoms of the world? Matthew wanted to tell a miracle.

4. The Miracles of Jesus in General.

Already in the Old Testament, Moses and Elias, besides others, were miracle-workers; in the New, Jesus and his apostles are their successors. The miracles of the Old Testament refer to entire countries and nations; those of the New concern most only single individuals; as a whole, they are imitations of the former, which are their models. The lame, blind, deaf and mute, the palsied, leprous, feverish, lunatic, demoniac, are here healed, nay, defuncts resuscitated, hungry ones wonderfully fed, tempests appeased, water changed into wine, etc. This summary already shows that among the miracles of Jesus the cures by far outweigh; this is a proof that the spirit of the New Testament has grown milder—Moses is an austere legislator, Jesus the meek, merciful Savior.

How must the miracles of Jesus be considered?

If any event is pretended to be a miracle, we are only to prove that it contravenes some general law of nature; the reporter of the miracle must prove that the exception of the law really took place; he cannot do this but by introducing trustworthy witnesses, who observed the narrated fact. But as the evangelies were written about one hundred years after the death of Jesus, such a proof by witnesses is impossible; for suppose even that the miracles really happened, still the witnesses who saw them could not have lived after so long an interval of time, consequently the evangelists could only from the third or fourth hand collect their reports, in a word, they could not tell but by hear-say. It is usually objected to this argument that the authors of these documents were guided by the Holy Ghost, during their compositions, consequently that they could not err. But this assertion finds no longer many advocates in our age, for it was evinced long ago that the authors of the Bible often contradict each other. Besides, many errors occur therein, concerning the truths of astronomy and natural science, of universal history, geography and other sciences. Therefore now-a-days the view is generally admitted that the contents of the biblical writings must be judged by the same rules which are applied to other books.

The origin of the belief in miracles also demonstrates its fallacy. How does, it take rise? Men would like to govern nature, e. g., to get rid of diseases to abolish even death, to cross rivers without bridges, to command storm and weather. The right way to reach this scope, are the knowledge of nature and the subjection of its forces; e. g., the force of steam is known, and employed for rail-roads, in order to move fast to a place. But this way is wearisome and protracted, and demands thousands of years, till mankind attains its aims by it. Imagination takes it easier: it skips the limits of nature, and likes the belief that this can be governed by witchcraft and miracles; it recurs to superstition.

If Jesus was the Lord of nature, it can be asked, why he did not heal every disease, and revive all the dead, or at least every young person who died. Why remained there yet hunger and thirst, poverty, in general, any evil in the world? He could surely extend his power to perform miracles over all countries, over all mankind. But this did not take place, nor is it related, because the common experience would have plainly contradicted; in single cases contradiction was less to be feared.

Furthermore, how was it possible that not the whole people, and even the priesthood believed his words? It is objected that Jesus did not operate his miracles in the presence of people. So the evangelists say in some passages; but in others they state to the contrary, namely that these miracles were performed in the presence of large crowds. The gospels, then, contradict themselves, and do not deserve any trust.

Many object also that Jesus would build the creed of men upon the excellence of his doctrine. Neither this assertion is true. When John's disciples asked him if he was the Messiah, he bade them to consider his miracles. He rebukes the incredulity of the towns which did no penance, though he had there performed the greatest number of his miracles. His disciples believed in him, because he had changed water into wine (as Matthew assures us); but John reports that the enemies of Jesus, after he had resuscitated Lazarus, even on account of his miracles, resolved to kill him. Therefore it remains incomprehensible how by the miracles attributed to him, the Jews were not persuaded that he was the expected Messiah, nay even the son of God. As this persuasion failed coming;

on the contrary, as they even murdered him: we justly conclude that those miraculous narratives are nothing but pious myths.

But how was it possible that so many contradictions crept into the reports of the authors? Every one composed his gospel for the circle of his readers, without knowing the other evangels, and without anticipating that their narratives would ever be compared, and that on account of their contradictions their purpose—to strengthen the belief in Jesus—would be frustrated.

5. His Miraculous Cures—Demoniacs.

Jesus healed every disease and bodily defect, in all towns and villages; his miraculous cures were said to be innumerable. He healed merely by his word or contact. Even from afar he is healing. The patients recover by touching his garment. He requires only faith. These cures are effected in a moment and thoroughly. The terrible and protracted disease of leprosy disappears in a trice by his word and touching. A man who had been suffering from gout, during thirty-eight years, had been bedridden, rises, encouraged by his word, and carries his bed home. Every one who acknowledges the laws of nature, and their necessity, conceives that such cures are impossible. (Cf. Views of the Univ., § 3.) These tales suppose total ignorance in matters of the human body, and medical science. So, e. g., Mark tells (7, 22,) that a man who since his birth had been deaf and mute, suddenly commenced to speak and understand human language. The evangelist likely ignored that the deaf and mute are disabled to learn a language, because they cannot hear it, that, therefore, they would neither be able to speak it, suppose that they at once obtained their hearing, because they never learnt to speak.

Some presumed that Jesus had acquired a superior knowledge of medical science. But no physician heals his patients with the mere finger and saliva, or with a few words. Neither did the bare faith in Jesus suffice to cure every disease, e. g., leprosy, blindness, deafness, gout. The authors of the Gospels want the cures to be miracles; they shall and must happen, in spite of nature's laws, and be incomprehensible, because also other men before the appearance of their hero had effected similar miracles, and Jesus ought to pass for the Messiah of the Jews, of whom the prophets had predicted: "Then the eyes of the blind, and the ears of the deaf are opened; then the lame jumps like a stag, and the tongue of the dumb exults" (Isaiah 35, 5). The ground from which the miraculous cures of the evangelics have sprung, is the expectation of a Messiah.

A particular species of patients, many of whom are healed by Jesus, are the demoniacs. According to the notions of the New Testament, sometimes unclean spirits, devils, demons, take possession of a man, and then dwell in his soul, and rule it. The effects of these spirits were considered to be: madness, melancholy, epilepsy, etc. Jesus expels them merely by his word, and they leave the demoniac usually with much bustle and cries. The strangest miracle of this kind is that which he works among the Gergesenes (Matth. 8., cf. Mark 5). A demoniac is possessed by a legion of devils (10,000—12,000); they ask Jesus to not drive them in the abyss of hell, but to suffer them to pass in a herd of hogs, which there was pastured. Jesus allows it; the demons rush into the swine, and the whole herd, namely 2,000 head, plunge into the lake of Genesaret, and are drowned. The Jews, indeed, found nothing wrong in this event, because they despised hogs, as being unclean animals; but what would the owner of so large a herd think now-a-days, if he should lose it in such a manner, and what sentence would our courts of justice pass if he should sue at law the abettor of such a damage? "If the proprietor of the swine came to demand justice, when Jesus was apprehended, it is clear that he was deservedly condemned, as there never was a jury in England that would not have found him guilty."—Woolston

6. Resuscitations of the Dead.

The Gospels narrate three resuscitations which Jesus is told to have effected. In Nain he revived the son of a widow, and delivered him to his mother. In Capernaum, Jairus, the chief of a synagogue, came to him, saying: "My daughter just died; but come, put your hand upon her, and she will be again alive." When Jesus came in his house, he ordered the people and the musicians to go out, approached the girl, seized her hand and she arose. So Matthew tells. But Luke and Mark say: "The girl lay a-dying, was about to die." According to Luke, Jesus took Peter, James and John, with the parents of the girl, to the room; then he sent the rest of the people away. Mark, on the contrary, reports: He let nobody follow him in the house, except Peter, James and John, put them all out, took the parents of the girl, and those who were with him, and entered the room where the dead was deposited. The three reporters, then, do neither agree mutually in this story. According to Mark, the girl was twelve years old. Both revivals are imitations of those which are attributed to Elias and Elisha. Even the words: "And he delivered him to his mother," which occur in the story of the youth of Nain, are used already in the model legend.

In the fullest detail John relates the revival of Lazarus. This was the friend of Jesus, and lived with his sisters Mary and Martha, in Bethany, near to Jerusalem. When he fell sick, the sisters sent for Jesus, and, of course, asked him to come and to restore the friend and brother to health. But he did not come, tarrying yet two days in the place where he was; not till then he went to Bethany. When he arrived, he found that Lazarus was already four days in the grave. It must, therefore, he concluded that Jesus was at least a two-days' journey from Bethany. It looks strange that the messenger could find him at such a distance. He proceeded to the grave; it was a cave covered with a stone. Jesus ordered this to be removed. Martha remarked that the defunct already smelled, because he had lain four days in the tomb. Nevertheless, Jesus cried: "Lazarus, come forth!" The dead came forth, bound hand and feet with grave clothes, and so also the face bound about with a napkin. Jesus ordered them to loose him and to let him go. Many Jews, who were present and saw this achievement, believed in Jesus, but some of them went to the Pharisees, and told them what Jesus had done.

Without urging the impossibility that a corpse which is already putrifying, could come again to life, it cannot be understood how a man, with his hands and feet bundled up, could walk, and it is incredible that some witnesses of the extraordinary miracle could turn spies and betray the Messiah. Finally, it cannot be explained why the three other evangelists do not mention at all the greatest miracle Jesus had performed. " A dead man restored to life would have been an object of attention and astonishment to the universe; all the Jewish magistrates, and more especially Pilate, would have made the most minute investigation. But so far from these wonders being mentioned, the world knew nothing about them till more than one hundred years had rolled away from the date of the events. Neither any Jewish, nor any Greek or Roman historian, at all notices these prodigies."—Th. Woolston.

7. Miraculous Feedings—Water Changed to Wine—The Storm Appeased.

Two evangelists report two miraculous feedings, the others only one. At one time 5,000 men (without counting the women and children) are fed and satiated with five loaves of bread and two fish, the other time 4,000 with seven loaves and a few fish; and there are yet many fragments left, the first time twelve, and the second seven baskets full. It has been supposed that among the people were many rich persons, who shared their provisions with the poor; but it cannot be believed that they were able to fill with them so many thousands; the reporters, too, mean certainly that the victuals were increased by a miracle. Their models were the flour-barrel, and the oil cruet of the widow in the legend of Elias (both were never drained), besides, a similar miracle, effected by Elisha with twenty loaves, and the feeding of the Israelites on manna in the wilderness. Jesus also operated his feeding in the desert.

As Jesus here provides food, so he procures a pleasant drink at the wedding of Cana, to which he with his mother and disciples was invited, by changing water into wine. The miraculous wine was, perhaps, not much in the taste of some guests, as the water from which it originated had been poured into wash-basins, in which they used to wash the feet. In the desert Moses furnished the Israelites water, by a miracle, from a rock; perhaps the transformation story took its origin from that myth.

Once Jesus navigated with the disciples on the lake, when a storm arose so that, while he was sleeping, they were much endangered. They awake him; he commands the storm and waves, and the lake is immediately appeased. At another time he follows his disciples who crossed the lake, and walks upon the waves. Peter descends on the billows in order to proceed to him, but sinks;

Jesus seizes his hand, and both mount on board. Both legends may be imitations of the myth of the crossing of the Red Sea, effected by the Israelites. The second contradicts the general law of the specific gravity of bodies. According to this law, a solid body, if immersed in water, displaces of the latter a quantity equal to its own volume; if the displaced quantity of water is lighter than the solid body, this sinks down; but if heavier, the body swims on the surface of the water. Now, we know from experience that the human body is somewhat heavier than water. Therefore it sinks in the latter to the bottom, even if it is lying flat upon it, as it happens in swimming, so that the swimmer must restore the equipoise of his body and of the water by the skillful motion of the hands and feet. But if he stands perpendicularly on the water (as this narrative reports), his body displaces perhaps only the twentieth part as much water as if he swims, and must, therefore, sink so much easier. Jesus, then, necessarily had to sink in the lake, for he, too, had a human body, neither could he save Peter from sinking by his offered arm.

8. Solemn Entry of Jesus into Jerusalem—His Last Supper.

A short time before his death Jesus traveled to Jerusalem. The reports of the Gospels, concerning this journey, are rather confused, and contradict each other in several particulars. He is said to have performed a solemn entry in Jerusalem, riding on one or, according to Matthew, on two asses, namely on a she-ass and her colt. The people spread their garments on the road, cut down branches from the trees, strewed them in his passage and cried: "Hosianna (hail) to the son of David; the coming reign of David be praised, the King of Israel be praised!" Even the children took part in these cries. In a word, the people proclaimed him their King. The whole city was terrified by his entry. In Isaiah (ch. 62) a similar passage is written: "Say to the daughter of Sion (to Jerusalem): Behold, thy King comes to thee riding on an ass, on a colt." The narrative of the entry of Jesus may have been occasioned by this passage of the prophet.

After the procession the cleaning of the temple followed. "Jesus (it is said) entered the temple, overturned the tables of the money-changers, and the seats of the dove-sellers, scattered the money of the bankers, made a whip of ropes, and expelled all sellers of bulls, sheep and doves, together with the money changers."

This action could not happen in the temple itself, but only in its yard, where the venders were permitted to offer victims for sale; even there it could hardly be executed, because the superintendents of the temple would probably have interfered with it, as it subverted the established order of the temple.

All evangelists mention a supper which Jesus is said to have eaten with his disciples the evening before his death. They speak of it with different words and considerable variations. One makes Jesus say: "That is my body, that is my blood;" another: "That is my blood which will be spilled for many, for the pardon of their sins;" a third: "Do ye that to my memory." The first Christians frequently celebrated the Lord's Supper, as it is called; but that soon an abuse crept in this custom appears from a letter of Paul, in which he blames the Corinthians that every one brought along his meal for himself, so that the rich ate and drank delicately, the destitute poorly. It is not probable that Jesus instituted a supper in memory of his death, nor that he declared bread and wine to be his real flesh and blood because John does not mention such things. How could he pass silently such an important institution of his beloved master? According to his report Jesus took his last supper one day sooner as the Jews used to eat the legal paschal lamb; therefore it was an ordinary repast. It is also only Matthew, who has the words: " For the pardon of the sins." In any case it is more probable that the disciples continued, to the memory of their dearest teacher, his custom to pass them bread and wine at their common repasts. In general, *posterity* institutes festivals in memory of eminent men, not these themselves.

At the last repast Jesus is said also to have revealed to his disciples that one of them, Judas, would betray him. The statements of the evangelists are also here contradicting each other; e. g., according to Matthew, Jesus says to the disciples: "He who dips his hand with me into the dish, will betray me." But according to John: " This will betray me to whom I shall give the morsel I dip." It cannot be seen, in what Judas would have committed treason. Thirty shekels (about $18.65) were indeed a too paltry profit, even for the greediest man, in order to sell for them the life of his friend and teacher. Why did the priests want the help of a traitor? Jesus appeared according to the evangelies, every day in the temple, and went every evening before the city to the mount of Olives, where he rested during the night in the open air. If they would not arrest him in the temple, they could easily espy his nocturnal sojourn, and seize him without any danger.

9. Arrest, Trial and Condemnation of Jesus.

After the hymn of praise they went out to the mount of Olives; but according to John, " over the brook Kedron in a garden." Here Jesus prayed that God might remove the cup of suffering from him. His mental agony was so great that his sweat broke forth, and fell to the ground as it were drops of blood. An angel appeared from heaven, and comforted him (Luke 22). (Who could hear the prayers of Jesus, and see the angel?) Meanwhile the disciples sleep, though Jesus had admonished them to watch, and predicted them that he would be arrested in that night. While he awakes them, and speaks to them, Judas arrives with the bailiffs, whom the high priests and the elders of the people had sent, furnished with torches, lamps and swords. Luke states that the high priests and elders themselves were present. According to Matthew, Judas had given the bailiffs a signal, namely, saying : " He whom I shall kiss, is the man, of him lay hold!" Forthwith he approached Jesus, kissed him and said: "Hail, master!" The words which Jesus is said to have then spoken to Judas, are differently quoted by the different evangelists; John does not mention the kiss of Judas at all. Jesus then was seized; but the disciples forsook him, and took to flight.

After the arrest of Jesus his trial followed immediately in the presence of the High Council and Pilate. Three evangelists report that the trial and the condemnation of Jesus took place the same night. Such a hasty proceeding of the tribunal would have been, to be sure, an extraordinary measure, for which hardly a sufficient reason could be alleged. Luke contradicts them, too, positively, saying that the trial and condemnation did not take place till the morning. Nay, the other evangelists also mention, contradicting themselves, a meeting of the High Council, held in the morning.

In the presence of the high priests false witnesses testify against Jesus; but their depositions do not agree (Mark). At last the high priest asks him, "Art thou the Christ?" Jesus affirms it. Then they tore his clothes, saying: "He has spoken blasphemy. What's the use of more witnesses? What do you think?" They answered: "He is guilty of death!" John represents the trial of Jesus in a way quite different from that of the three other evangelists. As the trial before the priests was done, Jesus was conducted to *Pontius Pilate*. He was Governor of Palestine, because this country then was a Roman Province The members of the High Council accompany Jesus even themselves to the Governor (?). They accuse him that he has revolted the Jewish nation and forbidden it to pay taxes to the Emperor, saying that he is the Christ, and a King. Pilate asks him: "Art thou the King of the Jews?" Jesus affirms the question, and consequently confesses to be a revolter, guilty of high treason. Thus he deserved to suffer death, and according to Roman law, even death by crucifixion. Nevertheless Pilate declares him guiltless! This declaration provokes the high priests and the multitude, and they repeat their accusation: "He excites the people, teaching in the whole country of Judea, commencing in Galilea till hitherto." Pilate perseveres in his first inconceivable sentence, declares again Jesus to be innocent, and tries to set him free. To this end he avails himself of the custom to release to the Jews a captive on Passover, and permits them to choose Jesus or Barabbas, who had been arrested on account of sedition and murder. As they demand the latter, Pilate still takes all pains to dispose them in favor of Jesus. He asks them: "But what must I do with Jesus?" They cry: "Crucify him!" In order to excite their sympathy, he orders him flogged, and presents him to them covered with blood. But they only cry more enraged: "Crucify him!" Pilate always continues to insist upon saving him; he deems him still to be guiltless. Finally, they threaten to accuse him as an enemy of the Emperor, and repeat their impeachment, saying: "He who makes himself a King is against the Emperor." Pilate at last pronounces the sentence of death, but at the same time he declares solemnly by washing his hands in the presence of the people, that he is guiltless of the death of Jesus. It is impossible to comprehend the proceedings of Pilate, as they have been stated, thus far; he could not have acted in that way, he could and dared, not act so as a Roman, and as the substitute of the Emperor. John probably perceived this inconsistency; therefore he lets Jesus also answer Pilate's question: "Art thou the King of the Jews?" in the affirmative, but by addition the explanation: "My kingdom is not from hence," to wit, it is a reign of truth. In this sense considered, Jesus must be to him a mere teacher, therefore appear innocent. The source from which this representation of the evangelists has emanated, is their attempt to lay the guilt of the execution of Jesus alone to the charge of the Jews and their leaders, and to burden the Jews with it for all times and generations.

10. Crucifixion of Jesus.

The sentence of the Governor is immediately executed: Jesus is crucified. Usually the hands of the criminals who were crucified, were extended upon the cross and fastened with nails. The crucifixion was one of the most cruel kinds of death man has ever suffered. The place of execution was called Golgotha; it is unknown where it was. Before the execution they offered Jesus wine of myrrhs or vinegar, mixed with gall. The first usually was presented to such criminals, because it contained a narcotic power. They say that Jesus refused the beverage. The soldiers are said to have parted his clothes among themselves, by casting lots. By virtue of the Roman law the garments of the executed criminals indeed belonged to the executioners; but may be, this incident, too, originated from a Psalm (22), where it reads: "They parted my raiment among them, and for my vesture they did cast lots." The coat was without seam, woven from the top throughout. The narrators recollected the woven coat worn by the high priest, according to the Mosaic law; for they deemed Jesus to be the high priest of the New Testament. On the cross, according to the Roman custom, an inscription was fastened, and read: "Jesus, King of the Jews." It was written in Hebrew, Latin and Greek. With Jesus two criminals were crucified; one on his right, the other on his left hand. This circumstance was again prognosticated, as the evangelists pretend, by the passage: "He was computed with criminals" (Is. 53). One of them declares Jesus to be innocent, therefore he is promised Paradise. The bystanders, among whom also the priests and elders were seen, insult and revile him, wagging their heads; but he prays for them, saying: "Father, forgive them; they do not know what they are doing." So in that Psalm also it is said: "All who see me, insult me, and wag their heads." Such conduct as this laid to the charge of the people Jesus had not offended, is against human nature; it is also not probable that the high clergy would have been present at the death of their enemy, only to the end to satisfy their vindictiveness. It is more likely that the evangelists accused the people, and their leaders of this almost diabolical barbarity, because from their indignation they believed them to be prone to commit any, even the worst misdeed. John also reports that Mary and "the disciple whom Jesus loved" namely himself) were standing close to the cross, and that Jesus recommended to the disciple to take care of Mary as of his own mother. But Luke says positively that the women who were devoted to Jesus, and his other acquaintances, stood afar from the cross.

Shortly before Jesus expired, he spoke some other words, as all evangelists state, namely: "Eli, Eli, (to wit, my God, my God) why didst thou forsake me?" "I am thirsty!" "Father, in thy hands I commend my spirit!" "It is consummated!" The executioners mistook the cry of Jesus: Eli, Eli, meaning that he called the prophet Elias. One of them ran to fill a sponge with vinegar, and presented it to the dying man. As they were likely Romans, and therefore the name Elias could not be familiar to them, this incident also turns very suspicious. All those words are taken from that Psalm (22), and from other prophetic passages. Therefore, it is uncertain if Jesus spoke even one of those "seven words" on the cross, as they call them. Who did hear them? The women and friends of Jesus, who alone could be witnesses, stood (as we remarked already) too far away to be able to hear them. The evangelists differ entirely in the report of the words spoken by Jesus; none has them all; who has the genuine ones? One states this, another that sentence to be the last. Such discrepancies cannot at all be reconciled. Think only of the horrible situation of a crucified man, struggling with the pangs of death; such an one certainly never was in the humor to utter many words; at the most he ejaculates single woeful accents.

Three evangelists relate yet extraordinary phenomena which accompanied the death of Jesus; John knows nothing about them. From 12 to 3 o'clock (from 6 to 9, according to Jewish horology) darkness reigned over the whole country (it was therefore a solar eclipse); as Jesus expired, the curtain of the temple rent in twain from the top to the bottom (in order to symbolize the end of Judaism), an earthquake shook the ground, the rocks rent, the tombs opened, many corpses of the saints arose, and appeared to many inhabitants in the city. This account contradicts the laws of nature too grossly, and is, indeed, too absurd to need a special proof of its untruth. Suffice it to remark that other writers of that time let the death of great men, e. g., of Julius Cæsar, be accompanied by earthquakes, solar eclipses and other similar miracles.

When Jesus had expired, Joseph of Arimathia, a rich man and counsellor, buries him. He requests the corpse from Pilate, wraps it in clean linen cloth, puts it "in his new grave, which he had hewn out in the rocks, and rolls a large stone before the entry."--(Matth.) To the contrary, John reports that in the place of execution there was a garden, and in the garden a new sepulchre; that Jesus was buried in this, because haste was needed, and the grave was close at hand. Thereby it is evident that John did not believe the tomb to be Joseph's property. He states also that one hundred pounds of myrrhs and aloe were procured for the sake of embalming the corpse (!).

What is, then, the result of the investigation regarding the death of Jesus? That we know nothing with certainty about it but that it was caused by crucifixion. This result is very natural, as hardly any of his followers were present at the execution. How could it be, otherwise, that the reporters gainsay each other in such a degree? If his partisans had been present as witnesses, the dreadful scenes of the bloody tragedy must have rooted so deeply in their memory that such contradictions and hallucinations had become impossible. Probably they did not know more about it themselves than we. They borrowed the materials of their traditions, likely, from the Old Testament, especially from Isaiah (ch. 53), where the prophet says: " He was despised and forsaken by men; but he loaded our pains upon himself; he was wounded on account of our sins. He did not open his mouth, like the lamb which is led to the shambles. They assigned him his grave with blasphemers, though he had not committed any wrong," etc. It was natural, and could not fail coming, that the disciples of Jesus tried to form themselves a definite image of the sufferings and death of their highly venerated Messiah, and adorned the real event with wonderful touches. The Ancient Testament assisted their efforts. Another reason of their exaggerations was their desire to prove thereby that Jesus has offered the most stupendous sacrifice for the sins of the world.

The hour and day of the execution is also differently stated by the evangelists. Mark writes that the crucifixion of Jesus commenced at nine o'clock in the forenoon, and that he died at three o'clock p. m. According to John, Pilate at twelve o'clock is still sitting on the tribunal. According to the three older Gospels, Jesus ate yet the paschal lamb with his disciples, and was executed the day afterward. The paschal lamb was considered by the Jews as a sacrifice, and was always eaten the evening before the Easter. But the first and the last day of the festival were to them the most holy ones; therefore it is difficult to believe that on the first day of the Passover criminals were executed. John deemed Jesus to be the truly sacred and divine paschal lamb; therefore he let the crucifixion coincide with the slaughter of the Jewish paschal lamb. For that reason he also reports that the bones of Jesus, just like those of the paschal lamb, were not fractured. Consequently, according to his report, the execution of Jesus happened one day sooner than as stated by the other evangelists. Nay, it is even possible that it took place neither on the one nor the other of these two days, but either in the middle of the Easter week, or in general about Easter-time. So we perceive again here the great unsafeness of the evangelical reports. Matthew and John are said to have been witnesses of this event; nevertheless the day of death of Jesus, which of all days of his life must have been deepest inculcated to their memory, and which, if it happened near the Passover, obtained a firmer hold even by this incident; not so much as this day, the most important and most impressive for the mind and creed of his followers, is stated to the same date in the Gospels! The year, in which the execution of Jesus occurred is also utterly unknown.

11. His Resurrection and Ascension.

The Gospels mention a resurrection of Jesus, which, as they say, happened three days after his death. This statement is untrue, for they all report that it chanced already the second morning after the execution of Jesus, after having rested in the grave two nights and one day, consequently about thirty-six hours. The contradictions in the account of this event are even more numerous than in any other. All evangelists indeed agree in the circumstance that those who received first the news of the resurrection, were women. But according to the one there were two; according to the other, three women; according to the third, only one. One states that the stone was rolled off in the presence of the women, another that they found it already removed. According to the one the angels address the women at their first, according to the other at their second visit of the grave; these mention one, those two angels. The words spoken by the angels are related in a very different way by the different evangelists. According to some, the women announce immediately the apparition, according to an other they keep silence, etc. From one we learn that Jesus sent word to the disciples to go to Galilee, from another that he forbade them to leave Jerusalem. In one evangel he appears to the disciples twice, in another three times, in John's four times; in one he appears in Galilee on a mountain, in two others in Jerusalem, in the fourth at the lake of Genesareth. The reports gainsay also each other with regard to the manner of his appearance. On the one hand he represents himself exactly in his former shape; the marks of the nails are left on his hands and feet, and the scar of the side wound; he permits to be touched, in order to prove that he is no spectre, and he eats in the presence of his disciples. On the other hand he appears ghost-like; his friends do not recognize him; Mary Magdalen first takes him to be the gardener, and at a sudden he appears, in spite of the locked doors, in the midst of the assembled disciples, refusing to eat and to be touched. The words he addressed to them at the several apparitions, are of very different kind in the several Gospels. Finally, neither the reports of the Acts of the Apostles and of the Apostle Paul agree with the Gospels; as to the former, Jesus appeared to the disciples yet during 40 days (therefore surely oftener than four times), and Paul enumerates five apparitions. The myth of the resurrection is an evident proof, how arbitrarily the writers of the New Testament modeled and remodeled their stories, according as it suited their particular purposes.

What can have occasioned the belief in the resurrection of Jesus? Paul lets us guess the reason of its origin; he says (2 Cor. 12) that he has had a vision of Jesus, having been transported to the third heaven (without being able to tell whether in or out of the body). Experience teaches that some men imagine they have seen their defunct friends appearing to them. It may be that the women, the feelings of whom are more irritable, first thought to see their dead friend, and that their example induced also the disciples to such visions; enthusiasm is contagious. The character of Jesus had affected so deeply their minds that they could not forget him so soon; his image was present to their eyes more lively as he was torn from their side by a horrid death. In later times the narratives of the Gospels might have been founded on such imaginary apparitions, and adorned as their authors pleased to do. They admit also themselves that some remained doubting the reality of the visions, till to the last moment, when Jesus ascended to Heaven. One of them was Thomas, the Apostle, who afterwards was called the incredulous.

Some believe that Jesus was only lying in a deep swoon, being apparently dead, when buried; that, in the grave, he awoke again, and found a secret asylum with friends. This supposition is very improbable, for it happened very seldom that crucified persons revived after having been taken from the cross. Among the Jews of that time the rumor was also rife that the disciples had stolen the corpse during the night, and then spread the report of the resurrection of Jesus. (Matth., 28, 11, etc.)

The ascension of Jesus is mentioned by Mark, Luke, and by the Acts of the Apostles. Mark lets him ascend when he is taking his repast (consequently indoors), while the others say he ascended in Bethania, from a mountain top. Luke reports (ch. 29) that Jesus ascended on the same day he rose from the dead; the Acts relate that he conversed yet during forty days after his rising with his disciples, and then add: " A cloud took him away from the sight of the disciples, and two men stood with them in white robes, saying: ' Why do you stand here, gazing up into the heaven? This Jesus who in your presence has been taken up to Heaven, will so come again as you have seen him.' " Natural science and experience prove that a body which is heavier than air, cannot be elevated by itself in this element; but as Elias was said to have ascended, the Christians may have derived their fable from that. Greeks and Romans, too, had the superstition that men who were favorites of the gods had been taken to their Olymp; so, e. g., Hercules and Romulus.

These are the principal narratives the Gospels have communicated to us from the life of Jesus. He who attentively and impartially examines them, must be persuaded that they are altogether pious fictions. What *do* we, then, know of the life of Jesus with certainty? Very little; only about the following incidents: He was born in Nazareth, a town of Galilee. His father was a carpenter; the name of his mother was Mary. According to the unanimous testimony of the Gospels, he had several brothers; but these, and his mother, too, seem to have disliked the idea of his making the appearance as a prophet. John says distinctly (7, 1) that his brothers did not believe in him. They and Mary are said to have joined his adherents only after his death (Acts, 1, 14). He passed through the country as a wandering teacher, where he proclaimed the approaching kingdom of the Messiah, and gathered many scholars. Finally he went with them to Jerusalem, and there was put to death as a false Messiah, who had attacked the doctrines of the established religion, and the priesthood. It is also doubtful how long he has been efficacious as a reformer; may be only a few, or perhaps twenty years; neither is it known how long he lived. Some believ that he was born before the beginning of the common era. "The fundamental features of his mind must have been an uncommon combination of strength and meekness, of intellect and tender feelings."* This is evident from the Gospels; besides, only by this supposition the great sensation can be explained which he effected in his contemporaries and in the posterity. His person having become an object of the universal history, he was glorified by miraculous legends; for the biographies of common men no Gospels are composed.

There are also, in modern times, critics of the Gospels who assert that their reports are imitations of the Hindoo-mythology, that Jesus Christ is the Hindoo-Chrishna, that he has not been crucified, and has never existed, but that the Essens (Thereapeuts) have adopted him as the hero of their sect, and composed the Gospels, which from them were transmitted to the Christians. (See History of Religions, § 4.) This opinion is especially supported by Rob. Taylor in his works, "The Diegesis—The Syntagma," etc. Taylor was, therefore, confined to the goal (1829), and kept there for three years as a martyr of liberal views. William Jones says: "In the Sanscrit Dictionary we have the whole story of the incarnate Deity."

12. The Miracle of Pentecost—The Three Principal Festivals of the Christians.

Luke tells in his Acts of the Apostles (ch. 1, etc.), that Jesus still remained forty days on earth after his resurrection; during this time his disciples saw him, and he instructed them in matters concerning the Kingdom of God. Then he ascended, in their presence, from the Mount of Olives to Heaven, whereafter they returned to Jerusalem. Ten days later the miracle of Pentecost happened. They were all assembled in the same house. Suddenly a sound comes from Heaven, as of a rushing, mighty wind, and shakes the house. There appear to them cloven tongues, like as of fire; they sit upon the disciples, who become full of the Holy Ghost, and begin to speak in foreign tongues. The multitude assemble, for they heard the noise, and all are horrified and amazed, when every one hears the disciples speak his native language; there were Parthians, Medes, Egyptians, strangers of Rome, of Arabia, etc. Petrus delivers a speech, which affects the assembled multitude so deeply that at once three thousand men agree to be baptized, and to join the Christian association. Soon after, a second discourse of Petrus increases the number to 5,000 men. This would signify about an amount of 20,000 souls; for most of the men probably had wives and children,

---

*A. Wislicenus.

who may be supposed to have shared the creed of the husbands and fathers. But in contradiction to this statement, some chapters farther, it is said: "Of the rest none dared to join them" (ch. 5, 13).

The Holy Ghost, then, comes here from Heaven, to wit, as a roaring hurricane. This fiction is still conforming to the notions of the Old Testament. According to Moses the spirit of God passes over the water. Upon Christ the Holy Ghost descends in the shape of a dove, upon his disciples like tongues of fire, in order to signify that by this spirit they receive the faculty to speak foreign languages (for they ought to announce the doctrine of Jesus to all nations of the earth): an easy contrivance to teach foreign languages, indeed!

Both, the festival of Pentecost and of Easter, passed from the Jewish into the Christian Church. The first was really the festival of harvest of the Jews, because they gathered their crops at the time of Pentecost. The Easter feast was by them celebrated in memory of the exodus from Egypt, and of the return from the Babylonian captivity. But primitively (immediately after they had settled in Palestine) it was the festival of the vernal equinox and of the beginning of the harvest, at which they offered the premioes of fruit, animals, and even men as sacrifices. The Christian Church remodled both festivals according to its intentions. The same was done with the very ancient festival of the winter solstice (which commences the 21st of December), by transforming it in the feast of birth of Christ, because he ought to be the Saviour of the world, the spiritual sun of mankind. The celestial sun, which at that time is approaching again the Northern Hemisphere, is his model. Several ancient nations celebrated the birthdays of the gods of sun at the time of the winter solstice. The solar god *Mithras*, who was worshiped in the eastern part of Asia, was said to have been born in a cavern. His birthday was the 25th of December. In Egypt, on this day, the people collected from all parts of the land to celebrate the festival of the sun god *Osiris*, and cried: "We have found him, let us exult!" (Cf. Luke, 2, 10—20.) The feast of the nativity of Christ was primitively a worship of the sun, adopted from heathenism. Christ's resurrection is also in some relation to the worship of the sun; for it happens at sunrise on the first day of the week, the Sunday (dies solis), which since ancient time was consecrated to the sun, at the time of vernal equinox, when the sun shines perpendicularly on the equator, and illuminates equally all regions of the earth during twelve hours a day.

THE END.

SECTION THIRD.

VIEWS OF THE UNIVERSE FROM THE STANDPOINT OF THE MODERN SCIENCE.

In Questions and Answers.

" Nature considered rationally is one great whole animated by the breath of life."—*Alex. Humboldt.*

§ 1. Force and Matter. The Force—Imperishable.

Teacher. Illustrate the terms "matter and force" by examples!

Scholar. Matters are: gold, iron, earth; forces: heat, light, electricity.

T. Can force and matter be separated from each other?

Sch. No; force and matter are closely united; this can not be imagined without the other, and so inversely. There is no force without matter, no matter without a force. (1.)

T. Illustrate this principle by simile!

Sch. Matter is not like a vehicle before which the forces can be hitched and unhitched, just as we please.

What are the forces really?

They are qualities of matter, and forms of its motion.

What reciprocal relation does exist between the forces?

One force can directly or indirectly be changed into another, e. g., motion into heat, heat into electricity. If we, e. g., rub our hands, the friction generates heat. The rapid strokes of a sledge-hammer can ignite a wooden block. Sealing-wax becomes electric, if it is rubbed with a woolen cloth. The friction of the glass cylinder of an electrical machine elicits sparks (light). Inversely, heat can be transposed in motion, as it may be seen in the pistons and wheels of a locomotive, which are moved by hot steam. Again, in summer, heat excites electricity in the clouds. Electric force magnetizes a bar of soft iron, sets an iron wire melting, etc.

Consequently, can forces be lost?

No! They can only alternately be changed; they are imperishable, eternal.

§ 2. Matter—Imperishable and Infinite.

1. Is matter perishable?

Matter, too, is imperishable; that is, not its smallest particle can ever be lost; it only changes form. The quantity and species of the elements also ever remain the same. If, e. g., wood is burned, and if the products originated by its combustion are weighed, we find that its weight has not diminished, but increased, because during this process it has attracted also elements of the air. The elements of wood (carbon, hydrogen and oxygen) have remained; they are indestructible; only the form in which they appeared has past away. Evaported water retakes, if condensed by cold, its original form. The quantity of matter in the Universe remains always equally great, and can neither be augmented nor diminished.

What is the result of this view?

That the change between dissolution and origin, between decay and renovation of matter, is infinite.

2. Matter is infinite both in its infinitesimal and largest parts. In the hundredth part of a water-drop we discover through the microscope yet a world of creatures (infusoria), the intrinsic organization of which we don't know. The smallest particle of salt, the existence of which we can hardly guess by taste, contains thousands of millions of particles which no human eye will ever see. In the ethereal space of the Universe there are seen whitish, nebular spots, which, observed through the telescope, are resolved into a multitude of stars. Though light passes in a minute a distance of two millions of geographic miles, it requires 2,000 years to go from the galaxy on earth. Therefore, it is rather certain that the space of the Universe and its matter are infinite.

What view can be deduced from the stated qualities of matter?

This view, that also matter is eternal, namely, that it has not originated in time. To be sure, the eternity of matter cannot be comprehended; but from nothing, nothing arises; therefore it is more sensible to suppose that matter has always been in existence than that it has originated by creation from nothing. This was, long ago, the view of several ancient philosophers. Physical science, too, holds that matter is eternal and imperishable, because experience so far has never proved the origin or annihilation of the smallest particle of matter. (2.) If a God created the Universe, then, there must have been a time when he commenced to create. Back of this time, what was this God doing? He spent an eternity, so to speak, in perfect idleness!

What do they call the hypothesis that matter and force are closely joined?

Realism, Monism or *Materialism.*

Why do they call it Realism?

Because the Realist considers nature and all its phenomena as they really exist. (3.)

Why Monism?

Because, according to this supposition, matter and force form only one object (the monon). (4.)

Why Materialism?

Because Force is inseparable from Matter. (5.)

Are the precepts of Morals abolished, or endangered by Realism? (Materialism)?

No, for they rest upon the unchangeable nature of man. (6.) (Cf. 2. Sect. Morals, § 2.)

§ 3. The Universe—Uniformity and Necessity of the Natural Laws.

What is the Universe?

The tenor of all what exists.

What is the nature of the laws by which the Universe is governed?

They are uniform and unchangeable. E. g., for all celestial bodies the same laws are valid: the law of gravity, the law of centripetal force, the law of impenetrability of their matter, of the effect which light and heat has on them, etc.

Are there exceptions to the natural laws?

According to experience, there are no exceptions to them; they are strictly necessary; e. g., every stone falls according to the same law of gravitation; every seed-grain is developed in the same way; lightning is always attracted by metals, etc.

What follows from the fact that the laws of nature are invariable?

It follows that miracles are impossible.

Why are miracles impossible?

Because they are exceptions to the natural laws. "No arm grasping out of the clouds can raise mountains, transpose oceans; feed man, etc. All phenomena of nature are stamped by stern necessity." (7.)

How is the conservation of the Universe effected?

It is effected through the same forces of nature, and according to the same laws, as in the past. "One common, lawful, therefore eternal tie, clasps round the whole, living nature," says Alex. Humboldt.

What's the meaning of the term, "Special Providence?"

It means that God for the benefit of some men suspends a natural law; e. g., if by a compassionate rich man he suddenly furnishes bread to a poor man, who is almost dying by starvation.

Is there such a Providence conspicuous in life?

No, experience refutes the belief in it. E. g., if two solid bodies clash violently together, both are shaken, according to the general law of velocity. Therefore, if two locomotives moved by steam, going in opposite directions on the same road, are propelled, swift as lightning, and then strike each other, the cars, hitched to them, must be crushed, and the passengers in them injured, without any distinction whether they be sinners or saints. The tempest works according to the same law, and consequently by its violence destroys entire fleets which are sailing on the sea. (8.)

May, then, man, while in distress, hope for wonderful help of God?

No; he must exert his own faculties, he must endeavor to help himself. A proverb says: Help yourself, and God will help you.

How, then, must the progress of men be considered, when they implore God to prolong their life, to grant them good health, their livelihood, good crops, victory, virtue, etc.?

Their prayers are useless and unreasonable, because they ask God to suspend the universal, everlasting laws of nature.

§ 4. The Starry Heavens.

What bodies do we perceive in the celestial space?
The stars.
How are the stars divided?
In fixed stars, planets, moons and comets.
What are fixed stars?
Stars which shine with their own light. They can easily be distinguished from the planets by their tremulous light. However, the light of some planets is also scintillant, e. g., the light of Venus and Mercury. (9.)
What is the origin of the name "fixed stars"?
The ancients believed that these stars are, as it were, fixed to their places, and never change them. But since, it is known that they also are moving, as in the case of the Pleiades (the Great Wagon, or the Great Bear), which have since 2,000 years changed their position towards the nearer, smaller stars, more than 5,000 miles. (10.) By far the most stars are fixed ones. About 6,000 of them are visible to the naked eye. The galaxy (the milky way, as it is called,) is quite crowded with them. W. Hershel believed that by means of his large telescope, eighteen millions could be seen in it.
What are planets?
Planets are stars which turn around a fixed star, and receive their light from it.
What are moons?
Moons (secondary, concomitant planets) are stars which turn around a planet, and with it around a sun.
What are comets?
They are shining, celestial bodies, which consist of a nebulous, luminous nucleus, and a bright, capillary tail. Many of them come also forth without a tail. There are many comets. Their tails are millions of miles long. Their orbit is irregular, and sometimes crosses even that of the planets. (11.) So far their nature is little known; there are about 200, the orbit of which has been computed; only 14 of them are known more particularly.
What is the sun?
It is the fixed star around which our earth with many other planets revolves; it forms with them our solar system, which advances towards a certain point of the firmament. (12.)
What is the theory called, by which the sun is supposed to be the center around which the planets are revolving?
It is called the Copernican, from its author, Nicholas Copernicus (1553).

What opinion was held before his time?

The opinion that the earth was resting, and was the centre of movement of the sun and of the planets.

Which two forces cause the planets to turn around the sun?

The centripetal and the centrifugal force. (13.) By dint of the former, the bodies which fall to the earth are attracted to its centre; by the latter, they move on a plane always in a straight direction, when they are once put in motion, and when there is no obstacle on their route.

But what line does a body describe in its fall, if obliquely thrown into the air?

It then describes a curve.

What effect would these two forces take, if each would alone determine the course of the planets?

The attractive power of the sun alone would drive the planets directly to the centre of this fixed star, and their own centrifugal force would keep them continually in the course they have taken at the first impulse.

How is their course shaped, since both forces act simultaneously on them?

Elliptically.

How many planets of our solar system are already discovered?

Eight larger and more than 100 smaller ones.

What are the names of the planets which are accompanied by moons?

The earth, with one moon; Jupiter, with 4; Saturn, with 8; Uranus, with 6 moons; Neptune has at least one moon.

Which are the two largest planets?

Jupiter and Saturn; their diameters are ten times as large as that of the earth; but the diameter of the sun surpasses the diameter of those two planets also ten times in length. (14.) The mean diameter of the earth is 7,912 miles.

What planets are nearer to the sun than the earth? Which is the most distant from it?

Mercury and Venus are nearer to it, Neptune is the farthest distant; therefore the light of the first is the brightest, that of the latter the weakest. The light of Mercury is six times more intense than that of earth; but that of Neptune is only the hundreth part as intense as that of the latter.

In what ratio is the volume of the sun to that of the earth?

More than a million of terrestrial globes could be made out of the sun. But its matter is only one-fourth as solid as that of earth. The sun turns in $25\frac{1}{2}$ days around its axis. Its light requires 8 minutes and 17 seconds to pass from it to earth.

How great is the distance of several stars from earth?

Almost immeasurable, for their light must travel 30 millions of years, before it reaches our earth. (cf. § 2.)

What hypothesis have the most natural philosophers and astronomers accepted with regard to the matter of the solar-system?

They suppose that the matter of the solar-system was, before immemorial time, dispersed in the celestial space, and that according to the law of gravitation, it was more and more condensed, and by-and-by devoloped from the nebulous into a gaseous, and from this into a solid state.

§ 5. The Earth and Its Gradual Transformation. (15.)

How is the origin of the earth explained?

The most eminent natural philosophers of the time suppose that the earth, too, like the other planets, has been developed from gaseous matter; during the process of its formation it evolved heat, and became a fiery fluid, which by degrees passed into a solid state. Its uppermost layers first grew cool and solid.

To what degree must, according to this hypothesis, its surface have cooled, before the gaseous vapor could be transformed into water?

As far as to 212 degrees, Fahr.

Has the earth, since it has started in existence, grown a thoroughly solid body?

Probably not; there is a belief that towards its centre it continues to be in a condition of fiery fluid; for the deeper they penetrate into its crust, the higher in crease the degrees of the inner heat.

What more justifies this opinion?

The hot vapor and water springs of earth, the volcanoes and earthquakes, which often shake large tracts of land and sea.

What do they conclude from the great number of extinct volcanoes?

That once the inner fire of earth has reached still nearer to its surface.

How deep have they, thus far, penetrated into the inside of earth?

About two geographical (equals 9.2 Engl.) miles.

How thick is the crust of the earth?

Only about fifty geographical (equals 230.5 English) miles (according to the statement of the geographer Ch. Ritter).

In what way did earth continually gain dry land?

1. By volcanoes. They vomit ashes, sand, lava and rocks. So, by their repeated eruptions, new tracts of land are gradually formed.

2. By earthquakes, by their concussions sometimes new islands and mounts are brought to appearance.

3. By brooks, rivers and torrents. Namely, in water always earth, mud, sand and stones sink to the ground. Brooks, rivers, torrents convey and put them down partly on their banks, partly at their mouths. Thereby the banks of rivers grow higher, and at the mouth of large streams new tracts of land are formed, sometimes in the shape of triangles (deltas), like the delta of the Ganges, Mississippi, Nile, Rhone and Po. The Po delta has during 2,000 years grown twenty miles in width. By the depositions of the Nile, opposite to the island of Pharos (at Alexandria) the sea has entirely disappeared, and the island forms now part of the continent. Likewise, the ancient lake Mareotis in Egypt has been laid dry by the mud of the Nile. Rapid wood-brooks carry rocks and large bulks of

stones down into the valleys, and build up there hills and mounts. In a similar way the downs and sandbanks of the ocean are originated.

4. By many species of the smallest animals. To these the corals (a species of the polyps) belong, being only of the size of a pin-head; their bodies represent only a bag, which on the outside forms the skin, on the inside the stomach, and have many arms, by which they catch their food. One polyp commences every coral-stem at the bottom of the sea. Many animals on which it feeds have calcareous shells, and it is lime which it abundantly casts off. It forms a little knot, on the top of which it is seated; this grows into a twig, a stalk; out of the mouth of the mother-polyp, new animalcules are developed; the stem grows stronger, and is not much dissimilar to a leafless shrub. By degrees the oldest parts die, and the descendants are building higher up, until they reach the surface of the sea, which puts a limit to their growth. These animals defy the waves of the ocean which are too powerless to hurt their life. They belong to the oldest inhabitants of earth. The lime of the Jura mountains is mostly formed from corals. In the Indian, in the Pacific ocean and in other seas they have built innumerable islands and riffs; and entire chains of mountains owe their existence to them.

Moreover, there are muscle-like infusoria, the shells of which by the naked eye can hardly or not at all be noticed, and are composed either of lime or flint. The mountains of all zones contain these petrified; e. g., Paris, together with the surrounding towns and villages, Berlin, Richmond in Virginia, the Pyramids of Egypt are built with their shells; even in Victoria Land (in the Antarctic Ocean) they have been found. There are already 2,000 species of them known. Even in the undermost of the known layers of earth, they are frequently extant; neither fire nor water, nor the pressure of whole mountains, could do them any harm. They have a larger share than any other creature in the formation of earth. (Cf. § 7, 2, 6.)

§ 6. The Earth's Mountains—Periods of Its Transformation. (16.)

Which forces gave rise to the mountains of the earth?

Water and fire. The formations caused by the force of water, are called *Neptunian*. They are very extensive on the earth, and appear for the most part in horizontal layers.

Does experience confirm this mode of their origin?

Yes, for even now-a-days the oceans, lakes and rivers are forming continually new layers of earth and stone.

What species of stones do the Neptunian mountains contain?

Sandstone, flint, limestone, clay-slate, etc.

What do they call those Neptunian formations of earth which did not originate till in more recent time?

They call them, usually, *Alluvial-land*. Examples of this formation are the large deltas of Nile and Mississippi, which these rivers have formed at their mouth.

What mountains came by the power of fire into existence?

The Volcanic, the Plutonic, and the Neptune-Plutonic.

How did the Volcanic mountains originate?

By the inner fire of earth, which worked *near* or *on* its surface. Specimens of volcanoes are *Ætna* and *Vesuvius* in Europe, and *Cotopaxi* and *Popocotapetl* in Mexico. Volcanoes are spread all over the earth, though they be not as numerous as in times of yore.

How did the Plutonic mountains originate?

Also by subterraneous fire, but this worked in a very profound depth of the earth; there the solid parts of earth were melted, changed into lava and slowly cooled. These mountains lie also horizontally, still not above, but below the Neptunian mountains. Sometimes they were pushed through the crust of the earth, and very highly elevated, as, e. g., the summits of the Andes, of which *Chimborasso* is 21,000, *Sorata* 21,200, and *Auancagua* 23,900 feet high.

From what species of stones are the Plutonic mountains composed?

From the hardest, e. g., granite and porphyry.

How is the origin of the *Neptune-Plutonic* mountains explained?

Their ingredients were probably by the water floated over layers of rock, and in later times crystalized by fire, hot water or steam?

What species of minerals do they contain?

Gneiss, the red sandstone, extensive layers of coal, etc.

What are Plutonic mountains frequently called?

Primary mountains?

Why?

Because the geologists formerly believed that these, with regard to their origin, are the oldest kind of rocks on earth.

Is this assumption correct?

No, for though they form mostly the lowest layers, still part of them is, with regard to time, more recent than the three other kinds of mountains. All kinds of mountains have originated partly at the same time, and partly in different times. The inner parts of earth were often changed. The actual position of the mountains was not their original, but it was in different times different.

How did they formerly explain the origin of the Neptunian mountains?

Some believed that in the beginning the whole earth had been submerged by water, until the Creator separated them. Others asserted that the great deluge (mentioned in the Bible) formed those mountains during earth's universal inundation.

Can their opinion be proved to be true?

No! There is no good historical proof of their opinions, and experience, too, contradicts them. For in both cases they ought to admit that there was once a much greater bulk of water in the oceans than at present; then the question would arise, how the water could subside to its present low level, as we see it everywhere; a question which the defenders of these opinions cannot answer. (Cf. Bibl. Narrat. 1—4.)

How do the best naturalists of our time explain the origin of the Neptunian land?

Layer by layer was formed at the bottom of the oceans and lakes, and by the alluvions of rivers. By and by such land was raised above the ocean by the inner forces of earth, principally by fire, as it is still going on in many places, e. g., on the shores of Bothnic Bay, and in the southern parts of Patagonia.

What proves the correctness of this explanation?

The great number of petrified animals, especially of shells and fish which were found by digging into these mountains. They occur frequently in the Pyrenees, Alps, Cordilleras, and Himalaya mountains, even on places as high as 8,000—18,000 feet. Is it possible that the sea has ever reached such an elevated ground?

What do they conclude from these observations?

That the sea has not sunk, but the land has been raised.

Into how many periods does Geology divide the time of the gradual transformation of earth?

Into five; these are called: Primary, secondary, tertiary, diluvial, and alluvial periods. The older section of the diluvial period is also called the glacial time.

In what condition was earth's surface during the glacial period?

A coherent mass of ice, beginning on the North pole, covered the northern and middle part of Asia, Europe and America; in Europe it seems to have extended towards the Alps. From the South pole, too, the ice-cover enveloped a great deal of the Southern hemisphere. Only a small zone remained between the two sections of ice for organic life.

What country informs us of that period?

The Northeastern part of Germany; for there are still left numberless huge rocks (boulders), belonging exactly to the same species as the mountains in the Scandinavian peninsula, and which must have been floated from these to Germany during the ice-period; probably they formed part of those swimming mountains of ice which had been torn from the glaciers of that peninsula, and were carried by the waves of the sea to Germany. (18.)

§ 7. The Age of the Earth.

What facts impart information to us, with regard to the age of earth?

1. The evolution process of the earth. Until the earth, originally ignited, could cool from 2,000 to 200 degrees of heat, indeed millions of years must have passed away.

2. The age of the different mountains and of their fossils.

(a.) Neptunian (Tertiary) mountains. Three thousand shells, found in Neptunian mountains, have been compared with five thousand species of present time. In the lowest layers of the ground there were 3½ per cent. of the shells like those in the present time, 17 per cent. in the middle ones, 35—50 per cent. in the still higher ones, and 90—95 per cent. in the most recent ones. How many thousands of years may have elapsed between these formations? According to the computation of the most skillful geologist, 350,000 years. (17.)

(b.) Mountains of lime and chalk. Next below the Tertiary mountains lie the groups of the mountains of lime and chalk. They are partly built up from the petrified shells of little animals. The Suabian Alp owes its origin to the claws of crabs. Such a layer at Bilin (in Bohemia), extends through a large tract of land, and is fourteen feet thick. It supplies what they call polishing slate (tripoli), which is used to polish metals. It is mostly composed of petrified animalcules, and contains 41,000 millions of their shells in every cubic inch. (18.) Their corpuscles were bedded in small, round granules, which were like raspberries formed in balls, and represented pretty houses with many chambers. These animalcules have built in all zones entire chains of mountains. The chalk mountains in England, Ireland, France, in the middle part of Europe and Asia, which together comprise an area as large as that of Europe, owe to them their existence. What number of them, and what length of time were necessary, till so many mountain chains were constructed. Between the formations of the lime rocks and those of the Tertiary period may as many thousands of years have elapsed as between the construction of the Tertiary mountains and those of the present time. (19.)

(c.) Coal strata. They have originated by floods, which accumulated masses of trees and plants, and covered them with sand and clay; by and by these minerals hardened into slate, upon which new masses of organic matter was deposited. (20.) This process was repeated by nature several times, until coal mountains of surprising length and height were formed. They say that their formation has taken a million of years.

(d.) Plutonic and Primary mountains. In these no remains of animals are found, whereby we may conclude that, in general, they are still older than the other rock formations.

3. The structures of the corals (polyps). A learned geologist, James D. Dana, conjectures that they build one-eighth of an inch of their structures in one year. Now, there are some coral-reefs 2,000 feet high, the formation of which, therefore (computed ⅛ inch a year), required 192,000 years. Since the body of these polyps is only as large as a drop of water, and since an infinite number of islands, reefs, and rocks (of the mainland which some day was covered with water) is their work; the age of their creation can hardly be computed. (21.)

4. Discoveries in the valley of Nile. When in the Nile delta borings were attempted, they found in a depth of 60—70 feet tools and pieces of pottery. They have computed, how many inches the alluvium of land in the delta is increasing during 100 years, and the result of the calculation was that it rises 2½ inch or (according to the computation of others) 3½ " or 5." According to

these different suppositions the increase of 60—70 in depth would have taken about 33,000, or 24,000, or 16,100 years. Beside, it is known that, since there men have made their appearance, the alluvium has increased 200 feet high; therefore 50,000—100,000 years must there have passed away. *22)*

It has also been computed, how much ground the Mississippi annually conveys to its delta, and thereby concluded that for the accumulation of its alluvia at least 50,000, may be even 100,000 years were wanted. *23)*

5. The age of the human race. From the age of the human race also may be inferred that the earth must be many thousand years older than people formerly believed (cf. § 9).

What conclusion follows from the related facts?

From these facts the conclusion follows that the age of earth is higher than any calculation can define.

How old would the earth be according to the Jewish-Christian era?

Only 5,000—6,000 years.

What must we decidedly say with regard to this belief?

That it is erroneous. (24.)

§ 8. Organic Life—Doctrine of Descent.

What change on earth must have been accomplished, before organic life (animals and plants) could get existence?

Its crust must have been cooled and condensed, must have become solid and firm.

What forces have contributed in particular to development of organic life?

Heat and light.

What are the latest naturalists teaching with regard to all organic life?

That animals and plants originally, and both at the same time, have been developed from cells; therefore that they were not created. (25.)

Whereof descend the cells, in the opinion of some naturalists?

From still simpler elements, which they call *moneres* and *protoplasts* (primitive organisms.) (26.)

But how did the latter get existence?

So far, science cannot explain their origin.

Of which elements do both cells of animals and plants consist?

Of the same elements, namely: Oxygen, hydrogen, nitrogen and carbon; only the quantity and the arrangement of these are different.

What creatures originated on earth, when the mass of vapors in which it was enveloped, by precipitation was dissolved in water?

Such an ones which are fit for life in water, e. g., fishes.

When did plant-eaters make their appearance?

Since earth had produced plants and forests.

When could carnivorous animals begin to exist?

After the formation of plant-eaters.

On what condition, then, did the origin of the organic forms depend?

On the exterior condition of the earth.

How can the truth of this assertion be proved?

In this way: In the course of time different layers of the earth were formed; in every one the remainders of other species of organisms are found; only in the Plutonic strata, which mostly are the lowest, they are entirely missing. In the higher layers first appear coal strata; besides ferns, 40—50 feet long, occasionally also palm and pine trees, and other plants; but they don't much resemble the Flora of our time.

What species of animals are embedded in these layers?

Shell-fish, snails, oysters and many sea-fish, but neither mammals nor birds.

What fossils occur in the layers which are stretched above the coal strata?

Amphibia of immense length, as lizards which are 40 feet long; winged lizards, too, the wings of which measure over 16 feet; besides land and sea dragons, from 30 to 40 feet long; and in general, the most formidable beasts of prey; also petrified fish, but few mammals.

In which are the most fossils found?

In the layers which are yet much higher bedded, those of the Tertiary period (in the Neptunian mountains). In these, sea animals, especially shell-fish, change to the higher classes of animals. The mammals there found are often of gigantic size and strange form, as the mastodon, the giant salamander, and the mammoth-elephant. The latter is frequently found in Siberia, frozen up in the ice and mud of the rivers and islands; the mastodon, in North America, sunk in the clay and mire of the rivers and swamps (as that of the Ohio River). These species are now extinct. Of man there have been thus far found few remains; but in the most recent time they have found in these mountains bones and flint stones, in which there is indicated an artificial management. (27.)

Which gradation of origin do the remains of the organisms exhibit?

The oldest exhibit the simplest shapes; they belong to the class of shells and fish. Afterwards amphibia followed; after these creepers, birds and mammals; of the latter the lowest forms appear again the first. Man made his appearance the last. The same law is also conspicuous in the kingdom of plants. First the tangs took origin, after them the ferns, then plants with blossoms (phanerogamia), among which the trees with pointed leaves (as pines and firs) were the first. Still the transitions from one period of formation to another don't exhibit any abrupt contrast; they were effected by degrees. (28.)

What corollaries can be deduced from these observations?

1. The older a layer of our earth, the simpler; the more recent, the more perfect are the extant organic forms of our planet.

2. Organic life grows more perfect in the same degree as the planet itself has developed.

3. In every period many other organic bodies are found.

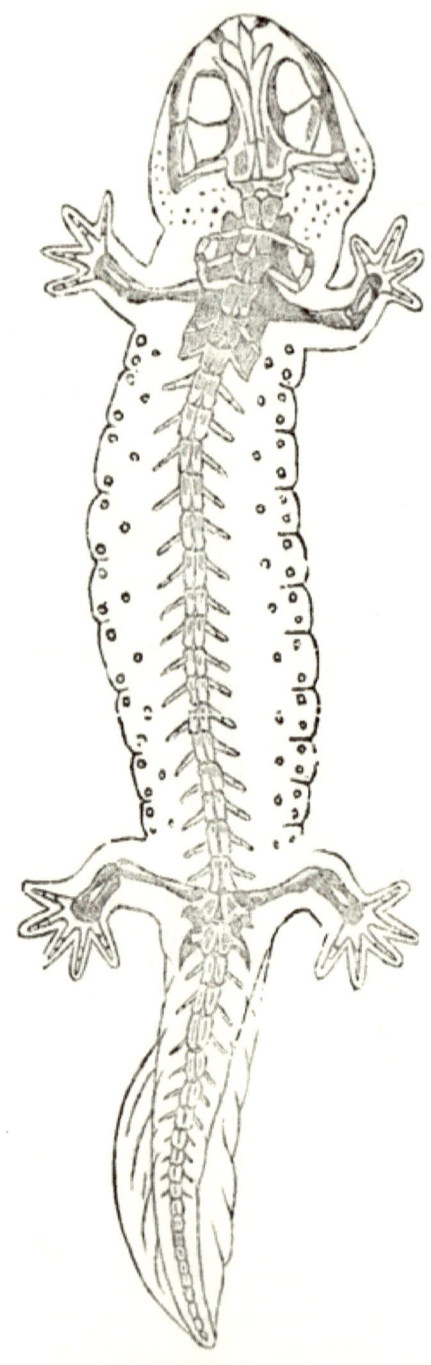

GIANT SALAMANDER.

4. As often as earth entered a new period of general mutation, the existing kinds of plants and animals partly perished.

What causes gradually effected the improvement of the organisms?

Principally these two causes: *inheritance* and *adaptation;* also the transformation of earth, the length of time which has elapsed from the beginning of organic life unto the present age, the struggle for existence, etc.

What's the meaning of *inheritance?*

The essential qualities of all kinds of organisms are transmitted to their descendants, e. g., the bodily and mental qualities of the parents to their children, and grandchildren.

How is *adaptation* working?

It works by the change of diet and of the way of living, by habitude and exercise, by migration, etc.

How does Nature act in the struggle for life?

All animals and plants have enemies who endeavor to destroy them. " In the course of hundred thousands of years the strongest plants and animals always vanquish the other ones."—Ch. Darwin. (29.) In this way new species and sub-species gradually come into existence.

What is the doctrine of the gradual improvement of the organic world called?

The doctrine of *evolution* or *descent.*

Who is the author of this doctrine?

Charles Darwin. Therefore it is sometimes also called *Darwinism.*

What observation suggested to Darwin the idea of his doctrine?

He noticed the proceeding of the gardeners, when they want to create new species of plants and flowers: namely, they select one of them which they want to propagate, and make use of it for propagation, secluding all the other species. (30.)

How is the importance of the doctrine of evolution manifested?

It throws open a new path to the moral accomplishment of man, by teaching him to return to nature. It ennobles family life by the knowledge of nature's laws. It initiates radical reforms in the education of youth, and in the social and political relations of the people.

§ 9. Man—1st, Age, and 2nd, Origin of His Species. 3d, His Primitive State. 4th, Human Races.

1. In which earth-layers first occur remains of man?

In the Tertiary layers. Since the time of forty years such remains (bones, skulls, etc.) were found in several countries of Europe, also in North America and Syria. They were mingled with the remains of extinct animal races, e. g., of the mammoth, with arrow-heads, battle-axes and hatchets. These tools are made from shells, whereby the jaws of the cavern-bear were used as instruments. In the Mississippi valley also petrified human bones have been discovered, the age of which are 40,000—50,000 years, as computed by American geologists.

What is the reason that man came into being later?

Nature's course of evolution. The farther earth's development advanced, the more its organic forms improved; therefore it is natural that man, the most perfect creature on earth, did not make his appearance but in a later period.

Is the opinion that the human race has existed only since 5,000 years ago, well founded?

No, because even earlier than 5,000 years A. C. Egypt, Babylon, Cashmere, China and Hindoostan were the seats of human civilization, and in the first of these countries the hieroglyphics were already used about 3,400 A. C. In that time in Egypt were built the pyramids, the palaces and the royal tombs of Thebes with their subterranean labyrinths, apartments and halls; besides, in India those gigantic temples, the roofs of which are supported by 1,000 columns, each thirty feet high. "Such culture supposes that men long ago must have lived in those countries." (31.) (Cf. also § 7, 4.) "Before man began to exist, probably millions of years, and since at least 20,000, perhaps several hundred thousand have passed away." (32.)

2. What is the prevailing belief with regard to the origin of man?

That he has come forth grown up, and finished from the hand of the Creator.

What does the modern science teach us in this regard?

It has not yet definitely answered this question. Many most learned natural philosophers believe that man has developed from one of the higher animal classes, and that he is descended from a class which, in perfection, was next to him. (33.)

From what reasons do they conclude that their belief is correct?

From the evident resemblance of man to that class of animals. Almost in every modern text-book of zoology we can read: "Man (homo) constitutes the first order of mammals."

How can it be demonstrated that man is related to mammals?

It can be seen that he is related to the mammals, nay, also to lower classes as they are, if he even cursorily only is compared with the animals. He lives like them on grains, herbs, roots, fruits, quadrupeds, birds and fish. He breathes and digests like other animals. He begins also to exist in a cell; if he dies, his body is decomposed into the same inorganic ingredients, like the body of other animals. "The arm of man, the wing of the bird, and the fore feet of the mammals and amphibia have the equal number of bones, and the same position." (34.) "They are built after the same pattern. All bones of human skeleton can be compared with corresponding bones in a monkey, a bat, or a seal. The same comparison holds good with regard to his muscles, veins, nerves and intestines. Brain, the most important organ, follows the same law." "The construction of the human skull and limbs on same plan with that of other mammals, and a crowd of analogous facts—all point in plainest manner to conclusion that man is co-descended with other mammals of a common progenitor." (35.) "The germs of a turtle, a chicken, a dog, an ape, and of man, are most similar to each other." (36.)

What is the cause of the conformity and of the disparity between man and animal?

The conformity is the effect of inheritance; the disparity is the consequence of adaptation.

To which species of mammals is man most similar?

To some species of apes of the old world (to the Orang, Shimpanzee, Gibbon and Gorilla). They have, especially, 32 teeth, like man, and their noses are divided into two nostrils by a narrow partition, like the human nose. Their brain resembles more the human than that of the inferior species of their own class. Nevertheless, every bone of the apes differs more or less from the corresponding one of man, and in general no ape resembles man in all parts of the body. (37.)

What may be inferred from this comparison?

That man cannot be a descendant of any species of apes still extant; his apelike progenitors have long ago died away. (38.)

What may be the principal reasons for the superiority of mind by which man surpasses apes?

The erect position of his body, and the considerable development of his brain.

Have we any reason to be ashamed of our low descent, or to grieve at it?

Not at all, for it is less ignoble than the descent from a clod, as the Bible relates. "Is the glorious poet, philosopher or artist degraded by the probability (not to say certainty) that he descends in last line of some naked, bestial savage, whose intelligence was just sufficient to make him a little more cunning than the fox, and by so much more dangerous than the tiger? Is the love of a mother vile, because a hen, too, shows it, or fidelity base, because also dogs possess it?" (39.)

On the contrary, what does the low descent of man demonstrate?

The excellence of his faculties.

And what may we hope for these?

That in the future he will yet rise to higher perfection.

§ 10. Continued—3d, Man's Primitive State. Lake Villages— 4th, Human Races.

3. What does science teach us with regard to the primitive state of man?

That he by degrees has risen from his rude state to civilization.

In what way is this assertion proved?

1st, By historic testimonies; and 2nd, by the experience of our time.

First arms and other tools, shaped in the primitive times of man, have been discovered; they indicate different periods of age and culture. The oldest are made of stone; after these others follow, made of bronze (tin and copper);

lastly, iron ones. Therefore, three periods of age and culture are assumed: a period of stone, bronze and iron. (39.)

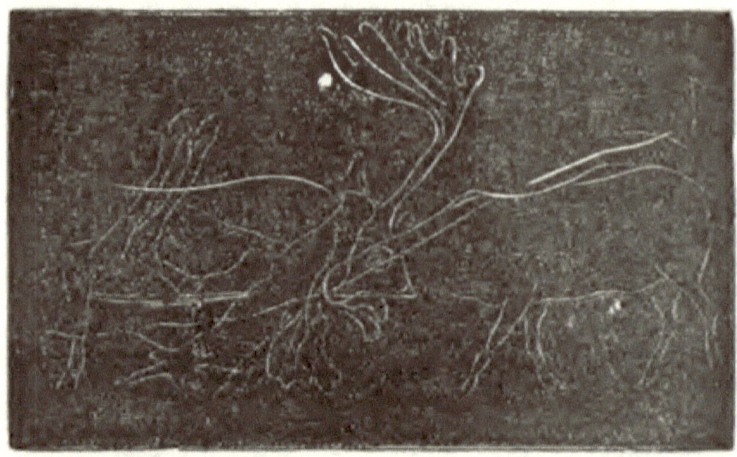

REINDEER GROUP SKETCHED IN THE STONE PERIOD.

Where are stone utensils yet found?

In the lake-villages of the Swiss and other lakes; such are: hatchets, hammers, chisels, knives, saws; beside arrow-heads of horn and bones; also dried fruits, wheat grains, etc.

In what manner were the lake-villages built?

In places where the water of the lakes was seven feet deep, piles were driven into the ground, trunks of trees put over them, on these wooden huts raised, and joined by bridges or skiffs to the shore. Several of these villages probably comprised some hundred huts with one thousand and more inhabitants.

What could be the aim of such structures?

People would probably protect themselves therein against the attacks of wild beasts or predatory neighbors.

What business did the lake inhabitants manage?

Hunting, fishing, and raising grain and flax.

How was the grain prepared?

It was simply crushed by pressing, and bread baked of it on hot stone slabs.

What do the weavings, found in these villages, signify?

That their inhabitants were able to spin and weave. Part of the webs was evidently fabricated on the loom.

In what periods were the lacustrine villages built?

In the stone period, and in the commencement of the bronze period.

Are there yet now-a-days rude tribes of men found?

There are still tribes, almost as wild as brutes; they are naked, eat raw meals, worms, insects, nay, even human flesh; they dwell on trees, do not know the use of fire, use stone weapons, know only a few words, are not able to count ove four, etc. But some tribes may have relapsed into their primitive rude condition, as can be conjectured from the regular construction of their language.

How does mankind rise to civilization?

Anyhow very slowly and by degrees.

Will it abide in the present degree of culture?

No, it will advance farther; to the iron age the age of reason and humanity will succeed.

4. Into how many species (races) do they class mankind, and which are their principal characteristics?

Usually there are assumed to be five races of man: the *Caucasian* (the white) with oval head and smooth hair, the *Mongolian* (the yellow) with smooth hair, the *Ethiopian* (the black) with crisp, wool-like hair, the *Malayan* (the brown), and the *Indian* (the red) race. Some naturalists assume less, others more than five races; e. g., 8, 15 to 63.

Are the distinctions of race primitive, or have they originated in the course of time?

In this regard, too, the opinions of naturalists differ from each other.

What arguments do they allege for the primitive plurality of races?

The differences in the formation of their heads, in the quality of their hair, and in the color of the skin advocate their opinion; besides, the great diversity in the three principal branches of human language (the Indo-German, the Semetic and the Chinese).

But what view do the most naturalists of modern time follow?

The opposite view; for those differences do not contain any firm characteristics, and can also be the sequences of exterior influences, e. g., of the climate. The races incline to each other. Further, the diversity of the species of other animals, e. g., of the dog, are much greater than those of the human race, though none believes that those species originally existed. (40.)

Is only the Caucasian race fitted for civilization?

No, for the experience of ancient and modern time teaches that by education individuals of other races also can reach a high degree of culture.

What races are dying away?

The races of the Indians, Hottentots, Australians, and Papuas.

Where is man's first home to be looked for?

It may have been in the Southern part of Asia, or according to another conjecture, in a Continent which has been submerged long ago, and where now the Indian Ocean is expanded.

§ 11. Human Body—Senses—Nerves—Brain—Human Mind. (41.)

What are the fundamental elements of the human body?

Albumen and fibrous matter in the muscles, the former, generally, for the most part in the firm textures, and in the blood; *jelly* in the skin, sinews, and bones; *fatty matter* in the brain, spinal column and nerves; *phosphorus* in the brain; *salt* in the blood; and *lime* in the bones. Blood contains 80 per cent. of water.

What are muscles?

Fine fibres (filaments) from which all the lean flesh of the body is composed.

What are sinews?

The tougher and denser ends of the muscles.

In what manner are the bones of the body joined to the muscles?

They are joined to them by sinews.

For what do sinews and muscles serve?

For moving the solid parts of the body.

What are nerves?

Tender, whitish or grayish filaments, which are distributed through all parts of the body.

Where do they all rise?

In the brain and the spinal marrow.

Of how many cords is every nerve composed? And what is their use?

Every nerve is composed of two cords; with the one we are feeling, with the other we start the motion of the limb to which it is joined. Therefore, the nerves of the latter kind are termed *motor nerves*.

To what are the muscles and sinews united?

To the nerves.

How many senses has man, and what are they?

Man has five senses, namely: Touch, taste, smell, vision and hearing.

What use does the sense of feeling subserve?

We learn by it, whether an object is rough or smooth, sharp or dull, cold or hot, soft or hard, etc.

Where does it reside?

In the nerves of the skin, and especially in the ends of the fingers.

What are the uses of the senses of taste and smell?

To guide and warn us in the selection of food and odors.

Which are the organs of taste and smell?

The tongue and palate are the organs of taste; the nostrils, of smell.

With what nerves are the tongue and nostrils provided?

The former with the gustatory (or nerve of taste), the latter with the olfactory nerve.

Which are the two most important senses, and what are their organs?

The two most important senses are the sense of vision and of hearing; their organs are the eyes and ears.

How are their nerves connected with the eye and ear?

The optic nerve (or nerve of vision) enters the back part of the eye, the auditory nerve is expanded upon the inner side of the ear, and both nerves originate in the brain.

What purpose do the senses subserve?

They afford us a knowledge of all external objects.

In what organ does this knowledge originate?

In the brain.

In what way is the perception affected?

External objects produce on the ends of the nerves impressions, which are conducted to the brain; so, by its office, our perceptions and notions of objects are produced.

What do external impressions leave behind in the brain and generally in the nerves?

They leave their traces (pictures) in the brain. (42.)

When can these traces (pictures) be revived and renewed?

When similar impressions are again made.

What is the result, when we find the new impressions to be similar to the past?

We *remember* or *recollect*.

What do they call the faculty of remembering perceptions we have had before?

Memory.

What do strong excitements of the brain and nerves cause?

They cause feelings or emotions.

Is man only capable of thinking and feeling?

No, he has also the ability of volition and action.

What is also the cause of our volition and of our actions?

The organism of the body. (43.)

Which part of our organism is particularly the source of our volitions and actions?

The brain.

How does brain cause our activity?

If we have resolved to begin some action, the brain incites the correlative motor-nerve, and the muscle which supplies it; forthwith the muscle contracts, and the part of the body which is connected with it begins then to act.

What do they call the force, by dint of which we perceive, think, recollect, feel, exert volition and act?

They call it in a word: human mind (spirit).

What else do they call the mind?

Soul, especially, if they speak of animals; for a mind is not attributed to them.

Is, then mind (spirit, soul) a real being?

No; these words signify only an imaginary being, like " intellect, memory, love, hatred," which also do not mean really existing beings, but only qualities of mind.

Why cannot the soul be an independent being?

Because till now nobody was able to discover what the soul is composed of, wherefrom it comes, how it is joined to the body, where it retires during a swoon and apparent death, and where it goes and resides after death.

§ 12. Relation between Brain and Mind—Human Will—Corollaries.

What is the brain, it being the organ of mind?

It is the source of the mind. Therefore, we are used to say of a man who overcharges his mental faculties: "He works too hard with his brain," and the consequences of his excessive exertion are headache, inflammation of the brain, loss of memory, insanity, etc. (44.)

What produces the mental functions of man?

The nervous system, and in particular, the brain. Mind developes together with the brain, it strenghtenes with it, is taken ill with it, grows old with it; in this case, too, force can not be separated from matter. (45.)

What is it that causes some expressions of activity which are usually attributed to the soul?

The nerves of the spinal column, and of other parts of the trunk. If, e. g., the head of a frog is cut off, and one of its legs touched with an acid, it stirs all its feet, and rubs the acid off with the other leg of the same side; and if this is also cut off, it uses the foot of the other leg, rubbing it off with that. If the cerebral hemispheres of a pigeon are taken off, and it is then thrown in the air, it will fly; it will follow with the head the movement of a burning candle, etc.

What is the ratio of the force of mind to the brain?

The force of mind depends upon the size of the brain, e. g., animals which instead of brain have only knots of nerves, thus stand on the lowest step of mental ability. The brain of the great and celebrated naturalist, Cuvier, weighed four pounds, the brain of the German poet, Fred. Schiller, of Lord Byron, Cromwell, and Napoleon I. had almost as many pounds. The average weight of human brain is three to three and one-half pounds.

What is the principal reason of the superiority man maintains over animals?

The reason is that his brain is relatively larger and heavier than that of some other animal. (46.)

Upon what else does the force of brain depend?

Upon its shape and the manner in which its parts are arranged. No part of the human body is so delicately constructed as the brain. (47.)

What is the ratio of the female brain to the male brain in weight and magnitude?

"The brain of woman is lighter and smaller than that of man; but in proportion to her height, she possesses as much brain as man does." (48.)

Can there be mental force without brain and nerves?

No; mind and brain cannot be separated; they influence each other, e. g., to the same extent that the brain of a bird or another animal is taken off, its mental faculties are lost. By feeding such an animal, it can conserve its life during several years, and grow fat and heavy; but it rests motionless, like as in sleep, and its senses are blunt. Brain diseases often cause insanity. Spirituous liquors affect our thoughts, and increase their activity, because the alcohol the liquors contain raises the activity of brain; but when it is too much excited, the mind finally grows slack. Inversely, mental occupation increases the strength and magnitude of brain. (49.)

Does this mutual action take place, too, between special faculties of mind and brain?

Yes, e. g., between brain and memory. "In the brain the organic records of memory are never forgotten, but they last as long as life; a fever, a dream, a blow on the head sometimes recalls them unawares." (50.)

How do the emotions of the mind affect the organism of the body, especially the muscles of the face?

Lively joy or hope is manifested by the brightness of the eyes, by a quick pulse and breathing, by laughing and singing, jumping and dancing. We turn pale from fear, and blush from shame or anger. Some tremble from wrath; it can also cause cramps and epilepsy. Grief dims the eyes, slackens the veins, weakens heart and liver, hinders digestion, elicits sighs and tears. Sudden fright can palsy the tongue, nay, all limbs, can turn the hair gray or white, can effect swooning, epilepsy, insanity, and even instantaneous death.

Is the last cause of the mental functions known?

No; we do not know more about it than about the last cause of electricity, gravitation, and other forces; it seems to be inscrutable. The essence of brain, too, has been thus far but little investigated, and the last cause of the mutual relations existing between mind and brain, will be yet a long time, if not forever, a mystery.

What important principle follows from the fact that the perception through the senses is the foundation of all human knowledge?

From it the principle follows that man ought to acquire many and correct perceptions by means of the senses. This principle is the first and most important for the promotion of education and instruction. *Nature* ought to be man's Bible.

By what is our faculty of perception limited?

By the bounds of our senses.

What follows from this fact?

That we never shall be able to know the last causes of objects; e. g., as far as we do not yet know the cause of gravitation. Still, with the progress of science are also more remote causes discovered.

Is it wise to despise the body, or to estimate it less than the mind?

No; for we owe all our knowledge to the senses and nerves of the body, and in particular to the brain, its most considerable part; our existence and welfare depends generally on the body; it is of equal birth with the mind. They are from each other inseparable; the former is matter, the latter is force and attribute which arises from it. All natural and mental forces are in matter.

How long is the weight of the brain increasing?

Until to the 25th year; from this time it remains the same till to the 50th; thereafter it gradually decreases.

Is human will absolutely free?

No, for man is a creature of nature; therefore also his will and actions depend on the same necessity as the whole fabric of the Universe. (51.)

To what aim does man, conforming to his nature, necessarily exert his faculties?

For his welfare. Our nature urges us to search for that which is pleasing, and to shun that which is noxious to us.

Wherein, then, does human liberty consist?

In the faculty of endeavor for welfare.

What are the conditions that influence and determine man's will?

The qualities of his body, his innate faculties, his sex, temperament, education, company, the climate of the country in which he lives, etc.

Has the doctrine of a limited volition not a tendency to destroy the welfare of civil society?

Not at all; for if the individual man is necessitated to feel, think and act, as he does, it must not be overlooked, on the other hand, that the society is necessitated to feel, think and act likewise, and that, if the individual is necessitated by the laws of his nature to do wrong, the social body is also necessitated by the laws of their nature to restrain him from or to punish him for doing wrong.

By what means does man increase his welfare?

By improving himself.

Does the history of mankind prove that this view holds true?

Yes, for we know that man, from his original state of rudeness, has gradually arisen to higher civilization, and that he has thereby increased his welfare. (52.)

What science rests on this view?

The science of morals.

In what kind of association can the welfare and civilization of man best be effected?

In the State, while its members afford each other mutual assistance.

What ought to be the aim of the State?

The common welfare of all its citizens.

§ 13. The Soul of Animals.

How does the human soul differ from that of animals?

It differs from the animal soul not in kind, but only in degree. (53.) The animals are also capable of love, faith, gratitude, pity, pride, vindictiveness, etc. The hen warns her chickens, if any danger threatens them, and even fights and dies for their safety. The spider carries her eggs in a little bag, and rather suffers to be caught and killed than to give them up. The animals reflect, gather experience, provide for the future, like man. They build houses, nests, dams and paths; they understand each other by peculiar signs and sounds. Some ones form also States, e. g., the bees. As examples of the faculties which animals enjoy, the dog, the ape, the elephant, the bee, the ant and the beaver may be mentioned. With the stories of the ingenuity of these animals whole volumes are filled; in this place only some intimations of them can be admitted. The *dog* varies the sounds of his voice in different ways, according as he gives notice of strangers, is angry or cheerful, playing or fighting, asking for food or suffering pain. His faithfulness towards his master has become proverbial; he has often sacrificed even his life for him. Admirable is his faculty to trace the tracks of of the game, and to find again his lost home, even in the night time and in the greatest distance. The *wood-bee*, in order to provide for its brood, bores a hole, in which it lays the eggs, and then carries pollen, dead caterpillars and spiders to them, in order that the maggots, when they creep forth, may find food. The *paper-wasps* build their dwellings of wooden filaments several stories high, while they knead them with water, form balls of the pap, and with the mouth and feet build thereof hexagonal cells. The most intellect is manifested by the *honey-bees*. Their queen's destination is to lay eggs. If she dies during the time the hive has got a young brood, the working bees break off several work-cells, build thereof a cell for a new queen, feed there maggots with the food of the queen-bee, and keep one of the hatched young queens, and the others are expelled and killed. The *ants* carry their eggs, if the sun shines, in the open air, and, if rain impends, back again to their cells. If the young ants creep out, they feed them in the manner of birds. The *white ants* (termites) of Hindoostan, Africa and South America, build their houses of clay like ovens, which are 8—20 feet high, and so firm that they can bear ten men standing upon them. Part of these ants are laborers, part warriors. The royal chamber is in the centre of the house, and has two small openings, through which only the working ants are fitted to pass. The king and the queen are kept prisoners therein. It is surrounded by many cells of servants, to which the storerooms adjoin. These animals are working below covered galleries. If their house has been destroyed, they restore it. If a hole is broken, the warriors make their appearance, biting around. If the enemy retreats, the working ants come with mortar in their mouths, and fill up the breaches.

Do animals always act by instinct?

No, it is not always blind necessity which forces them to activity; they have feeling and perception, often also reflection and choice; still the liberty of their choice is often almost equal to nothing. They can be drilled. Not by instinct are older animals smarter than the young ones, but by experience. Not pushed by instinct does the fox steal the chickens, when master and servant, as he knows well, are at the table, but from conviction of need. Apes (and other animals) put out sentinels, when foraging; from time to time they call each other; at the first sign of alarm all make a halt and listen, till a second call of a different tone follows; thereafter all set out marching. If some of them are off on the retreat, other ones return and begin the fighting anew, in order to free their weaker fellows from the demands of their enemies. Baboons are used to build huts, and to shelter themselves by screens against the sun and rain. A swallow which having returned in spring, was looking for its old nest, but found it occupied by a sparrow. It began to close up the opening, and thereby forced the intruder to evacuate the nest.

By perception and experience animals, too, form habits which in part are propagated. In this way some species of ants establish slave States, by catching in war other species of ants, which they subject to their service. It is known that young spaniels frequently the first time, while they are taken along a-hunting, announce the nearness of the game. In other dog-races the disposition of saving those who are in danger, is a hereditary quality; as it is also the habit of the shepherd's dog to run always round the flock.

In order to prove that some species of apes possess higher faculties which in the intercourse with men easily can be developed, the history of two Chimpanzees, reported by the renowned naturalist, Dr. A. E. Brehm, is here recited.

"When I showed the Chimpanzee my child, she presented him kindly the hand. She played with another child, without ever using her teeth. She knew the ducks, after they had been shown to her twice. If she would raise her whip against girls, it sufficed to say: 'Fie, Molly! these are girls,' and she immediately dropped it and offered them her hand."

"Another Chimpanzee behaved like the most obedient child towards his waiter, who during his disease had carefully nursed him. In a short time he contracted human manners and habits, e. g., he ate with knife and fork, used the spoon like us, stirred up the sugar in tea, and took with the spoon every morsel, because he was forbidden to take it out with his fingers. One day, being in company with my friends, he behaved in a manner which will be forever to the credit of his race. First he took a bottle in order to pour wine in his glass; then he seized the glass, and hobbed and nobbed the glass of his neighbor to the right and left. Now he drew near a plate, and when he was helped to food, he used knife and fork very cleverly, according to the manner he had been taught. He performed gymnastics with an admirable ability, and not after the manner of apes, but the way we were used to do them. Every day he devised a new exercise, and knew to apply every tool of gymnastics in the best way; in so much, that it was a pleasure to look at him. Besides he was very sensible of praise and blame. If some of us came, he practiced as zealously as a scholar during the examination: he liked to show what he knew. He knew the parrots pretty well, and could not help quizzing them sometimes. He stole quietly to their cage in order to raise up suddenly the hand. But because the waiter resented this wantonness by saying repeatedly: 'Stop!'—it did not take much time till the parrots learnt the word, and then said themselves: 'Stop!'—and now he drew the hand down quickly. When he fell sick, and ought to take medicines, the single word of the waiter: 'You must take this!' was sufficient to induce him to comply with the order."

How differs the human from the animal mind?

It is the inventor of arts and sciences; it represents its thoughts and feelings by language; it is able to admire nature, to muse upon the cause of all things, and to exhibit a love which is sacrificing for others' benefit. "Its distance from the animal soul is infinite." (54.)

§ 14. The Law of Evolution in the Universe. (55.)

By what law are all phenomena of the Universe bound?

By the laws of successive evolution.

What dominions of the Universe are especially ruled by this law?

The celestial bodies, the earth, the organic life and the social state of man.

By how many principal directions does it manifest itself in each of these dominions?

By three directions.

1. *In all dominions of the Universe there prevails a progress from a diffused to a more contracted state.*

Science supposes that all celestial bodies (the earth too) originally were gaseous, then liquid, and gradually grew solid. We observe stars of all degrees of solidity, misty forms of stars in all degrees of condensation, and solid masses up to the thinnest clouds which by the most powerful telescopes hardly can be discerned. And if another hypothesis of science be correct, namely, that the matter of the astral system is attracted by the force of gravitation, then it must be more concentrated by degrees.

In particular, as long as the earth mostly existed in a liquid condition, and only had a thin crust, it could not contain but small tracts of land and water, large mountains presuppose a solid earth crust, and only when this one grew enough condensated, continents and oceans could start into existence.

Organic life develops, if parts of matter which before were scattered in a larger space, aggregate in *one* body. So e. g., the plant grows by absorption from the surrounding gases. In the child the parts of the same bone grow by degrees together, and, even in the adult, bones join which before were separated from each other. The sections existing in the body of the caterpillar, disappear in the butterfly, and are then so closely joined that they cannot be distinguished from each other. In general, all organisms depend mutually upon each other, and so far integrate one another; e. g., all animals indirectly or directly live on plants, and plants on the carbonic gas which those evolve; the carniverous animals cannot subsist without the plant-eaters. Some plants and animals of one district of nature even die away, if transposed among the plants and animals of another.

In the rude state of nature man roves restless in woods and deserts; in the civilized state many are joined together by the ties of common government and laws. Towns are founded, in which men form different ranks according to their professions. Manufacturing towns draw the laborers from afar to a center. The social connections are growing firmer and closer. Nations form alliances; the barriers to commerce are broken down, and the mutual intercourse is more and more enlarged. Finally, States, animals, and plants, all depend upon the light and heat of the sun.

2. To the first general formula must a second be added: *With passage from incoherent to coherent there goes on a progress from uniform to multiform.*

Where once gaseous matter filled the celestial space, there we see now an immense quantity of suns, planets, and moons, so different in circumference and gravity, mass and solidity, heat and illumination, inclination of their orbits and axes, and in their physical constitution. Some stars (e, g., Mars) have a red, other ones a green or yellow (e. g., the polar star), or a whitish light. There are astral groups, the stars of which are dispersed, and again such ones, the stars of which are in every degree more or less closely concentrated. There are groups, consisting only of two, others of 1,000 or still more stars. In some places of the sky they are in crowds, in others they are missing entirely. How heterogeneous are the star mists! Some having a regular, others an irregular form; and those are arranged in the shape of a spiral-line, or of a ring, or an ellipse, etc.

On our earth from century to century layers of rocks were deposited, one above the other, the parts of which are so diversified, and through the fissures of which frequently pass metallic-veins. From mile to mile it assumes another aspect. Its surface has partly grown higher; the oldest mountains are the lowest; the highest, as the Andes and the Himalayas, are the youngest. Since it has grown cool, it has changed climate in many countries; thus now icy coldness rules towards its poles. The climate changes sometimes in a short distance of one place to another; thus on the southern side of the Alps prevails the warmth of spring, on the northern the coldness of winter.

Almost all plants are in their germ similar to each other, but the more they grow, the greater becomes their difference, both in their general aspect and in their parts. Some cells are changed to marrow, others to wood or bark. How diverse are the plants according to their height and duration of life, to their leaves, fruits, stems and trunks!

With animals the same law holds good. Thus e. g., the cells of different animals first resemble each other in their eggs; but soon they grow dissimilar. The feet and wings of the same bird are in the beginning also of the same size. It is known that all the different classes, families and species of animals develop from similar cells.

Man, too, has in the course of time experienced manifold changes. Proof for this assertion are the different races. The bones of the skull of the civilized man are larger, and the jaw-bones smaller than those of the savage. Quite as considerable is the variety of the degrees of civilization to which men have risen. The more they were civilized, the more arts and sciences were improved since the rudest beginning which we notice among savages. Languages branched off in principal and secondary ones, in innumerable dialects; the stock of vocables increased from generation to generation. The art of writing was invented; first they formed images, by and by letters. The sculptor cut his gods, men and animals, at first in walls, then in a block, finally he chiseled them in stone. The art of painting, which in beginning formed only outlines, comprises now divers branches, and has divers names, according as it represents historical objects, or landscapes, or flowers and fruits, or real persons, animals, etc. In the musical department various instruments were invented; in song the three other parts were added to the first; from the battle song of the savage music advanced to the hymm, to the social song, as far as to the opera. In social life, too, the law of the multiform prevails. The chieftain of a wild tribe hardly differs from its members in dignity and in the way of life. In well organized States the Government enjoys power and authority. The citizens divide the labor, and perform mutually various actions for each other. According to their vocation they are joined in divers classes, and start religious, scientific, economical and other associations. Some people, especially, practice agriculture, some commerce and navigation, other trades, fabrication and arts.

§ 15. Concluded.

3. *Evolution advances from an indefinite, incoherent homogeneity, to a definite, coherent heterogeneity.*

The system of stars, and of the earth, too, must (according to the hypothesis of natural science) first have an irregular shape, and by degrees get more regular forms; for a gaseous body of ovale figure has not so definite limits as a fluid or solid one. The movements of the solar system must also originally have been indefinite, and in the lapse of time become regular. Now-a-days the time is determined in which the planets and their moons revolve around the sun and on their own axis. As long as earth, surrounded with a thin crust, had only small lakes and seas, water could make but short rotations. After the formation of the continents and oceans, water also commenced to move from the hot to the frigid degrees of latitude (e. g., in the Gulf Stream of Mexico); and this movement grew more definite, as the expansion of the surface of the land increased.

If we consider the organic creation, we see that, the higher one of its classes stands, its functions also are the more definite and perfect. The simplest animal forms have only an alimentary canal; the well organized ones possess organs for the mastication of the food, a stomach and intestines; in that the chyle moves irregularly to and fro; by the latter it is conducted into the viens and mingled with the blood, which flows through the heart, lungs and veins, and in this way diffuses in all parts of the body. Animalcules which we only see with the aid of the microscope, move in the water by means of trembling eyelashes which cover their surface; the more perfect animals, to this end, enjoy one or several pairs of feet. The heart is first only a wide blood-vessel, later a partition is formed in it, by which it is divided in two halves (ventricles).

The functions of the human organism also gradually are getting more definite. The infant first stammers inarticulate sounds, by degrees it learns to pronounce the easier consonants, then the more difficult and the compound ones; at first monosyllables, after these dissyllables and polysyllables. In such a degree as the functions of the organs of speech grow more perfect, the mental evolution becomes more definite too. The child is yet poor with regard to ideas; its observations are volatile and superficial; it makes always mistakes in speaking, reading, ciphering. If we compare with it a public orator, a Demosthenes, a Newton, or Humboldt: what a difference! Likewise the savage has only a narrow sphere of conceptions; his language is very poor; he is not acquainted with the exact sciences, arithmetic, geometry, astronomy, etc.

The same effect of the evolution is also conspicuous in the civil association. A rambling tribe of savages has no permanent home, their public relations are confused, the affairs of the individuals not defined. On the contrary, men living in a State, build residences; the rights and duties of the citizens are defined, and the laws which at first are rude, rendered more distinct. If there be resistance and defense wanted, the savages fight in disorder, every one for himself. But the organized army of a State is divided in batallions, regiments, and companies; some fight on foot, others on horse-back; others discharge the cannons; the duties of the private soldiers, of the officers, and the General are defined; during the battle each occupies a definite place, and executes definite actions. Whereas barbarians only trade in the way of barter, in the State daily millions of dollars are circulated by purchase and sale; the articles of the trade, and their value are of endless variety, and every enterprise which refers to commerce, is exactly computed.

What direction must the further evolution of mankind mainly take?

The direction of a higher intellectual and emotional development.

Does the evolution of the Universe alternatively succeed in one of these four dominions after the other?

No, it takes place simultaneously in them all. While the individual man develops, the evolution of the whole society, too, is going on, because it is composed of individuals; and with the metamorphosis of the earth and the solar systems, the human association also changes. The evolution of the Universe effects simultaneously the general change of things.

What is the last result of the evolution of the Universe?

Mankind is by and by so transformed by it that it will be able to adapt itself more and more to the relations of nature and life.

To what will man finally attain in this way?

To the highest accomplishment and happiness.

Is nature's evolution boundless?

There are limits it cannot overstep. The rolling stone comes at last to rest. Water pouring from the clouds in the form of rain, gathers in rivers, where it is stopped by the resistance of other particles of water. The string which by the bow or hammer has been set swinging, comes again to rest. Every development finally arrives to a state of equipoise.

By what influence is it then controlled?

By the influence of its environs.

What's the necessary consequence of this influence?

The dissolution of the object, the evolution of which is finished. The dissolution can already happen in a few days, or it can be postponed for millions of years; but some day it *must* happen, and indeed happen in all dominions of the Universe. (56.)

State associations are dissolved by the attacks of enemies or by revolutions. The evolution of organic beings is ended by death (in the more general signification). After death their ingredients are decomposed in gases. This process happens slower or quicker, and depends much on the degree of temperature. It occurs faster in summer and in hot countries, than in winter and cold regions. Carcasses of mammoth elephants that have died long ago, and were buried in ice at the mouths of Siberian rivers, were found unhurt, wherefore their flesh, if dug out, is eaten by wolves. Inorganic bodies often remain a long time without any perceptible change. Masses of alluvial earth and stones harden from the pressure of new alluvions, and become rocks, and so can rest unchanged millions of years; but by rain, and frost, and air they also can crumble, and by fire even be volatilized into gases. Some natural philosophers (57) and astronomers even assert that the earth and whole system of stars—of course only after an immeasurable series of years—must again return into a gaseous condition; but that after every universal dissolution a new evolution will follow, because the creation of the Universe had neither a beginning, nor will have an end. Greek philosophers maintained already this opinion.

COROLLARIES.

What follows from the doctrine of the evolution of the Universe?

If this doctrine is correct, the belief in a personal God, who stands outside of the world, in divine revelations, in miracles and supernatural forces, in everlasting religions, in the different stories of the origin of the Universe and of the creation of the organisms (of plants, animals and men), in merely spiritual beings, in a personal immortality, in heaven, and hell, etc., loses its hold, and Darwin's theory of man's origin is vindicated.

§ 16. The Unknowable in the Universe.

The unknowable in the Universe. (58.)

Whereby are the sensations, the objects effect in us, necessarily originated?

By causes; e. g., the sounds we hear are the effect of the oscillations of air, which touch our organ of hearing.

What do we find, if from a next cause we investigate farther?

We find a cause more remote; e. g., the oscillations of the air can be caused by discharging a cannon, or by a tempest.

How long must we continue to inquire from cause to cause?

Until we arrive at last cause; e. g., in order to understand the process of respiration, we notice that the air is rushing into the lungs. The condition of this movement is the expansion of the chest; but this expansion depends on another cause and this again on another, etc. Thus we are obliged to proceed from cause to cause, until we arrive at one which we must suppose to be the last; for if it were not the last, another must yet follow after it.

Is this only so with some things?

No, the existence of everything depends on an ultimate cause.

What does oblige us to admit this hypothesis?

Our *common consciousness*. It is to be found in every man and all people who are tolerably well civilized. It is the essence of every religion.

How does history confirm that this consciousness is correct?

That all men hold it in common.

What creed do all religions hold in common?

The creed that there is a last, unknown cause of all phenomena.

Is it possible to adduce proofs of the existence of an ultimate cause, in the proper sense of the word?

No, for it transcends the sphere of our intellectual faculty. Its correctness is merely a fact of consciousness.

Where is the last cause of things manifested?

It is manifested in all phenomena of nature and human being.

How must all matter and force of the Universe be considered?

They must be considered to be the effect of this first cause; it is the eternal, persevering force which lies at the bottom of all forces, both the physical (e. g., of heat, light, electricity), and moral (e. g., the faculty of perceptions, of the intellect, of the volition).

What is its relation to the evolution of the Universe?

It is the cause of every evolution proceeding in general, and especially in the organic life, in the human mind and in society.

Is it limited or unlimited?

It is unlimited in space and time.

Is the last cause of all reality to be looked for within or without the Universe?

It is existing within it, because it is also a force. There are no forces without the Universe.

How far does its efficacy reach?

As far as there is any phenomenon of nature.

Is it physical or spiritual?

Neither the one, nor the other.

What, then, is it? How can it be known and explained?

Being unlimited and absolute, to human intellect and finite understanding, it remains forever an unknowable, inexplicable, nay, even unthinkable mystery. It is that veiled image of Sais. (59.)

May we give the ultimate cause particular attributes, e. g., personality, omnipotence, infinite benevolence, or other qualities and feelings in the highest grade?

No! for by every attribute it would be limited and humanized.

How far do all historical religions contradict themselves?

As far as on the one hand they confess that the last cause cannot be understood, but on the other they give it definite attributes.

Why ought we not to confess any religion?

Because all religions contain unprovable doctrines.

Against which spirit does he act who teaches untrue dogmas, and commands us to believe that the ultimate cause of all things exists in any definite manner?

Against the spirit of genuine piety.

Which people are generally called pious and religious?

Those who pretend to stand behind the unknown *Power*, and to know the conditions according to which it is obliged to act.

To which object can such men be compared, if they call their opponents atheists?

They can be compared to the pert clock, which believed that the watchmaker, like her, is moved in his actions by springs, wheels and scapements, and called every other clock, which did not assent to its opinion, atheistic.

What is, then, wisdom and religious duty?

To consider the ultimate existence which causes the subsistence of all things, as the Unknowable and Unthinkable. (60.)

What reasons do several German philosophers object to the hypothesis of an ultimate existence?

They say: As nature has neither a beginning nor an end, this hypothesis cannot be admitted. The foundation of any object lies deeper, and was sooner extant than the structure which reposes on it; therefore, if there were a first cause of the Universe, it would have been extant before the latter, and so the Universe would be limited in space and time, while it is unlimited in both regards. The series of causes is infinite, like Nature itself. Experience teaches only the existence of an almighty Power in Nature, though with our limited intellect we cannot understand the way and manner of its existence. (Cf. § 2.) (61.)

§ 17. The Conception of God. 1.—In the Christian Church.

In what do the Christian Churches believe?

In an almighty, all-wise, all-bountiful and all-just God, the creator and conservator of the world.

What is the foundation of their belief?

A presupposed revelation of God.

What does science answer them with regard to this belief?

It answers: 1. The Christians believe in God's existence, because he himself has revealed it to them; herewith they presuppose already his existence, which they first ought to prove. True, in order to prove that a revelation really has happened, they appeal to miracles, asserting that these did concomitate the revelation; but they are neither able to prove the genuineness of the miracles. Jesus Christ himself lamented that his cotemporaries would not believe him, though they saw his wonders. Besides, miracles are impossible. (Cf. § 3.)

2. With the benevolence, wisdom and justice of God, the many evils on earth, e. g., diseases, wars, famines, earthquakes, etc., are at variance. We see often the innocent pine in misery, and the criminal revel in abundance. Thousands of generations live and die in wretchedness. Useful species of animals have died away; pernicious ones (e. g., locusts, migratory pigeons, field-mice), prevail to excess, tormenting men and beasts; some men are born blind, etc. (62.)

Does, then, the law of conformity to the purpose rule in nature?

No, the alleged facts testify to the contrary; nature's works neither manifest intelligence or design, nor are they consequences of a blind chance; but it creates everywhere according to definite, immutable laws. (63.)

3. The doctrine of the Christian church contradicts itself; for, according to it, God has damned mankind for ever, because Adam and Eve had transgressed his command; God's son had to propitiate him by his death, and suffered it on a cross; nevertheless the most men continue to be damned, because God has predestinated them to damnation; the damned must for ever burn in the fire pool of hell, etc. Such dogmas can not be reconciled with the idea of an all-kind and all-just God.

4. The expressions " Creator, kind and wise God " signify a personal being, similar to man, though infinitely more perfect than this. The word " God " literally means: the good one, and attributes to the supreme being even a peculiar sex. (64.)

From what being are all notions man forms of God, derived?

From man.

What would the bird imagine God to be, if it could get an idea of Him?

"He would imagine Him to be a bird, only larger, finer and stronger than it is itself." (65.)

How do different men and people always imagine God?

According to their grade of culture, to their passions, to the properties of their race and country, therefore rude people adored an elephant, a cow, a crocodile, a tree, and even a stone. (66.) The cheerful Greeks formed themselves merry gods, the stern Hebrews an ireful Jehovah, the negroes—gods with black skins and curley hair, the Mongolian—with a yellow complexion. Zeus was a perfect Greek, and Jove looked as though a member of the Roman Senate. The gods of the northern countries were represented warmly clad in robes of fur; those of the tropics were naked. Everyone changes his conceptions of God according to the degree of culture to which he advances. (67.)

How are also the sacrifices adapted which man offers to his gods?

They are adapted to his habits of living. The Heathens sacrificed meat and wine; the Roman peasants cakes of milet; the Hebrews only " clean " animals, no pork, because they themselves were not used to eat it; the peasants in Lithania flitches (to the thunder-god Perkune); the peasants in Prussia parcels of hogs, geese, chickens and calves (to the god Ziemienic); the Ostiake stuffs tobacco in the nose of his god, etc.

How do others contrive to prove the existence of God?

By asserting that all people on earth believed and continue to believe in a highest being.

Is this assertion true?

No! Many people had and have no idea of God, e. g., many Indian tribes. (68.) The original religion of Buddha is ignorant of God and immortality, (69); besides, two of the religious systems of the Chinese have no expressions for the idea of God and immortality in their language. Individual men, too, who grow up without education, have no idea of God. (70.) Moreover, according to that assertion there must exist, too, demons, because the belief in them is still wider spread, than that in an all-kind being.

From whom did the Christians and Mohammedans receive the conception of a personal God?

From the Jews.

When did the belief in a personal God originate?

At the time when men yet stood in the lowest degree of civilization; for then they did not know the causes of the phenomena of nature. (71.)

Which doctrine of astronomy did shake the belief in a personal God?

The doctrine that the fixed stars are similar bodies to our sun; hence he has no more home in heaven. (72.)

§ 18. Concluded. 2.—From the Standpoint of Modern Science.

What's the view of modern science with regard to the notion of a God?

Its adherents form several classes. One of them, indeed the most numerous, discarded those ideas of God, which too grossly contradict the advanced culture of our age, and now imagine him as the infinite being, infinite in power, sanctity and benevolence (73): as the law-giver of Nature.

Can this notion of God be correct?

No, for it also contains the feature of a personal being. His attributes, though conceived to be infinite, contradict each other. Being infinitely just, he must punish every sinner; being infinitely merciful, he must pardon every one. The evil on earth contradicts his infinite benevolence and power; for it exists either by or against his permission; in the first case he is not infinitely benevolent, in the second he is not omnipotent.

Is there a law giver of Nature, like law givers of States?

No; the words "law" of Nature and "law" of any State have different meanings; the latter is the expression of the will of a superior; the former, the generalized expression of the manner in which certain phenomena occur.

How does another school define the divine idea?

It defines God as the invisible, first cause of all existence and life. "As sure as a living spirit dwells in man, we must in the Universe recognize a living, forming, disposing highest spirit: this is God." (74.)

On what foundation does the divine idea of this school rest?

On the religious sentiment. They say: "Man feels his dependence on a first cause; that is a religious feeling. Every more diffuse description is defective. Even the phrases, 'God is the father of men, the spirit of the Universe, the supreme intellect,' cannot afford any sufficient representation of the first cause of all things. The religious sentiment approaches the notion of God closer than language."

How is (according to their view) the religious feeling manifested?

By amazement, reverence, joy, confidence, and resignation in God.

How do they continue to define this sentiment?

They call it the most powerful, for it sacrifices even life; it created the splendid temples and statues of the Greeks, etc. Still (as they say) its condition depends on education; therefore it differs so widely in diverse times, both in the individuals and nations; e. g., some worship only one God, others several gods, etc.

Which error does also the doctrine of the religious emotions contain in common with the two preceding ideas of God?

Its foundation is also the representation of a personal being; for it uses, too, the words "God" and "gods." Besides, the religious sentiment is not to be found in every one; it is missing in the rude and uneducated man.

What does this school reply to that reproach?

That at least the faculty of it exists in every man; but that it must be developed.

What other reasons are there why religious emotions cannot be the safe foundation of religion?

Because they often misled men to follies and to the most ferocious actions, even to kill their own children for their gods, to burn heretics and atheists, to believe in a hell, to adore a piece of dough (which they called the holy host), etc.

In what countries are the most and worst crimes committed?

In those where the religious feelings have the highest sway, e. g., in Italy. Such crimes are: murder, robbery and theft.

Does the religious feelings abandon the criminals during the perpetration of their misdeeds?

No! With all fervor of a devouted mind they pray "God's mother" to assist them at their criminal action; in the most profound humility they cross themselves in the presence of "the holy image," behind which they kill a traveler in the next moment; with the most scrupulous conscientiousness they confess the committed sins. (75.)

What notion of God has a third class of the representants of the modern view of the Universe?

None at all; they do neither believe in a historical God (i. e., in such an one, as men hitherto imagined), nor in a personal God generally. Theirs are also the same objections which so far have been propounded. (76.)

Do they profess a new idea of God?

No; for 1st, from the statement of this idea, hitherto given, it is evident that the notions which men until now devised of God, always were erroneous, nay that they even contradicted each other; therefore it is not probable that man ever will succeed to form a correct idea of God.

2d. The word "God" always implies a personal being.

3d. If by it the power, manifesting itself in the Universe, is meant, the expression is however erroneously chosen. But it was already before (§ 15) proven that this power will remain inscrutable forever; therefore it will be always impossible to form a representation of it. (77.)

4th. Man is the highest standard wherewith we can measure the infinite Power; as soon as we outstep our nature, the conception and word fail us. God, as men can imagine Him, will, then, always be a humanized being.

5th. As we can know only such things, as we are able to perceive with our senses, and as God is said to be a supersensual (transcending) being: we can never acquire any knowledge of Him. (78.)

6th. The only object of science are nature and her laws; science cannot acquire any knowledge but in the sphere of experience; whatever transcends this, remains precluded from its comprehension. Must we search for information from theologians and philosophers? They do not know any more. The wisest of them are teaching: "A God who could be comprehended, would be no more a God at all." "It is blasphemy to think that God exists in the manner as we believe that he must exist." (79.)

What corollary is to be derived from these reasonings with regard to humane prayers?

That they are of no use, because they are addressed to a person who does not exist.

Which men are usually called atheists?

Those who do not believe in the ruling notions of divinity. In this way the Greeks and Romans called Socrates and other philosophers, and even the ancient Christians, atheists, because they believed not in the gods of their countries; and again the Christians used in all times to call so those who uncovered the errors of their creed. (80.)

§ 19. The Religions.*

What is religious belief?

The belief in one or several gods.

What is usually added to this belief?

External rites and ceremonies, e. g., visiting the churches and temples, prayers, etc.

What do most religions hold in common?

They teach nearly the same morals; beside, they profess supernatural, incomprehensible opinions, which men must believe to be true; moreover they relate many pious legends, transmitted from the olden times.

What verdict do many of our cotemporaries pass on religions?

Many intelligent men think that they are not needed, some even assert that they are obnoxious.

What reasons do the latter allege?

1. That the religions contain several absurd, inconceivable and erroneous dogmas, e. g., the dogma that three divine persons make one God.

2. That they contradict each other.

3. That they always have engendered hatred and persecution, bloody wars and barbarous actions among men. So the Jews have exterminated such people who would not adore Jehovah; the Christians have burned millions of men on the pretext that they were heretics; and the Mohammedans have made war against the infidels (as they called the Christians and Jews); nay, even among themselves, one sect was fighting the other. (81.)

What do those desire who adhere to the latter view of religions?

They desire that the State religions (as they call them) ought to be abolished, or at least separated from the governments of the States. In the latter case the States should not appoint and pay the clergy, and not enjoin Sabbath laws; the

---

*This word is here understood in the historical sense.

property of the churches should not be exempt from public taxes; the public schools not be controlled by the churches, etc.

What do they wish with regard to the religious instruction of youth?

Youth ought not to receive any religious instruction; for experience proves that such an one is detrimental to their education.

What detriment does it usually effect?

1st. The juvenile mind receives an erroneous impression of the Universe, is crammed with superstition, incited to sectarian hatred and fanaticism, and is subdued to the sway of the churches.

2d. The time of instruction is wasted by it, and such branches which are necessary and useful to the scholar, are neglected by it. Only the history of the religions ought to be taught in order to warn and protect the youth against the aberrations of human intellect.

§ 20. Death and Immortality.

What are the effects of old age?

In old age the brain shrinks, the veins grow impassable, the senses dull, the muscles slack, the hair white, the head and back bent; the weight of the body decreases, body and mind become incessantly weaker, and finally nature like a mother receives us again in her lap.

What symptoms announce death?

The body is not able to move, and the limbs to stir any more; by and by the breath stops; at last the heart, too, ceases to beat, and the circulation of blood is at an end. By degrees putrefaction sets in, and the different parts of the body are changed in gases, salts and earth.

Is death a necessary result of human life?

Yes; for every moment, with every draught of breath and with every drop of sweat a particle of ingredients by which the body is composed, returns to the realm of ever changing nature. So e. g., a part of the blood forms nerves and bones, and another already leaves again the body, dead and transformed in breath and sweat. Death is born with the man, and is dwelling with him since his birth (cf. § 14).

What truth is no longer doubted in regard to the body of man?

It is no longer doubted that man's body in a certain meaning is immortal. The existent matter of the Universe is eternal, consequently the matter of the human body too. True, it is by death decomposed in its different primitive ingredients; however, none of them is ever lost, but they are only united with other forms of matter. Not the smallest particle of the body is ever lost (§ 2).

In what sense is the human mind immortal?

That which man creates, invents, teaches, becomes an heritage of his children and grandchildren, and even of mankind in general. The succeeding generation receives and increases the heritage. The literary productions of great geniuses, and the generous actions of good men continue to live in the memory of posterity. "Thus far the human mind is also immortal." (82.)

Is there also a *personal* continuation of mental life?
No, a continuation of conscious mental life is impossible.

What reasons does the science of our age allege for this assertion?

1st. The mind, in general, is a product of organization; therefore it must perish with organization, as the flower perishes with the gem.

2d. The mind is, especially, a product of the brain. It has its origin in the brain; its faculties develop as the brain develops, and decrease with it; it is inseparable from it (see § 10 and 11). Man becomes conscious of himself only by the influence which the external world exerts on his senses; now if the organs of the senses, the nervous system and especially the brain get inactive or even are destroyed, the consciousness and therefore the mental life must also cease for some time or for ever. The first case happens during swooning and sleep. During profound sleep man has no dreams, they do not begin but in passing from sleep into the state of awaking. In the second case we say that man is dead. Therefore sleep and death are called twins. In this way the clock also stops, if its wheels are hindered to turn, or are disjoined. (83.)

3d. Every object which began to exist, must one day perish; soul did not exist once, therefore it is perishable.

4th. Force and matter are closely united together, that is a quality of this; it disappears, when the material parts are separated and otherwise rejoined. The soul is the force of the brain; if, then, the latter is dissolved, and enters other combinations with other matters, the former must loose, too, its existence. This happens in death. (84.)

5th. The human soul differs from that of animals not in kind, but only in degree of essence. (§ 12.) Now, if man's soul is immortal, we must also grant immortality to the animal souls. But, we do not doubt that animals are mortal; therefore man neither can be immortal.

Which objections do the advocates of the doctrine of immortality produce, and how are they answered?

They say: 1. "Human soul is of spiritual, not material essence; therefore it cannot be destroyed." But if soul is no species of matter, it has neither the attributes of matter: it is neither partible, nor extensible, nor ponderable, nor visible, etc., like that; but such a being is nothing at all. Think of the innumerable quantity of souls, which since the creation of man (according to this theory) must continue to exist! (85.)

2. "To think of our annihilation is unnatural, hurts our feelings, and contradicts our desire, for every one wishes to live forever." (86.)

Man fosters still many other desires, of which many must remain unaccomplished; therefore it is at least doubtful, if that wish for immortality will be satisfied. He who does not believe in immortality, neither desires to be immortal. (87.) The child, on its mother's arm, crying for the moon, ought on the same principle to have its wish gratified.

3. "Many men are suffering innocently on earth, others live in abundance, though they are sinners ; consequently there must follow another life, in which to the first then must be recompense, to the last punishment dealt."

From this reason it would not follow that all, but only that several men had to live on after death ; and even these must therefore not be immortal; suffice it, if they continue to exist as long, until they will have received the right measure of their deserved recompense and punisnment. "The compensation of a future life comes too late, for it heals the sick man only after he has died ; it refreshes the thirsty, after they have perished ; it feeds the hungry, when they are already starved." (88.) Besides, according to this argument, many animals, too, would be entitled to be immortal, for many of them, especially of the domestic, must very often innocently endure human roughness and cruelty.

4. "The human mind develops from the lowest degree of culture to an astonishing perfection : therefore it must be everlasting, in order to evolve itself more and more."

We do not know to what degree mental culture may advance, but certainly not infinitely ; on the contrary, it decreases in old age, as it has been observed in the greatest scholars ; e. g., Kant, the eminent German philosopher, grew, when being old, so childish that he crept again on all fours ; and Newton did not understand any more his own mathematical works which he, when younger, had composed. Ought we after death to be seated again on the school-benches ? (89.)

5. "All people believe in the immortality of soul."

They do not all. The Jews were ignorant of this doctrine before the captivity in Babylon ; and one Jewish sect, the Sadducees, rejected it entirely hereafter ; neither do the millions of votaries of Confutse and Buddha confess it. Among the educated Greeks and Romans, too, many individuals, and several philosophic schools refused to believe in it. So also in modern times, many respectable, celebrated men deny the belief in it. (90.) Are the Christians really believing in immortality ? No ! Proof of it is the fact that they dislike to die as much as infidels, and endeavor to conserve this life as long as they can.

6. "If men do not believe in immortality, sins and crimes are more likely to result." It is only the few who would be retained from doing evil by it ; or if not so, there would not be so many sinners and criminals among Christians. Nay, many commit the more sins, because they believe that they can yet secure their salvation, if they confess and repent their sins in the last moment of their life ; for Jesus promised paradise to the crucified murderer. To be sure, his blood purifies all sinners. This doctrine makes Jesus a scapegoat for rascality and wickedness. The thief, the robber, and the murderer, may go straight to heaven, and cheat the devil out of his dues, by repentance at the last moment. Man who

shuns sin only for fear of hell, and only does his duty for love of heaven, is greedy of gain, and not truly virtuous.

7. "Men will indulge in the basest sensual enjoyments."

They will not do so, because they know that in this way they would act against the higher demands of their nature, and render themselves unhappy, as every folly and vice is punished by itself. (Cf. Morals, §§ 3, 8 and 9.) Besides most crimes are detected and punished. (91.)

8. "The belief in immortality comforts children and parents; the first, if their parents, the latter, if their children die."

It cannot help children to meet again their parents after death, for they want them in this life; and for the parents the loss of good children is a misfortune lasting as long as their life.

Which other bad sequels causes the belief in immortality?

He who is constantly contemplating imaginary glories of another world, is not the man to give us great discoveries and inventions, or to take a lively interest in the affairs of this world.

How ought we to consider the earth, because human life is transient?

We ought to consider it as our home, and to transform it to a paradise.

How can this be done?

In this way that we earn some fortune by industry and parsimony; that we enjoy wisely the life, and that by virtue and humanity we make ourselves and others happy.

What ought to be the unique and general aim of our life?

Our mutual welfare. "The time to be happy is now, and the way to be happy is to make others so. This is enough for us. In this belief we are content to live and die."—Ingersoll.*

§ 21. Heaven and Hell.

What are heaven and hell?

According to Christian doctrine, heaven and hell are places where men after this life are forever recompensed or punished.

How did this superstition originate?

From the erroneous idea which men had formed of the movement of the earth and sun; namely, that the latter revolved around the former, and that the earth was a perfect plane.

Where was heaven and hell located, according to their opinion?

They represented heaven to be above, and hell below the earth.

When did this superstition lose its support?

Since Copernicus proved that the earth is revolving around the sun.

Where has superstition since removed heaven to?

To the large space of the Universe or to some star. (92.)

---

*"For the rest, he who can and will, or rather must believe in an eternal life, may do so, under the blessing of God; but he ought to permit also others to believe the contrary."—L. Feuerbach.

What results plainly from these opinions regarding heaven and hell?

That they are totally erroneous; for they are ridiculous, revolting and contradicting each other; e. g., the Indian, when thinking of heaven, means large hunting-grounds, where he can freely ramble and find an abundance of game. The ancient German hoped to drink in his Walhalla plenty of beer and mead. The Mohammedan deems heaven to be a paradise, a flourishing country, in which every kind of enjoyment is waiting for him, and the Christians call hell the place in which eternal fire burns in order to torment the damned for ever.

What other article of Christian faith is gainsaid by the belief in hell?

The article of faith which teaches that God is the holiest, kindest and merciful being, the father of all men.

§ 22. The Evil in the World.

What do people often complain of?

They complain of the many evils, which happen on earth; they call earth the abode of misery, and hope for a blissful future life.

What answer can be returned to such complaints?

1. Many things are regarded as evils which really are not, or appear to be greater than they are. E. g., for a long time they believed that thunderstorms were a chastisement, inflicted by God for human sins; but natural science demonstrates that generally they are beneficent. The agony of a dying person seems to signify dreadful sufferings, but in most cases the senses are stunned before man dies.

2. The sum of joys outweighs or equipoises that of sufferings in human life, like the number of bright days during the year is larger than that of the tempestuous and dull ones, or equal to them.

3. Man himself causes many of his evils by his follies and vices, e. g., the most diseases, the ravages of war, etc. (Cf. Morals § 8.)

4. Human nature has only few true wants, and these can be easily satisfied. Even the poor is not destitute of all enjoyments: hunger seasons his frugal repast; a tranquil sleep strengthens his tired limbs, and permanent health is the reward of his troublesome labor. " There are only two real boons of human life: good health and a clear conscience."—J. J. Rousseau.

5. Sundry evils are a necessary and salutary effect of natural laws; e. g., the heat of summer is annoying; but it ripens grains and fruits. Hunger is a disagreeable sensation; but nature admonishes us by it to provide for food. But for the sting of hunger we should not think of providing food, and so always be in danger to lose life.

6. Nature teaches us prudence by sufferings, warns us by them against greater evils, and urges us to improve our condition by efforts and struggle. The child which burnt its finger, will be more cautious in the use of fire. He who has fallen sick from intemperance, is thereby warned to take better care for

his health. Nations smarting under the lash of tyranny, learn to fight for their liberty. Want is the mother of inventions.

7. "Perhaps all our pleasures take their zest from the known possibility of their interruption. What were the glories of the sun, if we knew not the gloom of darkness? What the refreshing breezes of morning and evening, if we felt not the fervors of noon? Should we value the lovely flower, if it bloomed eternally; or the luscious fruit if it hung always on the bough?" (93.)

8. Virtue is joined to sacrifices and afflictions; but it affords us the delights of a clear conscience. By this sentiment the fetters become easier to the captive patriot; by it a tender mother stands every privation; she loves her children. In this way every good action is rewarded by itself.

9. If the afflictions of fate cannot be remedied, man can at least blunt, if not avoid the sting of pain by quiet resignation and patience. True heroism is tested by afflictions.

10. As long as we entertain hope, and desire to conserve our life, our adversity has not yet reached its acme; for the worst chance nature itself has thrown open to us many ports of egression: but who is to decide, when this chance is at hand?

11. Even death is not the heaviest evil which can befall us. All men must once die: that's nature's universal law. But what nature has destined to all, cannot be an evil. The wisest and best of our kin have gone before us. We arrived unconsciously on earth, and in the same way we depart from it. "While we are, death is not, and while death is, we are not."—Epicurus. "It is our duty to meet death with ready minds, neither regretting the past, nor anxious for the future."—Epicurus. If the power of our body is exhausted by age or disease, its primitive constituents must necessarily be dissolved; ought a miracle be worked for our sake? Of what use would an immortal body be to us, if it were weak and sickly from old age? Do we desire to walk with it eternally on earth?

"Virtue Alone is Happiness Below."

Shall burning Ætna, if a sage requires,
Forget to thunder, and recall her fires?
When the loose mountain trembles from on high,
Shall gravitation cease, if you go by?
Whatever is, is right.—This world, 'tis true,
Was made for Cæsar—but for Titus, too;
And which more bless'd? who chain'd his country, say,
Or he whose virtues sighed to loose a day?*
"But sometimes virtue starves, while vice is fed."
What then? Is the reward of virtue bread?

---

*One evening, as Titus remembered that he had not conferred a benefit upon any man; he exclaimed: "My friends, I have lost a day!"

What nothing earthly gives or can destroy,
The soul's calm sunshine, and the heart-felt joy,
Is virtue's prize: a better would you fix?
Then give humility a coach and six,
Justice a conqueror's sword, or truth a gown,
Or public spirit its great cure—a crown.—
Judges and Senates have been bought for gold;
Esteem and love were never to be sold.—
Fortune in men has some small difference made,
One flaunts in rags, one flutters in brocade;
The cobbler apron'd, and the parson gown'd,
The friar hooded, and the monarch crown'd!
" What differ more (you cry) than crown and cowl?"
I'll tell you, friend! a wise man and a fool.
You'll find, if once the monarch acts the monk,
Or, cobbler-like, the parson will be drunk,
Worth makes the man, and want of it the fellow;
The rest is all but leather or prunella.—
Who noble ends, by noble means obtains,
Or failing smiles in exile or in chains,
Like good Aurelius let him reign, or bleed
Like Socrates, that man is great indeed.—
Know then this truth, (enough for man to know):
Virtue alone is happiness below.
—*Alex. Pope, Essay on Man, ep. 4th, v. v. 123—310.*

NOTES.

(1.) " Force is not a pushing god, not a being separated from the material foundation of things; it is the inseparable quality of matter, inherent to it from eternity."—Moleschott. " Matter and force are two names of the one artist, who fashions the living as well as the lifeless."—Huxley, Lay Sermons, p. 262.

(2.) " Where from is nature? It is from and by itself; it has no beginning, and no end. Beginning and end of the Universe are human conceptions which man transfers to nature, because he begins and ends his existence in a definite time."—Lud. Feuerbach.

(3.) Realism (materialism) is in the territory of natural science already so naturalized that no natural philosopher or chemist, no mineralogist or astronomer ever takes it into his head to gaze at the efficacy of a creator in the obvious phenomena, e. g., in the electric or magnetic; on the contrary, they see all, and without contradiction in them the necessary and inalterable effects of the physical and chemical forces which adhere to matter.

(4.) Followers of the monistic intuition of the Universe are, among the Germans: Fr. Haekel, Louis Buechner, Moleschott, Bartman, Radehausen, Dr. David Strauss, Louis Feuerbach, Schopenhauer, Ch. Vogt, and besides them many other eminent scholars; among the Englishmen: Ch. Darwin, Th. Huxley, Herbert Spencer, Tyndall, Stuart Mill, etc.; among the Americans: Draper, Rob. Ingersoll, Fiske, etc.

(5.) "In connection with the word 'Materialism,' we ought not only think of matter, but of matter *and force*, or rather of their identity. Thus far all systems have been dualistic, since they professed a separation between matter and force, matter and form, nature and spirit, Universe and God, body and soul." —L. Buechner.

(6.) "For the materialist there is only one obligation, this: to make himself useful to human society, to take more interest in its welfare than in its own, because he, as the individual, owes more to it, than it to him. For him there are no other sins than the violation of the property, honor, liberty and peace of his fellow-creatures."—Prof. Bockh. "If we unbiased glance at life and history, it is not difficult to observe that scientific materialism has nothing at all to do with practical. The latter strives violently for material goods, and a refined enjoyment of life; and the consequent moral degeneration is just found deepest in those spheres of society which most are boasting of their religious piety. On the contrary, it is least developed in the scientific materialists; for they know beforehand that, in opposition to the prevailing preconceptions, they can only expect material damage and personal aggression."—E. Haekel. "The term 'materialist' can easily be made to serve as a poisoned weapon, and there are theologians who do not scruple to employ it as such against the upholders of philosophic opinions which they do not like, but are unable to refute."—J. Fiske.

(7.) "Nature does not answer man's lamenting and questions; it hurls him inexorably back on his own help."—L. Feuerbach. "Help yourself."—Franklin. "For what purpose would God perform a miracle? He would then be supposed to say: I have not been able to effect my design by my construction of the Universe, by my eternal laws. This would be an avowal of his weakness."—Voltaire.

> "Whilst to the eye of shipwrecked mariner,
> Lone sitting on the bare and shuddering rock,
> All seems unlinked contingency and chance:
> No atom of this turbulence fulfills
> A vague and unnecessitated task,
> Or acts but as it must and ought to act."
>
> —P. B. Shelley, Queen Mab, VI.

(8.) "The providence which appears in the order, conformity and legality of nature, is not the providence of religion. This rests upon liberty, the former upon necessity; the latter is special, the first only extends to the whole. God does not especially govern the actions of men, and the doings of the rest of his creatures; the consideration of the natural laws contradicts this view. Nature cares little for the single members. Being so wealthy, thousands of them are by her sacrificed without regret; it acts in this way even with man. Hardly the half of human race reaches the second year of age. In the first year every third infant dies, in the fifth one of 25, in the seventh one of 50," etc. "Among savage tribes might goes for right; the woman is man's slave, beast of burden, merchandise which he sells for train-oil; among them no loving eye of providence is watchful for the woman. Where infanticide is considered to be a religious sacrifice, or new-born girls are buried alive (as in Paraguay), or are exposed to starvation, and to rapacious beasts (as the inhabitants of Madagascar are doing); where every time one child of twins is killed (as in Guiana), because their birth is believed to be an infamy; where no human heart and law is protecting children: there neither a heavenly father does protect them. The providence of mankind is only its civilization and culture."—L. Feuerbach.

(9.) Alex. Humboldt, Cosmos.

(10—12.) Alex. Humboldt, Cosmos.

(13.) Astronomy of Hershel.

(14.) This and the following statements, regarding the planets, are taken from Humboldt's Cosmos.

(15.) Zimmerman's "Wunder der Urwelt," pp. 98, 99.

(16.) The most of this section is taken from Lyell's "Manual of Geology for Students." Darwin, speaking of this work, says: "I have always considered this book as the best for a beginner in all the branches of natural science."

(17.) Lyell.

(18.) Lyell, Tyndall, Rossmaessler. "There were several ice periods. The last began some 240,000 years A. C., and terminated about 80,000 years ago—embracing a period of 160,000 years; the cold was most intense about 200,000 A. C.—' James Geikie,' the great ice age."

(19.) Ehrenburg and Rossmaessler; the latter in his book "das Wasser," p. 231.

(20.) Lee, Geology.

(21.) J. D. Dana: Corall Riffs—Manual of Geology. In the latter book he says (p. 272): "At the falls of the Ohio, near Louisville, there is yet a magnificent display of the old coral reef. Hemispherical Favorites five or six feet in diameter lie there nearly as perfect as when they were covered with their flower-like polyps; and beside these, there are various branching corals and cup corals (Cyathophylla); some of the species of the latter have a breadth of three inches, and one of six or seven inches."

(22.) Buechner, "Stellung des Menschen in der Natur."

(23.) Lyell.

(24.) "The stubbornness of the old, religious notions has by and by softened; public opinion has by degrees yielded to the knowledge that not since 6,000 years, neither since 60,000, neither since 600,000, but since aeons which contain uncounted millions of years, this earth has been the scene of life and death."—Tyndall.

(25.) Within twenty-five years the naturalists have examined the cells of plants with the aid of the microscope, and the result of their investigation is this: Every cell is first divided in two chambers; hereafter every one of these parts is separated again in two others, etc. The more perfect a plant: the greater is the number of its cells. The organs of animals are also composed from cells, and come forth too from that partition of the first cell. The animal cell is the same formation as the plant cell; there is only one cell and one life. "Nothing seems to prove that the life of plants sooner awoke on earth than that of animals, or that the latter presupposes the former. Even the existence of human tribes in the polar countries, who only live on fish, shows us the possibility to do without any vegetable food."—Humboldt, "Cosmos." The doctrine of the natural, common origin of all organisms is professed by Ch. Darwin, Th. Huxley, Herb. Spencer, E. Haeckel, Oken, Lamarck, Ch. Vogt, the poet Will. Goethe, and many other renowned scholars. Darwin says: "All animals and plants descend at the most from four or five original families. All living beings have much in common in their chemical composition, in the structure of their cells, in the law of their growth; therefore every organic individual proceeds from a common origin." Haeckel advances still farther by asserting that also these few primitive families have a common origin. He says: "Before immemorial time all life of our planet began with the generation of moneres, out of which the organisms of all groups constantly have improved and perfected themselves. The lower we descend in the layers of earth, wherein the remains of the extinct animals and plants are buried; the older these are: the simpler and more imperfect their shapes are." Another naturalist writes: "All the numerous life-forms of the animal and vegetable kingdom can have sprung from a few or a single prototype, so that the whole kingdom of animals and plants forms one large pedigree with many branches, in which both the animals and plants of the present day, and those of all preceding periods are ranged."—K. G. Reuschle.

(26.) This opinion is principally represented by E. Haeckel in his book "Natuerliche Schoepfungsgeschichte des Menschen."

(27.) Buechner, "Stellung des Menschen in der Natur."

(28.) "There are no great gulfs between epochs and formations, no sucessive periods marked by the appearance of plants, of water animals and of land animals, en masse."—Huxley.

(29.) "By the combat of nature, by hunger and death the highest problem is solved which we are able to comprehend: the generation of gradually higher and more perfect species."—Ch. Darwin.

(30.) " In nature all things took existence by development; man, too, is no exception of this law. The species of the organic beings must be changeable; if they were unchangeable, their development would be impossible. The theory of evolution closely united all beings of earth, and demonstrates that the present forms of evolution are the last remains of the former."—Buechner. "The truth of the evolution theory is acknowledged by H. Spencer, Huxley, Grove, Hooker, Carpenter, Prof. Gray, Prof. Cope, and indeed by the majority of the English, Scotch, German and American naturalists."—B. F. Underwood.

(31.) Humboldt, Cosmos.

(32.) Haekel.

(33.) To these philosophers pertain: Huxley, Tyndall, Haekel, Buechner, Ch. Vogt, Schafhausen, and many others. Darwin says in his celebrated work " Descent of Man :" " The main conclusion arrived at in this work and now held by many naturalists who are well competent to form a sound judgment, is, *that man is* descended from some less highly organized forms. He is a distinct species of it," 2d vol, p. 368.

(34.) Haekel.

(35.) Darwin, "Descent of Man," 2 vol. pp. 369, etc. "The surface of the brain of a monkey exhibits a sort of a skeleton map of man's, and in the manlike apes the details become more and more filled in, until it is only in minor characters that the Chimpanzee's or the Orang's brain can be structurally distinguished from Man's. It must not be overlooked, however, that there is a very striking difference in absolute mass and weight between the lowest human brain and that of the highest ape. This is a very noteworthy circumstance, and doubtless will one day help to furnish an explanation of the great gulf which intervenes between the lowest man and the highest ape in intellectual power." Th. Huxley, " Evidence as to Man's place in Nature," p. 124.

(36.) Haekel, " Nat. Shoepfungsgeschichte des Menschen."

(37.) " The naturalists of the past age called the apes four-handed. But the principal difference between hand and foot is this, that the foot has three muscles more than that. This difference is found in apes as well as in man."—Haekel.

(38.) Darwin himself remarked that the connecting link between man and animal thus far has not been found, but he believes that it will be yet discovered, and adds : " Perhaps the petrified ape,- like ancestors of human race, will once be found in the Tertiary layers of Southern Asia and Africa."

(39.) Cf. Buechner, " Stellung des Menschen," etc. " The earliest traces of art yet discovered belong to the Stone age. They were sometimes sculptures, if one may say so, and sometimes drawings or etchings made on bone or horn with the point of a flint."—J. Lubbock, " the origin of civilization and the primitive condition of man." The drawing of the reindeer groups is copied from this work, p. 26. With regard to gradual civilization of man, Lubbock says : " The facts and arguments mentioned in this work afford, I think, strong grounds for the conclusions that the primitive condition of man was one of utter barbarism, and that from this condition several races have independently raised themselves," p. 323.

> " Human kind ! By Nature cast
> Naked, and helpless, out amidst the woods
> And wilds, to rude inclement elements,
> With various seeds of art deep in the mind
> Implanted, and profusely pour'd around
> Materials infinite; but idle all.
> And still the sad barbarian, roving, mix'd
> With beasts of prey; or for his acorn-meal
> Fought the fierce tusky boar; a shivering wretch,
> Agast and comfortless, when the bleak North,
> With Winter charged, let the mix'd tempest fly,
> Hail, rain, and snow, and bitter-breathing frost,—
> A waste of time! till Industry approach'd,
> And roused him from his miserable sloth;
> His faculties unfolded."
> —J. Thomson, " The Seasons—Autumn," v. v. 47, etc.

(40.) "All races agree in so many unimportant details of structure, and in so many mental peculiarities that these can be accounted for only through inheritance from a common progenitor."—Darwin, " Descent of Man," 2d vol. p. 308.

(41.) This and the next § are composed according to Cutter's Physiology, Buechner's " Kraft und Stoff," Cane's Chemistry, etc.

(42.) "All the Faculties in the world will never prevent a philosopher from perceiving that we commence by sensation, and that our memory is nothing but a continued sensation. A man born without his five senses would be destitute of all idea. Sensation includes all our faculties."—Voltaire. " Nihil in mente, quod not prius in sensu" (nothing is in the intellect that not first was in a sense). —Latin proverb.

(43.) "All vital action may be said to be the result of the molecular forces of the protoplasm which displays it, and if so, it must be true, in the same sense and to the same extent, that the *thoughts* to which I am now giving utterance and *your thoughts* regarding them, are the expression of *molecular changes* in that matter of life which is the source *of our vital phenomena*."—Huxley, " Lay Serm.," p. 138.

(44.) According to the doctrine of Galenus, the most renowned physician of ancient times, in the brain is the origin of every sense, of all perceptions and notions, it is the seat of reason, and the organ of intellect.

(45.) "That no idea or feeling arises, save as a result of some physical force expended in producing it, is fast becoming a common place of science."—H. Spencer, " First Principles," p. 217. "As pride, ambition, fickleness, and other qualities of character are transferred by inheritance to the descendants: in the same manner such a transplantation of fixed ideas, melancholy, idiocy, and other mental diseases is valid. It becomes here evident and irrefutable that the human soul is entirely a sum of physiological, motory phenomena of particles of the brain."—E. Haeckel, " Natuerliche Schœpfungsgeschichte," p. 161. " The mind develops together with the body, with the senses, in general with man. Where the skull, the brain from: therefrom is also the mind; where the organ from : therefrom is also its function : from nature."—L. Feuerbach, "The Brain is Thinking." " Thought is a function of the brain. If a man has no legs, he has no going ; if he has no brain, he has no mind, no thoughts."—J. C. Fisher. " Thought is a form of force. We walk with the same force with which we think. Man is an organism, that changes several forms of force into thought-force. Man is a machine into which we put what we call food, and produce what we call thought. Think of that wonderful chemistry by which bread was changed into the divine tragedy of Hamlet."—R. Ingersoll, "The Gods," p. 47.

(47.) "The quality of the brain determines both the kind and the intensity of mental life. No other formation of nature is comparable to the brain. About 400 millions of nerve-fibres constitute the bulk of the brain ; between them those thousands of millions of cells lie which they call ganglia (knots of nerves). The convolutions of the brain, too, act an important part in the mental functions. In the brain of the astronomer Gauss (whom Alex. Humboldt called the foremost of the astronomers of his age), their area measured 342 square inches ; in the gorilla it amounts hardly to 80."—Buechner.

(48.) L. Buechner.

(49) "Growth of mental power means an actual addition of structure to intimate constitution of centres of mind."—H. Maudsley, " Body and Mind," pp. 28, 29. " With the advancing culture of mankind the fore parts of the brain grow larger."—Buechner. " Already the brain of the civilized man is larger by nearly 30 per cent. than the brain of the savage. Already, too, it presents an increased heterogeneity--especially in the distribution of its convolutions."—H. Spencer, " Princ. of Biology," 2 vol., p. 502.

(50.) Maudsley, p. 28.

(51.) " It is utterly impossible to prove that any thing whatever may not be the effect of a material and necessary cause, and human logic is equally incompetent to prove that any *act* is really spontaneous. A really spontaneous act is one, which (by the assumption) has no cause ; and the attempt to prove such a negative as this is, on the face of the matter, absurd. Progress of science means the gradual banishment from all regions of human thought of what we call spirit and spontaneity."—Huxley, p. 142. " Statistics enable us to prove how completely the volition of individual men is controlled by their antecedents, and by the circumstances in which they are placed. The antecedents exist either in the human mind, or in the external world."—H. Th. Buckle " History of Civilization in England," 1st vol. p. 596. Statistics prove e. g., that, in the same country, or in the same city, annually about the same number of murders, suicides, marriages, etc. takes place. "Will means spontaneity, but within Nature's determination, which is independent from human will."—L. Feuerbach. "Human will is never absolutely free, but is always determined by inner or external influences. Every apparently free action is caused by antecedent representations."—Hackel.

(52.) "If the past history of man has been one of progress, we may fairly hope that the future will be so also; that the blessing of civilization will not only be extended to other countries, and to other nations, but that even in our own land they will be rendered more general and more equable, so that we shall not see before us always, as now, countrymen of our own, living in our very midst a life worse than that of a savage."—Lubbock, p. 323. "By the ceaseless exercise of our faculties is insured a constant progress towards a higher degree of skill, intelligence and self-regulation—a more complete life."—H. Spencer, "Biology," 2 vol. p. 500. "As man gradually advanced in intellectual power; as he acquired sufficient knowledge to reject baneful customs and superstitions; as he regarded more and more not only the welfare, but the happiness of his fellow-men; as from habit, instruction, and example his sympathies became more tender and widely diffused, so as to extend to the men of all races, to the imbecile, the maimed, and the other useless members of society, finally to the lower animals—so would the standard of his morality rise higher and higher; and it is admitted by moralists that it has risen since an early period in the history of man."—Darwin, "Descent of Man," 1st vol. p. 99. "Looking to future generations we may expect that virtuous habits will grow stronger, becoming perhaps fixed by inheritance, and—in this case virtue will be triumphant."—Ib.

(53.) "It is by no means my intention to suggest that there is no difference in faculty between the lowest plant and the highest, or between plants and animals. But the difference between the powers of the lowest plant or animal and those of the highest, *is only one of degree, not of kind*, and depends upon the extent to which the principle of the division of labor is carried out in the living economy."—Huxley, "Lay Serm.," p. 12. "The difference in mind between man and the higher animals, great as it is, is certainly one of degree and not of kind."—Darwin, "Descent of Man," 1st vol. p. 101. "The mental faculties of man are different from those of animals only in multitude, not in peculiarity, only in quantity, not in quality."—Ch. Vogt, "Bilder aus dem Thierleben," pp. 430—438. For examples illustrating animal faculties and mind, see Darwin, "Descent of Man," 1st vol., and *Dr. Brehm*.

(54.) Darwin "Descent of Man," 1st vol., p. 100.

(55.) This doctrine is here communicated according to H. Spencer's "First Principles," pp. 287—538. He is in England generally, and especially by Darwin, considered to be the most eminent philosopher of our age. His views of the Evolution of the Universe and of the Unknowable are professed by many egregious thinkers.

(56.) "The organic world is continually in the state of originating and perishing."—Humboldt.

(57.) E. g., Imman. Kant in his book " Allgemeine Naturgeschichte und Theorie des Himmels."

(58.) The contents of this section are also taken from Spencer's " First Principles."

(59.) A poem of Fr. Schiller, by which he teaches that no mortal is permitted to see the face of the image covered by the veil; the image is the emblem of the Deity.

(60.) " As concerning divine power, the understanding can perceive little or nothing, it would be more seemly for those who pretend to a familiar knowledge of the attributes and character of that Being, whom no man has seen, at any time, to confess their ignorance at once, that thereby we might hope to have peace from the long continued strife which has prevailed amongst men concerning the unknown."—Mackintosh, " Phys. and Mor. Philosophy," p. 402.

(61.) " The uninterrupted series of final causes (as they are called) was considered by the ancient atheists to be *infinite*; the theists call it *finite*."—Feuerbach, "Vorlesungen ueber das Wesen der Religion." "The cause of the Universe is Necessity."—Th. Bayrhoffer. " Whenever we are told that God is the author of any phenomenon, that signifies that we are ignorant how such a phenomenon can be produced, with the assistance only of the natural powers or causes with which we are acquainted. It is thus that the generality of mankind, whose lot is ignorance, attribute to the Deity, not only the uncommon effects, which strike them, but even the most simple events."—Shelley.

(62.) "Can the intelligence of man discover the least wisdom in covering the earth with crawling, creeping horrors that live only upon the agonies and pangs of others? Who can appreciate the mercy of so making the world that all animals devour animals; so that every mouth is a slaughter house, and every stomach a tomb? Is it possible to discover infinite intelligence and love in universal and eternal carnage?"—Rob. Ingersoll, " The Gods," pp. 70, 71.

(63.) " The air is not created to the purpose to be inhaled by men, but men inhale it because it exists, and they could not live if it were another thing as it is."—Feuerbach. The deer did not receive long legs from nature in order to enable it to run fast, but it runs fast because it received long legs. Animals living in the North have a tighter fur than in the South, and generally, in winter, tighter hairs than in summer. This quality of animals is a sequence of the state of temperature, not a premeditated management of a higher providence. Since the diver-bell was invented, we are told that, on the bottom of the sea, a gorgeous Flora, and an animal-world not less splendid exists. Now, to what purpose is this display of beauty and magnificence in a depth which only the diver's eye pierces? " The miscarriages (e. g., goats without heads or men with six fingers on one hand) are popular proofs already quoted by the ancient atheists that the formations of nature are products without any definite purpose."

—Feuerbach. "Religious people see nothing but design every where (in the Universe); they point us to the sunshine, to the flowers, etc. Did it ever occur to them that a cancer is as beautiful in its development as is the reddest rose? By what ingenious methods the blood is poisoned so that the cancer shall have food! See by what admirable instrumentalities it feeds itself from the surrounding quivering, dainty flesh! See how it gradually but surely expands and grows! By what marvelous mechanism it is supplied with long and slender roots that reach out of the most secret nerves of pain for sustenance and life! What beautiful colors it presents! Seen through the microscope it is a miracle of order and beauty. All the ingenuity of man cannot stop its growth. Is it possible to look upon it and doubt that there is design in the Universe, and that the inventor of this wonderful cancer must be infinitely powerful, ingenious and good?"—Rob. Ingersoll, "The Gods."

(64.) "It was not God who created man according to his likeness, but it was man who created God according to his likeness."—Feuerbach.

(65.) L. Feuerbach, "das Wesen des Christenthums."

(66.) The Arabs worshipped a lava-like, blackish stone in the temple of Mecca, until Mohammed took it away. They believed that it had dropped from Paradise.

(67.) "Man's likeness is reflected in his gods."—Schiller.

(68.) "Sailors, traders and philosophers, Roman-Catholic priests, and Protestant missionaries, in ancient and modern times, in every part of the globe, have concurred in stating that there are races of men altogether void of religion, e. g., the Hottentots, the Californians, the Caffirs, some of the Esquimaux, Canadian, Brazilian, Polynesian, Hindoostan and Eastern African tribes."—Lubbock, pp. 121, 122. "One hundred millions of savages in Asia, Africa, America and Australia have no gods."—Th. Hofferichter.

(69.) "At present time about 1,350 millions of men live on earth; more than the sixth part of them (over 225 millions) confess the Buddhism, which ignores the belief in a God."—Hofferichter.

(70.) "Even now-a-days children have no knowledge of God, till it is inculcated in their minds by parents and teachers"—Feuerbach, "Erlæuterungen zum Wesen des Christenthums."

(71.) "The primitive faith of man is the faith in the truth of his senses, the faith in the visible, audible, sensible nature, but what he cannot help to assimilate to himself, to humanize, to personify. But in the course of time he separates this unvoluntary personification of natural objects from these, changes them in independent persons, and finally, when he rises to the conception of the unity of the Universe, he comprises them in one personality or essence which differs from nature. So finally, out from his belief in the reality of nature, grows a quite abstract being, that issued from thousand years old traditions, is the object of his faith, to which he clings from habit as to his second nature." "God as a moral being is nothing but the idolized human mind; as the author of nature nothing but the idolized personified nature." " The gods are the personified wishes of man."—Feuerbach.

(72.) " Since men have known that the fixed stars are bodies, similar to our sun ; since the Universe dissolved in an infinity of celestial bodies, heaven in on optic vision : the want of a home troubled the old personal God. Now they cannot imagine more a God sitting upon a throne surrounded by angels. But the company of angels is necessary, if man will imagine a personal God ; for a ruler wants also his servants. No heaven, then, more for a palace ; no angels more, assembled round his throne ! Beside, thunder and lightning are not more his missiles ; war, pestilence and famine not more his scourges, but effects of natural causes! Since he lost all attributes of a personal existence and government : how could we still conceive God as a personal being?"—Dr. Fred. Strauss, " Alter und Neuer Glaube."

(73.) Theod. Parker (" lectures on Atheism," etc.) and others, among both the English and German theologians and philosophers. Aristotle, already called the first cause of existence: *Theos*, to-wit, disposer of all changes of matter which is separated from him. From that word the name Theist is derived. J. J. Rosseau, Voltaire, and, in general, the French philosophers of their age were Theists ; so was also Thomas Paine. The free-masons, too, belong to this school, for they imagine God to be the *architect* of the Universe.

(74.) Fr. Muench (" Materialism and Dualism "), Dr. Boehner, Schleiermacher and others.

(75.) " Religion in Italy has no necessary connection with any one virtue. The most atrocious villain may be rigidly devout, and, without any shock to established faith, confess himself to be so."—P. B. Shelley, " Preface to the Cenci."

(76.) To this class belong most of the German philosophers and naturalists, e. g., L. Buechner, L. Feuerbach ; and among the Englishmen H. Spencer ; besides most of the members of the German free congregations.

(77.) " He who uttering the name of God, only thinks of the cause or principle of the laws of astronomy, natural philosophy, geology, mineralogy, physiology, zoology, and anthropology, ought to be also honest enough to forbear this name ; for a natural principle is always a natural being, not such an one that constitutes a God. By shyness or fear to contradict opinions sanctified by their antiquity, men retained old names, but join to them quite different notions only acquired in the course of time."—Feuerbach.

(78.) " Of matter and force, of mind man can inquire and understand ; but of ultimate nature, essence or cause of matter, force or mind, man knows nothing ; these things are buried in impenetrable mystery. Every religion setting out though it does with the tacit assertion of a mystery, forthwith proceeds to give some solution of this mystery ; and so asserts that it is not a mystery passing human comprehension. But an examination of the solutions they severally propound, shows them to be uniformly invalid."—H. Spencer, " First Prin.," pp. 45, 46.

(79.) "Besides the evidence of his own existence man can only be sure of the existence of nature, not of the existence of a God, namely, of a being which individually differs from nature and man. This being rather rests (at least originally) on a conclusion, to wit, on the conclusion that nature cannot exist by itself, but supposes another being; it is therefore not at all an unquestionable being. It is missing all attributes of a sensible being; it is not a real, but only an abstract being."—"To believe in God imports to reject the necessity of nature; either God, or nature: there is no other alternative; for if God is governing, natural laws are not wanted, or they are deceits and lies."—"If actually no God is the fulcrum of the earth and stars, if the agent of their movement is mechanical, necessarily the first cause of the movement also is mechanical or, generally, natural. Which shallowness of mind to reject the second causes of superstition, the miracles, the devil, the demons as causes, in explaining the natural phenomena of nature, but to leave the first cause of all superstition untouched! God as first cause is a mere hypothesis in order to explain the first beginning of nature, and particularly the origin of man."—" Just as a republic without princes, nature also can subsist without a God."—Feuerbach, "Vorlesungen ueber das Wesen der Religion." " To be sure, science has not yet succeeded to establish the last causes of the Universe; but as the only object it knows are the Universe and its laws, it is the safest way to put the Universe on the place of God."—Th. Bayrhofer. "The time is surely coming when the very inadequacy of human language to express Divinity will be regarded as a reason for deeper faith and more solemn adoration."—J. Fiske, Cos. Philos., 2 vol., p. 451.

(80.) Among the Greeks as Atheists were declared: Thales, Pythagoras, Socrates, Plato, etc.; among the Romans: Cicero, Lucrece and the ancient Christians; among the Christians: Galilaei, Kepler, Locke, Kant, Schelling, Hegel, Feuerbach, Buechner, Haekel, and many others.

Here may also be quoted the opinion which Alex. Humboldt pronounced with regard to the attempts to discover the first cause of the connection of all forces and phenomena in the universe. In his celebrated work "Cosmos," he says: " History has preserved the different attempts which were made to perceive a single, universal force, penetrating and moving the whole Universe. Of all attempts to reduce the changes in the visible world to a single first principle, Newton's doctrine of gravitation is the most extensive and the most promising. The proofs of all empirical laws less surely, and partly not at all, can be deduced from the theory of the attraction of the atoms. Newton himself does not affirm that gravitation is the fundamental force of matter. The imperfect state of our knowledge of nature, especially in certain departments, oppose invincible difficulties to the problem to represent the whole natural science as an organic total. The infinity of empirical knowledge, and the illimited sphere of observation make the problem that would explain the changes of matter by the forces of matter themselves, an indefinite one. Still it does not behoove our age to condemn every generalization of the conceptions, and the intellect which scrutinizes the causal connection of things."

(81.) "Whence did all those horrible murders of whole nations of men, women and children, with which the Bible is filled up, and the bloody persecutions and agonies and religious wars which since have desolated Europe with fire and sword—whence did they originate? From that impious object which they call revealed religion."—Th. Paine, " Age of Reason." " I have come to the well considered view that all religions, none excepted, contain too much error to be of any use upon the present high decree of culture of the human mind."—Rob. Owen. " Unfortunately for Faith, happiness has not been its fruit. Ireland is full of Faith, and full of misery. In Spain and Portugal Faith and Bigotry reign triumphant, whilst strife and wretchedness cover the land. Wherever superstition has lighted her fire, and put on her seething-pot, the passions of men have boiled over like the lava from Mount Ætna, scattering misery, death and desolation around. The very names of vice and virtue have been made in many instances to change places. Horrible crimes have been committed under the supposed sanction of a merciful God, whilst the most sacred duties have been neglected under the apprehension of his displeasure."—T. Mackintosh, " Phys. and Moral Philosophy," p. 348. " Long have I sought the mainspring of human folly and crime; I have found the first link in the chain of evil; I have found it—in all countries, among all tribes and tongues and nations—in—Religion! It is not that Religion is merely useless: it is mischievous. It is mischievous by its idle terrors; it is mischievous by its false morality; it is mischievous by its hypocrisy; by its fanaticism; by its dogmatism; by its threats; by its hopes; by its promises."—Epicurus, in " A Few Days in Athens," by Frances Wright, pp. 199, 203. " Like the Paganism of Rome, Christianity is destined to become an obsolete faith—a worn-out superstition."—B. F. Underwood.

(82.) Bernstein, " Reich der Naturwissenschaften."

(83.) "Theology teaches that the soul is an immaterial principle, which dwells in the body and remains, when the latter perishes. But natural philosophy does not acknowledge such a principle; if the soul's organ, the body, perishes, itself, too, is at its end; this science has no knowledge of an individual continuance of the soul's life."—Ch. Vogt, " Bilder aus dem Thierleben," pp. 442, 443. " The most painful truth is death; how, then, should we acknowledge it? Therefore, we deny that death is the end of man; and still, this end is a truth quite as common, evident, testified by the sensés, as man's birth, proved by the same witnesses, the senses, as his commencement."—Feuerbach.

(84.) " Under whatever disguise it takes refuge, whether fungus or oak, worm or man, the living protoplasm (physical basis or matter of life) ultimately dies, and is resolved into its mineral and lifeless constituents (carbon, hydrogen oxygen and nitrogen)."—Huxley.

(85.) Experience states that one individual of human race dies in every second; therefore, on an average, annually 31,536,000 souls would be separated from their bodies; this sum amounts in 100 years to 3,153,600,000 souls. But their number becomes quite unimaginable, if we suppose that mankind already exists ten thousands of years, and that it, probably, will continue to exist yet millions of years. Where would be room enough for such an uncountable number of souls?

(86.) Fr. Muench, Th. Parker, etc.

(87.) "Immortality is only a concern of visionaries and idlers. The active man, who is busy with the objects of human life, has no time to think of death, and, therefore no need of immortality; if he sometimes thinks of death, he only beholds in it the monitor to invest wisely the received capital of life, and not to squander the precious time with naughty things."—"The Greeks entertained moderate wishes; they did not want to live forever; only, they did not like to die by a premature, or violent, or painful death. They did not sigh, like the Christians, to be subjected to the necessity of nature, to the wants of sleep, food and drink; they adapted their desires to the limits of human nature. The Christians want to be happier than the gods of the Olymp; they desire a heaven where all wishes are accompiished."—Feuerbach, "Ergænzungen zum Wesen des Christenthums," p. 483.

(88.) Feuerbach.

(89.) Many men have no propensity to science and art, and think it to be folly to care for objects so distant as stars, mosses, infusoria, etc. Neither does that propensity exert itself farther than the egotism of men. Nobody desires to know more than it does good to him." "The rationalistic Christian removes the goal of accomplishment infinitely: therefore man always has to remain an imperfect being; but a goal which never can be reached, is an illusion."—Feuerbach, "Vorlesungen ueber das Wesen der Religion."

(90.) Such ones were: The philosophic school of the Epicureens, Homer, Plinius the senior, Horace, Seneca, Voltaire, Mirabeau (the greatest orator of the first French revolution), King Frederick II., and others. Of our contemporaries belong to them: Burmeister, Ch. Vogt, Dr. Strauss, L. Buechner, L. Feuerbach, most of the members of the free German congregations, etc. In general, since Kant, only few German philosophers discuss the theme of the immortality of the soul. "Reinhold in his letters on Kant's philosophy, remarks that even, since Descartes established the rational idea of the soul's spirituality, the doctrine of immortality is doubted by the best philosophers, or at least silently passed by."—Feuerbach, "Gott, Freiheit, Unsterblichkeit," p. 223. Kant, immediately before his death, was asked what he hoped of the future; he answered: "Of this state I know nothing."

(91.) "Luther says: 'If man dies as a tree or a cow falls down, let us revel.' Luther's utterance furnishes a strong evidence how rude Christianity is, which only in a future life finds the difference between a man and a cow, between eating and revelling. But the conclusion which Christianity deduces from mortality, is not only rude, it is also silly. Even for the reason that we shall be dead to-morrow, we will not kill us already to-day by excess in eating and drinking; we will not destroy mutually our lives by robbery and murder (as Luther also says); we will not gall our lives by follies and mischief."—Feuerbach, " Gedanken ueber Tod und Unsterblichkeit," 3 vol. p. 394.

(92.) "How superficial and foolish is the modern rationalistic Christianity, if it makes, yet now-a-days, the stars the fulcra of its phantastic other world, after they were degraded in the class of ponderable, corporeal, empirical objects."—Feuerbach.

(93.) Epicurus in " A Few Days in Athens," by Frances Wright, p. 126.

CONTENTS.

Page.

PART SECOND—Religious Enlightenment.................................... 3
SECTION FIRST.. 5—87
OUTLINE OF THE HISTORY OF THE PRINCIPAL RELIGIONS............. 5
§ 1. Introduction—Definition—Division of the History of Religions... 5—6
CHAPTER FIRST... 6—23
THE RELIGIONS BEFORE THE CHRISTIAN ERA AND THE ISLAM............. 6—23
§ 2. The Ancient Religions in General—Priests—Sacrifices—Prayers
—Oracles... 6—7
§ 3. Religion of the Arians—Zend-Avesta.................................. 7—8
§ 4. Religion of the Hindoos—Brahmanism—Buddhism................. 8—13
§ 5. Religions of the Chinese—Confutse................................. 13
§ 6. Religion of the Egyptians.. 14
§ 7. Greek and Roman Religions..15—16
§ 8. Religion of the Ancient Germans.................................16—17
§ 9. Judaic Religion..17—20
§ 10. Mohammedan Religion—Arabian Culture........................20—23
CHAPTER SECOND...23—87
CHRISTIAN RELIGION.. 23
FIRST PERIOD (1—1024)..23—30
§ 11. Origin of the Christian Religion—Causes of Its Fast Propagation 23—24
§ 12. Origin of the Gospels—Life and Character of Jesus—His Doctrine
—Paulinism..24—27
§ 13. State of the Church—Ecclesiastic Councils—Clergy—Monks....27—30
SECOND PERIOD (1024—1300)...30—44
§ 14. Germany—Henry IV. and Gregory VII............................30—32
§ 15. Frederick I.—Arnold of Brescia—Frederick II.—The Albigenses..32—34
§ 16. Crusades (1096—1300)—The First Crusade—Capture of Jerusalem..34—36
§ 17. Continued—The Three following Crusades—Emir of Saladin......36—37
§ 18. Concluded—The Rest of the Crusades—Frederick II.—Louis IX.
—Effects of the Crusades...37—39
§ 19. The State of the Church—Anathema—Interdict.....................39—40
§ 20. Continued—The Inquisition Tribunal................................40—42
§ 21. Concluded—The Clergy—The Popes—Gregory VII.—Innocent III...42—44
THIRD PERIOD (1300—1518)...44—47
§ 22. War of the Hussites—Philip IV......................................44—45
§ 23. State of the Church—Wycliffe—J. Huss—The Popes................45—47
FOURTH PERIOD (1518—1648)...47—64
§ 24. Causes of the Reformation of the Christian Church—M. Luther...47—49
§ 25. Diet of Worms—Confession of Augsburg—War of Smalkalden—
Religious Peace of Augsburg...49—51
§ 26. The Thirty Years' War—Restitution Edict............................51—52
§ 27. Concluded—Gustavus Adolphus—Battles of Leipsic and Luetzen
—Westphalian Peace..52—55
§ 28. Switzerland—Zwingli—Calvin......................................55—57
§ 29. Spain—Revolution of the Netherlands..............................57—58
§ 30. France—War against the Huguenots—The Saint Bartholomew—
Henry IV.—Edict of Nantes—England—Episcopal Church
—Henry VIII..58—60
§ 31. Outline of the Ecclesiastical Reforms—Their Effects—Distinctive
Doctrines of the Single Churches...................................60—62
§ 32. State of the Church—Expulsion of the Unitarians—The Popes
—Order of the Jesuits...62—64

FIFTH PERIOD (1648--1789)..64—71
§ 33. Germany—Frederick II.--Emperor Joseph II.—France—Persecution of the Huguenots—England.................................64—67
§ 34. State of the Church—William Penn—Sects—Puritans............67—69
§ 35. Beginning of Rationalism—Voltaire—J. J. Rousseau—Lessing—Woolston—Dr. Paullus—Abolition of the Order of the Jesuits....69—71
SIXTH PERIOD (1789--1877)..71--87
§ 36. Effects of the French Revolution Exerted on Religion and Church—Epoch of the Restoration.....................................71—72
§ 37. The Revolutions in July, 1830—Origin of the Historic Criticism and of the Modern View of the Universe—Dr. Fred. Strauss—Reaction...72—73
§ 38. The Revolutions in 1848—The German Catholics—Origin of the Religion of Humanity—Free Religious Congregations in Germany—Reactionary Attempts...73—76
§ 39. America—Sectarianism—Religious Liberty—Thom. Paine.......76—78
§ 40. Continued—The Liberal Press—Liberal Orators—Transcendentalism in New England...78--81
§ 41. Continued—Liberal Associations—The Anti-Slavery Society—Free Religious Associations—The National Liberal League...........81—83
§ 42. Concluded—German Free Congregations—Their Organization and League..83—87
SECTION SECOND...87—118
BIBLICAL NARRATIVES AND THEIR CRITICISM...................87
CHAPTER FIRST..87—100
NARRATIVES FROM THE OLD TESTAMENT............................87—100
 1. The Author of the Mosaic Documents..............................87—88
 2. The History of the Creation..88—89
 3. The Garden in Eden..89—91
 4. The Great Deluge...91—92
 5. Abraham..92—93
 6. The Egyptian Plagues and the Emigration of the Israelites.....93—94
 7. Legislation on Mount Sinai—The Two Tablettes.................94—95
 8. The Tabernacle..95—96
 9. Conquest of Canaan—Joshua—Samson............................96—98
10. The Prophets Elias and Elisha..98—100
CHAPTER SECOND...100—100
NARRATIVES FROM THE NEW TESTAMENT...........................100—118
 1. The Birth of Jesus..100—102
 2. The Baptism of Jesus..102
 3. The Temptation of Jesus...102—103
 4. The Miracles of Jesus in General..................................103—105
 5. His Miraculous Cures—Demoniacs.................................105—106
 6. Resuscitations of the Dead...106—107
 7. Miraculous Feedings—Water Changed into Wine—The Storm Appeased..107—108
 8. Solemn Entry of Jesus into Jerusalem—His Last Supper......108—109
 9. Arrest, Trial and Condemnation of Jesus........................109—111
10. His Crucifixion...111—114
11. His Resurrection and Ascension....................................114—116
12. The Miracle of Pentecost—The Three Principal Festivals of the Christians..116—117
SECTION THIRD..118—175
VIEWS OF THE UNIVERSE FROM THE STANDPOINT OF MODERN SCIENCE...118
§ 1. Force and Matter. Force—Imperishable........................118
§ 2. Matter—Imperishable and Infinite................................118—120
§ 3. The Universe—Uniformity and Necessity of the Natural Laws.120—121

12*

§ 4.	The Starry Heavens	121—123
§ 5.	The Earth and Its Gradual Transformation	123—124
§ 6.	The Earth's Mountains—Periods of Its Transformation	124—126
§ 7.	The Age of the Earth	126—128
§ 8.	Organic Life—Doctrine of Descent	128—131
§ 9.	Man—1, Age, and 2, Origin of His Species	131—133
§ 10.	Continued—3, His Primitive State. Lake Villages—4, Human Races	133—135
§ 11.	Human Body—Senses—Nerves—Brain—Human Mind	135—138
§ 12.	Relation between Brain and Mind—Human Will—Corollaries	138—141
§ 13.	The Soul of Animals	141—143
§ 14.	The Law of Evolution in the Universe	143—145
§ 15.	Concluded—Corollaries	145—148
§ 16.	The Unknowable in the Universe	148—150
§ 17.	The Conception of God—1. In the Christian Church	150—152
§ 18.	Concluded—2. From the Standpoint of Modern Science	152—154
§ 19.	The Religions	154—155
§ 20.	Death and Immortality	155—158
§ 21.	Heaven and Hell	158—159
§ 22.	The Evil in the World	159—160
Notes		161

ERRATA.

The kind readers are respectfully requested to excuse the Errata, because the author, living in California, could not review himself the proof-sheets.

PART FIRST.

Preface, page 8, line 3 above, instead Feike read Fiske.
Preface, page 8, line 5 below, instead book read lack.
Page 17, line 10 below, instead Gravicus read Granicus.
Page 23, line 20 above, instead dead read deed.
Page 24, line 13 above, instead Aegin read Aequi.
Page 25, line 2 below, instead grouping read groping.
Page 28, line 1 below, instead friend read fiend.
Page 28, line 13 below, after "And" read "I".
Page 38, line 6 below, instead "I" read "A".
Page 50, line 10 above, instead deputied read deputed.
Page 53, line 16 above, instead beastial read bestial.
Page 54, line 3 above, instead bark read back.
Page 56, line 5 below, instead taked read taken.
Page 58, line 21 above, instead Bonmer's read Bonner's.
Page 67, line 16 above, instead bondage read freedom.
Page 88, line 12 below, instead write read excite.
Page 98, line 3 below, instead a read no.
Page 100, line 19 above, instead Kown read Know.
Page 114, line 2 below, after "we" add "not".
Page 132, line 24 below, instead Cincinnatius read Cincinnatus.
Page 132, line 16 below, instead Illustratious read Illustrious.

PART SECOND.

Page 8, line 4 below, instead didatic read didactic.
Page 13, line 10 above, instead exits read exists.
Page 13, line 10 below, instead Sao read Tao.
Page 13, line 9 below, instead It read Its.
Page 14, line 2 above, instead dieties read deities.
Page 16, line 15 below, instead sacrifice read sacrifices.
Page 17, line 9 below, instead servile read sterile.
Page 20, line 16 below, instead adversed read adverse.

Page 24, line 13 below, instead preservation read persecution.
Page 24, line 6 below, instead Gabrius read Galerius.
Page 25, line 9 below, instead lie read lies.
Page 27, line 8 above, instead he read be.
Page 33, line 3 below, instead Beriers read Bezier.
Page 41, line 2 above, instead services read sorceries.
Page 48, line 9 below, instead boy read bag.
Page 49, line 15 below, instead E. K. read Eck.
Page 55, line 7 above, instead He read It.
Page 56, line 5 above, instead pastorate read pastor.
Page 58, line 3 below, instead who read whom.
Page 67, line 5 above, instead Scots read Sects.
Page 70, line 2 below, instead Uraguay read Uruguay.
Page 78, line 7 below, cancel " Frothingham ".
Page 90, line 22 above, after " cause " add " of ".
Page 90, line 7 below, instead reminds read remind.
Page 92, line 10 above, instead therefore read therefrom.
Page 94, line 15 below, instead epoch read epos.
Page 98, line 14 above, instead one read ones.
Page 98, line 18 below, instead then read them.
Page 104, line 1 above, instead he read the.
Page 110, line 16 above, instead they read he.
Page 111, line 6 above, after " addition " add " of ".
Page 117, line 17 above, instead premioes read premices.
Page 121, line 1 above, instead progress read prayers.
Page 123, line 12 below, instead island read islands.
Page 125, line 17 above, instead Platonic read Plutonic.
Page 128, line 1 above, instead of 70 read 70'.
Page 128, line 4 above, after " away " add (22.)
Page 128, line 7 above, after " wanted " add (23.)
Page 133, line 14 below, instead (39.) read Huxley.
Page 135, line 16 below, instead diversity read diversities.
Page 146, line 5 above, instead viens read veins.
Page 156, line 7 above, instead gem read stem.
Page 165, line 10 below, instead " ape, like " read " ape-like ".
Page 174, line 15 below, instead Plinus read Plinius.

www.ingramcontent.com/pod-product-compliance
Lightning Source LLC
Chambersburg PA
CBHW030020240426
43672CB00007B/1025